THE NEW BEGINNING
(2002 and Beyond)

Kryon
Book Nine

66 International Kryon Books

See (www.kryon.com) for more info

Spanish
Kryon Books - One, Two, Three, The Parables, & The Journey Home - more below

Hebrew
Kryon Books - One, Two, Three, The Parables of Kryon & The Journey Home

Hebrew
Kryon Books - Six, Seven, Eight, & The Indigo Children books One & Two

Italian	Finish	Danish	Russian
Kryon Parables & Book One	Book One	Kryon Book One	Indigo Children

Finish Book One & Indigo Children (coming)

Russian The Indigo Children (coming)

Turkish
Kryon Books - One, Two, Three, Six, & Seven - more below & on facing page

Spanish
Three more Kryon Books & The Indigo

Turkish
Indigo Children

Dutch
Indigo Children - Parables of Kryon

Spanish
Book Six
Book Seven
Book Eight
(coming)

66 International Kryon Books
See (www.kryon.com) for more info

French
Kryon Books - One, Two, Three, The Journey Home, & Kryon Book Six

French
Kryon Book - Seven, The Indigo Children, & Eight

Japanese
Kryon Book One & The Indigo

Hungarian
Kryon Books - One, Two, & The Indigo Children

Chinese
Kryon Books - One & Two (3 coming)

German
Kryon Books - One, Two, Three, The Journey Home, & The Parables of Kryon - more below

Turkish
Kryon Book Eight & The Journey Home

Greek
Kryon Books - One. Two, Three

German
Kryon Books - Six, Seven, Eight & Indigo Children Books (2)

Greek
Kryon Books 7 & 8

French
Indigo Book Two

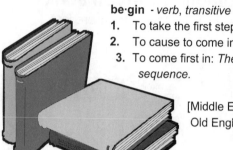

be·gin - *verb, transitive*

1. To take the first step in doing; start.
2. To cause to come into being; originate.
3. To come first in: *The numeral 1 begins the sequence.*

[Middle English *biginnen*, from Old English *beginnan*.]

THE NEW BEGINNING
2002 and Beyond

Kryon Book Nine

Publisher: **The Kryon Writings, Inc.**

1155 Camino Del Mar - #422
Del Mar, California 92014
[www.kryon.com]

Kryon books and tapes can be purchased in
retail stores, or by phone. Credit cards welcome.
(800) 352-6657 or e-mail kryonbooks@kryon.com

Written by Lee Carroll
Editing by Jill Kramer
Copyright © 2002—Lee Carroll
Printed in the United States of America
First Edition—First Printing—July 2002

ISBN# 1-888053-09-7 : $14.98

Table of Contents

Table of Contents . . . continued

From the Writer
"The New Beginning"
Kryon Book Nine

Lee Carroll

Preface

Preface
"The New Beginning"
Kryon Book Nine

From the Writer . . .

Greetings to the readers of the Kryon series, and also to those who are just beginning the Kryon experience. This is the ninth Kryon book, and perhaps the most profound in the series, as far as fitting into the new paradigm of Earth energy is concerned.

For those not familiar with all of the Kryon information, it's important to provide a brief explanation. Kryon is an angelic entity . . . an Earth helper, and not an energy that has ever been a Human on our planet. His purpose (we refer to Kryon with a male pronoun simply for ease of usage) is to explain how things are changing, how things work, and also to honor and celebrate the Human experience. Every message contains instructions and explanations about what is happening. Each parable is about us. Each channelling is uplifting, loving, and helpful.

Many feel that it's just too weird to have a Human Being channel messages from an angelic being. Even though angels have been speaking to Humans all through recorded spiritual history, if you report that you're speaking to entities and angels today, then it somehow puts you into the "spooky group." I often wonder what all this will look like in 100 years. Will it then become sacred and acceptable?

Somehow, historic events, no matter how unrealistic they seem to be, are often completely accepted as spiritual history. Present experiences of the same exact kind will often put you in the loony bin. I guess it's just Human nature to discount anything that doesn't have the stamp of approval of historic significance.

To me, Kryon has given us the blueprint for the exact energy we find ourselves in right now. All of the information leading up to our millennium, plus the recent events of the last year, have been given to us as hints, parables, and especially as numerological metaphoric energies, ready to be interpreted.

Twelve years ago in *Kryon Book One, The End Times,* Kryon told us that we had changed the paradigm of the future on Earth. We had voided the Armageddon as prophesied, and were headed toward the potential of a new consciousness on the planet . . . one of great promise. He indicated that the magnetic grid of Earth would change to accommodate our new abilities (it did—see page 209), and he told us that all the wars in the coming times would tend to be tribal (they seem to be).

Then he said that up to one percent of Earth's population might have to leave to accomplish all this—hardly a feel-good fact (*Kryon Book One,* page 97)! Do you remember this statement on page 101 regarding the future?

". . . many will terminate and return with new powers. Also, the transition to this new age of self-determination and power will be filled with changes. Things will not remain the same for any of you . . ."

He also gave us a date of 1999, telling us that this was a time when we might have an unbalanced leader creating chaos (*Kryon Book One,* page 23). This could have referred to Bosnia, or to what recently happened on 9-11. All of this was given within the first Kryon book more than a decade ago.

Indeed, communism fell over all by itself in the late 1980s, and there was no nuclear war. The time line for the Armageddon as prophesied, passed, and many were aware that we were headed in a new direction—one that nobody had foreseen.

As these books unfolded into the new millennium, Kryon gave us a great deal of personal information and methods for finding the divinity within ourselves. He always indicated that peace on Earth began with individual work, and gave us invitations to change our DNA. Within the books, he told us of the profundity of the 11:11 many times, where Humans had given permission to change the prophesied end. Then came *Book Eight,* the last one, *Passing the Marker.*

As I've indicated before, *Kryon Book Eight* probably gave us more information about what we're experiencing now than any other. Kryon told us that in the coming times there would be "no more fence sitting" (*Book Eight,* page 217). This meant that there could be no more "in-between" attitudes regarding what was happening on the planet—that the old vs. the new would create this.

Many would be "torn off the fence," Kryon said. He also indicated a "pull backwards" of apparent stability and peace, and even predicted the potential of the uprising of Israel in 2000 (*Kryon Book Eight,* page 182). He used the term *spiritual rage* for the first time as well, and also told us that we were in for a battle between the old and new. He said, "Don't be shocked and surprised if that war is not over. In fact, in some cases, the battle has just begun" (*Book Eight,* page 183)!

I think all of us were shocked and dismayed at the events of 9-11 (11-9 to Europeans and many others). For America, this is a new measuring point . . . a place in time where many will see an ending or a beginning. You don't have to be New Age or metaphysical to see the profound energy that this event has created in our society. Many are calling it the "Pearl Harbor" of this generation, and from here on, events in current American history may be looked at as "before and after the 9-11." Just the date itself has now become an icon, an abbreviation of indescribable sorrow, horror, anger, change, and even perhaps, promise.

Although there wasn't one 900-number psychic or drug-store tabloid that predicted it, many have asked if there were hints from Kryon over the last decade that perhaps we were in for this kind of change. I now feel that 9-11 was on our "radar screen" of potential since 1987. Now we're beginning to realize the significance of our 11:11 experience, where we were asked as a group of humanity if we would give permission to move Earth into the next level (as described in *Kryon Books One, Three, Six,* and *Seven*). Could we have helped to create this tragedy? Could we have actually collectively given permission for it? This is a tough question to ask. It's a hard thing to consider . . . that we might all have a spiritual, cellular responsibility for what happened.

In August, a few weeks before the 9-11 tragedy, the Kryon channelling in Vancouver was about world unity (reprinted in Chapter 6 in this book). Listen to what Kryon said about the United States (full transcription on page 169):

"The United States is currently in its greatest learning period. Things cannot remain the same. Honored are those who understand that changes that are important are afoot. The biggest changes in

*all of these places will be the old vs. the new. We're
here to tell you that the Human Being who sits here
and who reads these words is the one who can
change this. It cannot stand as it is. The potential for
the most profound creative changes come in the
year of the three" (2001).*

I personally feel that hints were given all along regarding
the potentials of our 11:11 permission, resulting in the 9-11
event. I have been told that there is no such thing as
predestination. Instead, there are "manifested potentials."
Since there is no future to Spirit (God), and no past, then the
very thought of predictions are moot. Yet prophets cooperate with our idea of linear time, and still give them. They are,
therefore, giving potentials, not absolutes. To Kryon (a
premise given later in this book), everything is in the "now."
What happens is a potential, waiting to be manifested or not,
and is an energy that develops into our reality . . . in our linear
time frame . . . which is based upon a combination of our past
and future intents. We totally control it.

Along with many others, I received the facts below on the
Internet right after the disaster. It's a short list of the obvious
"synchronicity of the 11's." Coincidence? Take a good look.

The synchronicity of the 11's

- The date of the attack: 9-11 (or 11-9) - 9+1+1 = 11
- September 11th is the 254th day of the year: 2+5+4 = 11
- After September 11, there are 111 days left to the end of the year.
- 119 is the area code to Iraq/Iran: 1+1+9 = 11
  (It's also the date in European denotation)

- Twin towers—standing side by side, look like the number 11
- The first plane to hit the towers was Flight 11
- State of New York—the 11th state added to the Union
- New York City—11 letters
- Afghanistan—11 letters
- The Pentagon —11 Letters
- Ramzi Yousef—11 Letters (convicted of orchestrating the bombing attack on the WTC in 1993)
- Flight 11 had 92 passengers on board—9+2 = 11
- Flight 77 had 65 passengers on board—6+5 = 11

Those in metaphysics always look at the numbers . . . always. Consider this: The only two numbers that were defined and explained in *Kryon Book One* in 1989 were **Eleven** and **nine**! The information given was about completion and permission. It's now becoming clear what this all means. Also remember this: The number of the "beast" was given as 666=18=9. Could it be that what we are seeing was also prophesied in veiled ways in scripture? Nine represents completion. Remember that most scripture is written in metaphors. According to author Gregg Braden, even the prophet Isaiah indicated that we had the ability to change the future.[1] I believe we just have.

Kryon has now indicated that through Human free choice, we have opted to advance the process of creating unity on the planet . . . that this tragedy will be seen in history as the turning point for planetary change. In this light, therefore, we see a glimpse of how heretofore unthinkable things might happen—that nations might come together and form coalitions to agree on what "civilization on Earth" will permit and not permit—that millions may have just been "torn off the

[1] *The Isaiah Effect* (decoding the lost science of prayer and prophecy), by Gregg Braden

fence" through spiritual rage, and that they will have to decide one way or the other what energy they are going to join or not join.

I was in a hotel room on September 30, where I watched two interviews at separate times on separate networks. One was with Secretary of State Colin Powell. The other was with the king of Jordan, His Majesty King Abdullah II. During these separate interviews, both men spoke the exact phrase: *"It's time to get off the fence."* I almost fell out of my chair! Here were Kryon's exact words coming to pass in current events. It's not the first time.

The energy we are seeing today is what Kryon spoke of time and time again, and over this last decade it has been published for all to read. Now that this new energy begins, and is of our own creation and free will, it will allow for that elusive phrase to come about . . . the eventual creation of The New Jerusalem. Kryon also said these words over and over: *"As go the Jews, go Earth."* Perhaps we are beginning to see how this all fits?

In Israel in 2000, I stood on stage during my afternoon lecture period and told an audience something that had been given to me by Kryon. I said that nothing productive would happen with their situation until the *"draw to zero."* I honestly didn't know what that phrase indicated. I got many questions and e-mails from Israel afterwards about exactly what those words meant. Did it mean a full war in their region? Did it mean annihilation? I didn't know. It was only after 9-11 that I fully understood that "draw to zero" meant ground zero. Nobody . . . not one person in that meeting, felt that the phrase would eventually relate to an event in Manhattan in the USA. Now it's clear.

If you have *Kryon Book Eight,* go take a look at the ISBN number (the computer code given on the back of the book). ISBN numbers are randomly generated and given to publishers by the book categorization industry to identify published works. The purpose is for inventory control and industry identification. The first part of an ISBN number is the publisher's "master number," and is always the same. The last two fields of the number represent the unique identifier for the book . . . or to a metaphysician, it's the energy of the book. The particular number identifying *Kryon Book Eight, Passing the Marker,* is 11-9. Coincidence? Maybe. But how many coincidences regarding these numbers are needed before we admit that perhaps messages are being given? When I did a final pagination on the book, look what random page the 911 information landed on in this book (182). That reduces numeroligically to 11. Now look at what page it ended on (189). That reduces to a 9!

What's next? We still have free choice. Suddenly, however, we must decide to either wallow in the old ways, or clean up our Earthly act. We have until 2012, according to Kryon. Whatever our energy then, will be our "stamp of intent" for humanity.

I have said it before: Someday I will go home. When I do, I wish to have a meeting with thousands of our family who were lost on 9-11. I want to tell them that what they did made a difference for hundreds of millions on Earth, for their future children, and for the Universe. Then I want to hug each one and sing a hero's song . . . one with lyrics about the 11:11 . . . the day that Humans decided what they really wanted on Earth, and took control to create it.

What's in This Book

This book is organized into sections with respect to what happened before and after the 9-11 experience. Just like the last book was organized before and after the millennium change, this one has a similar configuration, but for entirely different reasons. As in the past, the majority of the book is transcribed from live channellings from all over the world.

Just for Kids: What better way to start a book than with humor and fun? Here is a channelling from the past (formerly thought lost), of Bernie the Bird! This is one of the only live channellings done before children and given especially for kids (but really for all of us). We present a story about Bernie, the bird who was afraid to fly. This was first presented in the *Sedona Journal of Emergence* in 2001. It was originally channelled in 1998 in Dallas, Texas. I'm glad we found it!

Chapters 1 to 7 present the channellings before the event of 9-11.

Chapters 8 to 13 present channellings given after the 9-11 event, up through April of 2002.

Chapter 14 represents real questions from readers, something we originally published in the Kryon on-line magazine, *In The Spirit*.

Chapter 15 is a short article from Jan Tober about expanded consciousness. Did you ever feel you "stuck out" or actually called attention to yourself in a crowd because you vibrated at a higher level? If so, you're not alone. *The Rainbow Filter* may be the solution to becoming "invisible."

Chapter 16 is a real-life story of Fété and Clément, two Lightworkers who tell an amazing story about their escape from Africa. Theirs is a story of trust and faith in Spirit, and a touching tribute to what happens when you use your gifts of intuition and light. This was presented live in Montreal in 2001, at a Kryon conference given by hosts Marc and Martine Vallée.

As I write this Preface, I wish to invite you to our Website. It's a winner, with a brand-new E-magazine that's free to all. Designed and edited by graphic professionals Barbara and Rob Harris, it has become a favorite place for many Lightworkers to visit in the last year. According to our automated Website diagnostics, more than 12,000 unique visits a day are recorded on this newly designed site. In addition to the new magazine, there are channellings (or course) a chat room, an area to search for others in your area of like mind, information about people and books, a full schedule of all of our upcoming events, and much more. Our Website philosophy is a non-invasive one. We don't keep track of who visits; we don't ask for money (ever); we don't take e-mails or names, and there's nothing to join. We just want you to feel free to visit, read, explore, and come away with a loving feeling of family. Simple.

Contributing to the E-magazine regularly will be myself, Jan Tober (co-founder of the Kryon work and my presenting partner in the large seminars worldwide), Todd Ovokaitys, Peggy Phoenix Dubro, our editor Barbara Harris, and many others who are writing articles about science, pets, the law, humor, astrology, crop circles, energy work, and (of course) the Indigo Children. In addition, the magazine offers current and updated questions and answers from Kryon, current news, and a nifty scrapbook of photos taken at all our large seminars.

Go to [**www.kryon.com**] for this experience.

Here is something else some of you may not realize. Do you really have to wait a full year or more to read the latest Kryon channellings? The answer is no.

Every month, a publication called *The Sedona Journal of Emergence*, carries the latest Kryon channelling. So, you can have the best of both worlds: Each month you can read the latest Kryon channelling, and then when a book is published like this one, you can then have the best ones all together in one place, often with my commentary scattered around them.

The Website for *The Sedona Journal of Emergence* is: [**www.sedonajo.com**].

Dear reader, again I am filled with joy to be able to bring you loving information and compassionate words from a wonderful angel named Kryon. Non-evangelistic in nature, this decade-old work is meant to present concepts, not doctrine. It goes beyond organized spirituality and invites you to "peel the onion" of duality to discover the core of divinity in each of you. It is not meant to compete with organized religion, but to offer enhancements and further understanding of the Human spirit. The message is one of empowerment for the Human race and the individual.

Who is that? It's the individual whose eyes are on this page. Thank you for your support.

— Lee Carroll

Live Channelling

"Bernie, the Bird"

Channelled by
Kryon for Children
Dallas, Texas, 1998

Just for Kids
Illustrations by Michael Tyree

"Bernie, the Bird Who Was Afraid to Fly"

Live Channelling
Dallas, Texas, 1998
For Kids of All Ages

From Lee Carroll

For some years, many have asked if it was possible to have Kryon channel for children. Since the whole subject of the Indigo Children was first published in a Kryon book (*Kryon Book Six, Partnering with God*), it only seemed appropriate that Kryon could and would do such a thing.

Therefore, for those who have asked, we present one of two channellings that were recorded and transcribed from Kryon when sitting with children in a Texas Kryon seminar some years ago. In this case, a roomful of kids was present, ranging from three to twelve years old. There were also a couple of infants, and some parents and seniors who wanted to come, too! The presentation starts with my introduction, and moves right into Kryon addressing the children directly. First published in *The Sedona Journal of Emergence* in 2001, It has been buried in a closet all these years, and only recently has it been discovered and transcribed.

Lee Speaking Live . . .

Hi, kids! Welcome to all you children. I notice the youngest is about two months, and the oldest is about 74. Don't raise your hand if you're the older one, I know who you are! [Laughter] This is an unusual occurrence. I've only done this once before, and I imagine that eventually there will be a situation where this particular short channelling will be published someday in a book. If we do one of these a year, however, it will be decades before a book is compiled! [Laughter]

If you're here and you're between 9 and 20, I apologize that you've had to come to the children's channelling, because we all know you're not a kid anymore, don't we [wink, wink]. But this is really for all of us, even though the children are here just for this. [Child in audience screeches. Lee pauses and looks at the child.] Sometimes I feel just like you! But I can't do that! The adults won't let me.

Okay, this is just for the kids. I don't know if you know what channelling is about, but it's not spooky or weird, because even *you* do it sometimes, but you just don't admit it. I know you do! It's when you talk to your angels and you get answers. Some of you even *see* the angels, but you don't tell the adults about it. Here is what's going to happen now: I'm Lee Carroll, That's *my* name, and I'm going to join with an angel named *Kryon*. You might not see the angel or any big wings or stuff like that, but I'm going to shut my eyes, and we're going to have a special message for you from this special angel. You probably heard the name *Kryon* before, because that's why all these grown-ups are sitting here with you. In fact, they brought you here. But this is your time, so pretend they're not in the room. This is all about the special angel, Kryon, and a special message just for you. You don't have to close your eyes when I do. In fact, you don't have to do anything, but I invite you to just watch and listen. When Kryon comes, there may be a story for you . . . let's see what happens.

[The room gets quiet.]

G reetings, dear ones, and the little ones, I am indeed Kryon of Magnetic Service!

Don't let that fool you, because really I'm an angel, and there's something about me that's different for you than for the  adults here. That is because I've never been a Human Being—ever! Although it's hard to explain, that means that I have some of the feelings of a child. That also means that I can understand what you're thinking. It allows me to love you and to help you better!

Before we begin with our story, we're going to talk to the ones who are just a little older than you are, who are also in this room and reading the words on a page that will be printed someday. Be patient for a few moments while we talk to them. Then we will begin our story.

For you dear ones who are not children anymore but can remember a few years ago when you were, I wish to remind you of something: Remember when you were little and might have looked at adults? Perhaps you saw something in the grown-ups that you never talked about. It was because it was too private, but I know what you thought back then. You looked at adults and said to yourselves, *"I don't want to be that way because grown-ups have lost their fun! They don't laugh. They don't know how to play anymore."* So the message for you is this: Don't lose the fun of the child, for the fun of the ones who are small who sit here, is precious! It's the catalyst for enlightenment! It can be retained all of your lives. You can still play! It's a precious time for you, but it's a time when you're able to forget that fun, too. It's your choice.

There's a saying adults use that goes like this: "When I was a child, I spoke and thought as a child, but when I grew up, I put away childish things." Now we say to you, "Don't put the child away! Hold the fun that will always be there and is a secret to finding the angel that is invisible within you."

Now we come to the little ones. I speak to you now as an angel, and I have a message that even the grown-ups have never heard before. Did you know, kids, that angels never grow up? It's the truth! They're always the same age. Grown-ups see the big angels and they think they're grown-up angels, but they never are. They're always children in big bodies. They're always the same age. It's kind of a secret, but I think you know all about it, don't you? We have something else to tell you, and it's this: There's an angel with you all of the time. Did you know that? You might say, "I've never seen my angel. What do you mean, Kryon?" I'll tell you.

I know a story about a little creature who also had that same problem. He used to say, "I've never seen something, so how can I know it's there?" It's a story about unseen things that's just for you. This angel, Kryon, who is speaking to you right now, who is also a *child*, knows how to tell these stories with the help of my partner, Lee, who also never grew up! [Laughter]

We'd like to tell you the story about Bernie the bird. Now, Bernie the bird was the bird who was afraid to fly. We want to tell you the story of how this happened because it's a marvelous story, told over and over in bird-land. All the birds remember Bernie the bird, who was afraid to fly.

Bernie grew up in an extremely high nest. You might be aware of how birds are taught to fly. It's kind of spectacular, but kind of scary, too. Because Mom and Dad bird, when the children birds are ready, gently push them out of the nest when they're not looking! Did you know that? The birds fall naturally, but real soon they kind of know that they have to spread their wings, start flapping, and when they do, suddenly the wind will lift them, and up they go! It's kind of hard to fall before they spread their wings to fly, but Mom and Dad birdies can't train them how to fly in the nest. Think about it! There isn't much flying done in a small nest!

Well, Bernie didn't want anything to do with this process. Bernie saw his sister when she was pushed out of the nest one early morning and watched her fall down, down, down, down. At the last possible second, his sister spread her wings and flapped like crazy. Finally, she flew! But it seemed to Bernie that she almost hit the ground before she knew what to do, and Bernie got scared. He didn't want anything to do with flying! Bernie said, "There's no reason I should have to do this flying thing. There's something wrong with this whole system."

Bernie convinced his brother Bobbie that the whole flying thing was stupid. Bobbie didn't want anything to do with training to fly either, so he went to his mom to tell her about it. Bobbie announced that he didn't want to fly because he was afraid, and really he didn't need to, since the nest was kind of cool and he wanted to stay there. Mom took a long look at him and immediately pushed him out of the nest! Bobbie fell down, down, and right at the end, he spread his wings and flapped and flapped, and up he went.

Bernie saw all of this. He was the youngest, having been hatched at least two minutes after everyone else, and he knew he was next. He thought to himself, *I don't care if my sister and brother went through it. Nobody is going to push me out of this nest because I don't have to fly. This is not for me!* Bernie had to come up with a plan.

One night when everyone was sleeping, Bernie found a string. It was something that Dad had brought into the nest to help support it. Sometimes in building a nest, all kinds of things combine to make the nest strong, and there was a string buried within the sticks and straw that made the nest. Bernie decided to tie this string to his leg, and the other end to a stable part of the nest so that if his mom pushed him out when he didn't expect it, he would only fall about nine inches and be saved from falling. [Children laugh] Hey, it was a good plan!

The problem was that Bernie didn't go to any bird scout camp, so he didn't really know how to tie bird knots! He did his best, however, and tied a knot he thought would work and hid it carefully by always facing away from his mom when she was around. Sure enough, the very next night when he was sleeping, his mom pushed him out of the nest!

It worked! Over he went, and the string held. There Bernie was, hanging nine inches below in the air. It was kind of dark, and Mom, thinking that Bernie was below, flapping and learning to fly, went back to sleep. Bernie hung there silently, thinking how smart he was. He crawled up the string with his beak and nestled back into his warm 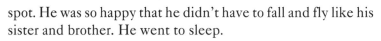 spot. He was so happy that he didn't have to fall and fly like his sister and brother. He went to sleep.

The next morning when his mom woke up, she saw Bernie there in their nest—string and all, and said to him, "Bernie! What are you doing here?" She pointed (with her beak) to the string, which Bernie had forgotten to take off his leg, and she was upset. "I guess it's time to have Dad take over!" she exclaimed. "He's going to talk to you about this whole thing."

Bernie thought to himself, *Stupid me! I forgot to take off the string! Now Dad's going to get involved. Drat!*

Dad, indeed, came back to the nest in due time. He was a very large bird with lots of feathers. Bernie was kind of afraid of his father due to his size. But Dad was a loving father and asked Bernie, "Bernie, what's up? All of the birds fly. Just look around here. Everyone is flying. It's a bird-thing, and you have to learn! Why don't you want to fly? Why?"

Bernie thought for a moment. "I'm afraid, Dad."

"Why are you afraid?" his father asked Bernie. "Look, your sister, your brother, me, your mom . . . we all fly. Take a look around. Your friends fly . . . birds fly, Bernie. You're a bird."

"I'm afraid, Dad, because there's nothing there! You talk about the air that's supposed to lift up our wings. It's invisible. It almost doesn't work, either. Did you see my brother and my sister when they fell? They almost didn't make it!"

His father thought for a moment. "Even though you can't see the air, Bernie, it will go under your wings. All you have to do is put your wings out on the way down, and the air will scoop you up. That's how we're all flying. It's invisible, but it's there."

"This is just magic," Bernie said. "You can't see air. You can't tell me there's air, because you can't see it. It's not there. Maybe the magic works for you and Mom and my brother and my sister, but I've got to see this before I'll believe it. Air is invisible. How do I know you're not fooling me? I don't know how you fly, but there's no such thing as air because I can't see it."

Bernie paused and then continued: "Dad, I've got this figured out. Look, why do I have to fly? I would like to start a new breed of bird, called *Walking Bird*." [Laughter] "Why do I need to be like all the rest? I'll have a nice life. I'll walk down the tree, I'll find the worm, and I'll walk back up the tree. I'll have a nice life. I'll find a Walking-Bird wife somewhere. We'll have Walking-Bird children. A new breed will be born. Someday they'll look back and say, 'This was the beginning of the great breed called *Walking Bird*.'"

Bernie's father looked at him for a very long time. He muttered under his breath, "Walking Bird?" He rolled his eyes. "Okay, Bernie, I can tell it's time to have Sigg see you."

"Who's Sigg?" Bernie asked a bit hesitantly.

"Well, that's the flock's bird, brain-doctor." [Laughter] "We're going to have to send Sigg to see you. But, Bernie, when the bird, brain-doctor comes, he's very sensitive. Don't call him *birdbrain* doctor." [Laughter] "Be sure you call him, The Bird, Brain-Doctor. No doctor wants to be called a birdbrain. [Laughter]

"Dad, it doesn't matter what Dr. Sigg tells me. Nobody can convince me that air is real. I can't see it."

Then it happened. Late that night when Bernie was asleep, his mother silently came to him and slowly gnawed through the string that he still wore for safety. Then she pushed him out of the nest! Things happened very fast. He fell and he fell, and it was a horrible experience! He was very frightened. He could feel himself frozen with fear. He watched the bark of the tree next to him race by, and he saw the ground race up. He thought to himself, *I have to spread my wings, but I don't believe in the air. I can't believe it because it's not real; I can't see it. I can't do this!*

Sure enough, he didn't spread his wings. He was headed right into the ground and he knew he was going to go in beak-first and he was going to end up like a stick in the ground . . . with his legs sticking up in the air! He was going to end up petrified in the ground, beak-down. Nobody would be able to get him out, and he would be like a statue in the park. He knew what birds did to Human statues, and could only wonder what Humans would do with a bird statue! Suddenly Bernie woke up. It was all a dream! [Laughter] What a nightmare that was!

Pant, pant . . .

In the morning, Bernie woke up as usual. Sure enough, there was the bird, brain-doctor. Sigg was there on schedule.

"Good morning, Bernie," said Sigg.

"Good morning, Mr. Birdbrain Doctor."

"That's Bird, Brain-Doctor," said Sigg. "Don't forget it, son."

"Okay, Dr. Birdbrain."

"Bernie!" The doctor exclaimed!

"I'm sorry, I'm sorry," said Bernie . . . but he wasn't. [Children laugh]

"Bernie, what are you afraid of?" the doctor asked sincerely.

Bernie went through it again. "I just can't believe in air. I can't see it, either. I know all of you are flying . . . flap, flap, flap. . . . Bernie was making fun of flying. But it's just not good for me because I've gotta see it! Mr. Birdbrain Doctor . . . sir."

Sigg frowned at Bernie again for the purposeful slip in speech. Bernie was having fun. He knew that Dr. Sigg didn't like to be called *birdbrain doctor*, yet every time he addressed him, he said "Birdbrain Doctor, *sir*." That kind of made it okay.

Sigg said to Bernie, " Bernie, you're afraid because you can't see the air. But what are you really afraid of?"

"Well, Doctor Birdbrain, sir, I'm afraid of falling and killing myself on the ground, which seems to race up very rapidly when birds fall out of nests. I'm afraid!" Bernie thought it was a stupid question, and he kind of answered it stupidly, too.

"What is it, exactly, that makes a bird fall?" Sigg asked his young student.

"Well, um, I suppose gravity does." Bernie said.

"Hmmm. Gravity." Sigg paused. "You know, Bernie, you can't really see gravity now, can you?"

Bernie thought a moment. "Well, no. No, I can't see gravity."

"But you believe in gravity, Bernie? Show me gravity."

Bernie thought, then spoke. "Well, I can show you gravity. If I leap out of the nest, I'll fall to my death. Ha ha! That's gravity." Bernie was proud that he had answered the difficult question.

"That's exactly right!" said the doctor. You can prove it exists as soon as you leap out of the nest. Bernie, you can also prove air exists when you leap out of the nest, because it's there just like gravity. You can't see it, but it really is there."

Bernie didn't like the way this conversation was going. Sigg, on the other hand, had finished his counseling session and then left . . . taking flight as he did. Instead of leaping forward and flying up, Sigg yelled at Bernie as he jumped out of the nest, straight down, seeming to fall.

"Gravity, Bernie!" yelled Sigg as he fell straight down. "Air, Bernie!" said Sigg as he straightened out with his wings in full extension. Then he gently flew away. You could hear the birdbrain doctor singing as he left . . . "Both are invisible… both are real."

Bernie was still for a long time. He thought and he thought. Finally he said, "You know, the bird, brain-doctor is right. Just because I can't really see it doesn't mean it's not there. Gravity is always there. Perhaps air is, too. That's what I'm really afraid of. I really won't know until I try."

Sigg, the Bird, brain-doctor, had pointed out to Bernie that it was interesting that there was something you couldn't see, like gravity, but that you knew it was there since you could die from falling. But he had pointed out that Bernie couldn't believe in something that was wonderful like flight, using invisible air. Bernie realized that he was really afraid of gravity! Perhaps invisible air would be something like invisible gravity, but would it save him? Bernie decided that tomorrow he was going to fly. He was going to be brave, and he told all the birds in the forest and the other nests. He told all the bird children who were watching, "I'm gonna do it! I'm gonna do it!"

The next morning, Bernie stood on the edge of the nest. Many were gathered, since the whole nest population knew of Bernie's problem. It seemed that anytime the bird, brain-doctor called on any bird, the whole group knew. That's a story for another time.

Bernie stood tall. He again announced to everyone that it was time to trust in the unseen thing called AIR! He spoke for a long time about trusting and about invisible things, and then with great courage and ceremony, he launched himself into thin air and began the plunge from the nest!

Bernie immediately found himself dangling nine inches from the nest. He had forgotten to untie the string! [Laughter] Bernie was very embarrassed and humiliated. The entire forest was laughing! Even the non-birds were laughing. Mice and squirrels, too! He could hear the forest echoing with the words, *"Walking bird . . . the great walking bird!"* Then Bernie knew that everything he had said had been spread around. He had to make this right.

He climbed back up the string, gnawed his way through it, took another breath of that invisible thing called air, and looked around. The forest was again quiet. Baby birds don't do this on their own, you know. They're normally surprised when sleeping and get thrown out when they don't expect it. They never do it by themselves. Somehow the other birds knew they were seeing something different. Somehow the adults remembered what it was like the first time. Bernie, the reluctant flyer, founder of the new breed called *"Walking Bird,"* was about to fling himself out of the nest . . . this time without the string.

Down he went. Fear took over right away as Bernie plummeted toward the ground. This was no dream. This time it was real! As Bernie watched the bark of the tree go flying by, and the ground came racing up toward him, he heard an internal voice saying, *Wings! Wings! Put out your wings!*

"I'm frightened. I'm scared!" Bernie yelled in his mind. Then finally, just like his sister and his brother had, at the last moment he put out those little stubby wings that had never been used and started flapping. Sure enough, that invisible support system called air took over. The magic of flight that had been good for his mother and father and his sister and brother took over. He felt the lift, and up he went!

Bernie couldn't get enough of it. He flew all day long. He flew and he flew. He flew as high as he could until his wings got tired, and then he celebrated the unseen thing that they all called AIR. He sailed around the trees and yelled, "Look I'm flying!" As though no bird had ever done it before! They all applauded Bernie—not because he was flying, but for the courage of the bird who had done it himself.

It's a simple story, isn't it? It's kind of fun, thinking about Bernie and his trust in the unseen. We're going to tell you now what this really means to all of you. Some of you already know, don't you? Little ones, there is an angel with you right now. There is an angel that was born with you, and you can talk to that angel anytime you want. It's a nice angel, and one who loves you. It has the mind of a child and even knows how you think. It's an angel who enjoys playing with the toys that you play with, and one who will grow with you as you grow. It's one who will always be available, and who can help you at any time.

Now, some of you might say, "I don't see any angel!" That's because it's unseen, just like the air was unseen for Bernie. We can also tell you that that this unseen angel will lift you up, even when you're in trouble, even when you're in sorrow and things aren't going just right. This is an angel who supports you with unseen energy, even when you're falling into the darkness of being afraid. We want you to remember this, because this child angel will be with you for life. It's beautiful. It's unseen, but just like Bernie found out, it's very, very real.

Perhaps you wish to know more about your angel? Just ask it! Even though you might not be able to see or hear the angel like a real person, the emotion of the love and friendship will be the "real" thing that proves that it's here!

Are you an adult here? Where did the child angel go? Is it still with you, or did you discard it as you grew up? Did it laugh at the story of Bernie? Perhaps it's time to find it, for it never left. It's yours for life, and beckons you to come out and play. Truly, then, this is the story for the adult, for it's the fear the adult has, not the child. It's the fear of one who doesn't want to leave the nest of intellect and seeming reality, in order to fly to the heights of being a child again . . . of playing again, and of the joy of believing in the unseen.

And so it is!   *Kryon*

Live Channelling

"The Catalyst for Miracles"

Channelled in
Chicago, Illinois
September 2000

Chapter One

"The Catalyst for Miracles"
The Beginning of Interdimensional Understanding

Live Channelling
Chicago, Illinois

*This live channelling has been edited with additional
words and thoughts to allow clarification and better
understanding of the written word.*

Greetings, dear ones, I *am* Kryon of Magnetic Service. We wish to hold the preciousness of this energy right now. In these precious moments, an entourage fills this area—one just large enough to encompass all the Humans who have come here through their intent in their disguised divinity. Surrounded indeed by a bubble of love, this place is precious! And the preciousness that is felt is due completely to those who are here. We have said this before: It is a reunion of souls—souls who you feel are singular, but who we know are many. For even as you sit in the chair hearing or reading this, there are "many of the one," yet you consider yourself as singular. It is part of the deception, dear Human. Dear ones, the energy that is being presented here is one where we indeed understand and feel the preciousness of family.

There is a tremendous remembrance when you get to the other side of the veil and experience the energy of who you actually are. There is the realization that you are part of the Ark of the Covenant, the Holy Grail, and the spiritual pieces that have been "missing," as the divine and mysterious parts of the Universe. All is not what it seems. This has been the message of Kryon since the beginning—finding the divinity inside. It has been my message all along, and the irony is that the children already know it! We speak of the souls of the Indigos who are "here," but not yet born [evidently Kryon knows of some pregnancies in the audience, and is addressing the mother(s) to be, including those reading this*]. Well, let me tell you, these children know what is taking place now. These precious souls, some of whom may represent a great challenge for the parents, come in by contract. Whatever happens next is by contract. You know who they are, and they know you. Mother, you are about to meet an old friend. Blessed is this day. Remember these words.

Dear ones, in these last months, we have spoken to you about the interdimensionality of Spirit. We have told you that the energy of this year [2000] is the beginning of a 12-year cycle, and we have invited you to discover the interdimensionality that is at hand. The grids have been shifted in such a way that at the cellular level, pieces and parts of who you are have been enabled. This enablement is such that there can now be an understanding of the interdimensional. And where there is understanding, there is action.

"What kind of action, Kryon?" you might ask. It's an action where individual Human Beings decide to raise themselves up from where they always were, to a level where they are peaceful with their lives—where they take and understand the responsibility for everything that is taking place around them, and where they are not afraid of the future. For now, they may stand tall and say, *"I am here as a piece of God, and while I'm on Earth, I will be a lighthouse and an anchor. I will be a source of refuge for my friends in trouble. I will be a peaceful place in a time of turmoil. I will be filled with solutions instead of challenge. I will be handling many things at the*

same time that others would never touch, for they seemed too difficult. I will have a 'Divinity overlay.' I'll be a lighthouse in the storm of life!' And that's what the work is about.

Dear *lighthouses*, there are many of you in the room. You know whom I speak to now, do you not? For you know of the principles here. This is a teaching session. It always is, and yet these are times when we'd like to sit and just love you. We would like to touch you in various places so you'll know we are here—starting with the head and the shoulders. We'd love to press upon you in a way that you'll know we are here. By the time you leave your chair, you'll know that Spirit was here.

There are those who would say that this is not real. They would say, *"It cannot be real. Spirit cannot do this. God doesn't do this."* Well, they are experiencing a 4D-reality block. God does this daily! In addition, God can do this in any place you wish. You don't have to come to a meeting like this, and you don't have to sit in front of authors or channels. You don't have to sit in front of healers and lecturers to have this energy presented to you. You can go into the smallest places in your house, and you can have divinity touch you! You can have a healing within your cellular structure because the angel in there is powerful indeed! Not one of you is any more powerful than any other. You are all equal—all divine. You are all spectacular in your potentials . . . that's the message of Kryon.

Let the teaching begin. The concepts we present this evening are not new. Some of them have been given before, even recently, but none of them have been transcribed. And so it is that we have chosen this meeting for the transcription. It is provided to give you information about part of you that you are not truly aware of. It's an interdimensional part of you, and one that is not fully understood for its potentials.

It's time to talk about how the Human Being works, where 4D touches multiple D. In the past, we have told you, dear ones, about the three-in-one, and we're going to give you information this day regarding some of the attributes of this threesome. Some of you have called it the *trilogy*, others have called it the *trinity*, and some have simply referred to it as the three-in-one. But all descriptions refer to the three energies that make up the whole Human.

We speak now of the *three*, and we have spoken of the number three before. We invite you to look at the three, which, of course, makes up a fourth of the twelve. It is no accident that there are three energy portions of the Human Being that we wish to speak of, for the three represents action. It is also a catalyst, for where the three exists, there is the potential for more. Although some of you may not understand this, there are others that understand it fully. The three-in-one is an interdimensional concept, but one where you live it in 4D.

"What are you talking about, Kryon?" We're talking about something that literally is part of the fabric of the belief systems around the planet, some of which are identified, and some referred to only metaphorically. We speak now of the three energies that are vastly different, that make up every single Human Being. We wish to speak of what some have called the Father, the Son, and the Spirit. We have renamed them before. We have instead called them the *adult*, the *child*, and the *Higher-Self*. So that is the nomenclature, the kinds of terms that we will use in this lesson. There is profound teaching around these three energies, and we are going to combine them tonight in a synopsis, as my partner would say. It is an overview—a great simplification of the energies of these three. We give them to you so that you will understand them, and also so that we can present some of the important aspects of what they represent. There are those here who need to hear this!

There is indeed structure here, and it needs to exist within the Human psyche. There is indeed divinity within the three, and there is indeed duality. All of these things come together in what we have called the three-in-one. Notice we call this the *three-in-one*, for none is more important than any other. Yet they have attributes of importance for your path at the moment, and one needs more explanation right now.

The Adult

Let us start by giving you the *adult*, or the father, as some of you have said—one of the three. Here are some attributes of the adult that you should hear. What is the adult part of the energy in the Human body responsible for? As you walk around, what can you expect from the adult portion? I'll give you some information. It is the father—the adult part of you that remembers. It is the adult part of you that has experienced lifetime after lifetime—the hardships, the karma, the heaviness. That's the part that awakens in spiritual ways. We sit in front of an awakening group of family members. We sit in front of those, dear ones, whom we know the names of! There are some of you only now beginning to remember that this is real and that it is true, for you are beginning to "feel" us.

It's the adult part that does the remembering and the *spiritual awakening*. The adult part is the structured part; it's the experienced part in this respect, which awakens. It is the adult part that deals with the contract [spiritual contract]. We have spoken of this before. The contract is the highest metaphor we can use for what the actuality of the situation represents. Notice in the word *contract* even in your language, it implies more than one signature. It is an agreement between at least two entities. Your main contract is to simply exist as a Human Being on the planet. We have told you before that the contracts, which are individual, have been changed within this new energy—indeed, they have been voided—and now what you are doing is building new ones. Some of you shake with vibratory energy.

You wonder what is going on in your life. The track in front of you is blank, and it's the adult who sees the potential and knows about contracts.

Responsibility is the next one. The adult energy is responsible. It's responsibility for recognizing that you planned everything that has happened, dear ones! We have told you this again and again. There are those here . . . (pause) . . . blessed be the angel disguised as the Human Being who sits in the chair hearing and reading, who has found what the gift of death is about! [Resuming] There are those here, and there are more than one, who have looked backwards into the sorrow of their lives and recognized the divineness of what took place. Well, we have some information for you today. Here is a gift for you, and perhaps you already knew this: The entity that left, the one that there was so much sorrow around, is with you for your entire life! Do you remember? If you felt the presence of this dear one, you're right. It was not an illusion! For so often the contracts of life do not end with Human death. They continue right on through your own life. The adult, at the interdimensional level, understands this. We will have more information shortly about how this actually works.

Whom have you lost who's important to you? Do you ever feel them around you? Do you think that it's your vivid imagination? It's not. Open your hearts to this interdimensional fact. Open your intuition to know that these feelings are real. These loved ones are indeed with you. They look down from a place slightly above your head—literally, slightly to the left. They are now part of you—part of your thought processes—and some of them are saying, "I love you." Some of them are saying, "Congratulations." Some of them are in awe of who you've become. Maybe you had to hear this tonight, as strange as it may sound to some Humans. Can we prove it? No. In your 4D, it's impossible to prove. And, by the way, we wouldn't have it any other way. For to prove it takes the incredible love and power away from it! It must be perceived beyond physics, and owned at the cellular level. Then it's real. It's like love—try to prove it. You can't. You can only own it and experience it, and know personally that it is real. That makes love interdimensional, too.

The adult is also responsible for ritual decision making—what we have called *vows* in the past. Briefly, as we have told you before, you are often in this newly awakened state [in the new energy] becoming aware of the shaman within you, represented within the lifetimes of the monks, nuns, and priests that you were. We have many of those in the room. We have told you before that it is the adult who makes those decisions to marry God, to focus on God and give a vow of celibacy—a vow to be alone, to be poor, to give away self-worth. It's the adult who does that. In all appropriateness, the adult makes those decisions.

Those are four attributes: awakening, contract, responsibility, and vows—four out of many that you will see as attributes of the adult, and one of the three energies of the Human Being. Now you can analyze those, and it will show you that they are all about structure. If you are a child in the room, and there actually are many here, you might say, *"That's the real boring part, isn't it?"* [Laughter]

Metaphor of the Bucket

We're going to give you the metaphor of the bucket, which represents the relationship between the three. Now you will see the whole picture, even before we have told you the rest. It's important for you to see the bucket. It is a pail, like a child's pail at the beach. And the actual part of the bucket that holds water is the *adult*, the *father* part, the *structure*. It allows for everything else to exist. It is the structure of the pail.

What is inside the pail is the *son,* or the *child* energy. It's water! And you'll notice that the structure of the pail contains the water so it will not flow out or leak. Instead, it is contained in a logical way, mathematically. The pail contains the water in such a way that it does not spill. It holds it steady. It provides for a way for the water to exist, does it not?

"What about the spiritual part?" you might ask. *"What about the Higher-Self? What part of the pail is that?"* That's the giant hand that holds it! So you have the structure, you have the substance, and you have sparks. Father, Son, Spirit—Adult, Child, Higher-Self—Structure, Substance, and Sparks. [Chuckle]

Let's talk about the *sparks* within the three-in-one. You might say, *"Well, Kryon the sparks have got to be the most important part, right? After all, that's the part we are studying today."* There is no most important part. There are parts that you have to know more about than others, and perhaps this is one. The Higher-Self is one of the subjects that is most commonly taught within the Kryon entourage energy. We speak about the *sparks* all the time, but tonight we are placing the spotlight on something else you must know about. But first, let us get past the *sparks*.

The Higher-Self

We will also give you four attributes of the Spirit, or the Higher-Self, although there are many. One is the *link to God*—the link to Spirit. We have told you this before, and you know this. For one of the attributes of the Higher-Self is within the vessel [Lee points to his body]. It is the vessel that links the Human Being to the Angelic Self. It is why you're here. There are not many of you who came to find out about the adult today. There aren't many of you who even came to find out about the substance—the child within, today. No, almost all of you want to know about the sparks, don't you? And the irony is that the sparks are who you really are when you're not here! No wonder you're interested.

I've told you this before, Lightworker—lighthouse: No matter what your age, no matter what you believe, no matter what your path is, no matter who you think you are, or if you happen to believe what is happening is real or not, I will see *all* of you again. A couple of you will say, *"Oh, no, you won't, I'm not coming back!"* [Laughter with Kryon] Remember that, dear one, when I stand in front of you along with the others, and your glorious colors shine. Remember what you said in all innocence when we congratulate you and welcome you back home. Remember that when you see throngs of applauding family [metaphorically], when you feel the love through the colors that we will show you, when you hear the colors that we will give you, and when we will say, "Welcome home." Remember that when you decide, with the mind of God, to return as fast as you can to be part of the new Earth.

I have seen you many times before, when you entered that great hall of honor and sang your name in light to us. What a celebration! Do you have any idea what that is like? You can't remember. If you knew what it was like, so many of you would leave now! [Kryon chuckle] This is the work, dear ones. This Earthly Human experience *is* the work. But you knew that, didn't you?

It's the spark that you came for today. We know that—the link to God is your longing. It's also the attribute that allows the Human Being to find incredible self-worth. It's the link to God that does that. We also know that within the profound challenges in this room, self-worth is one of them. It's always that way with the Lightworkers . . . it's from too many years on your knees, with your noses in front of altars!

You might ask, *"How am I going to get that link to work? I'm not one who gets up in the morning and looks in the mirror and sees the divine one inside me. I often see a Human in trouble, or one who is aging. How can I get the link? How can I understand this? Where is the self-*

worth answer?" I'll give you the catalyst for the self-worth issue in the next item of the single-trilogy explanation. But for now, let us say that although they are intermingled in some ways, the three: father, child, and Spirit, have separate, independent attributes. The self-worth challenge is one of them that we are giving you regarding the part of the Human called the Higher-Self. If you ever wondered which one was responsible for that inner longing, that's it.

Here's another one: true, sacred, divine *peace*—peace that has no understanding. When that phrase is given to you, it means this: How can you be peaceful when there's turmoil around you? It is through the divine; it is through the spark. It's the hand holding the pail. It's the Higher-Self. It's the angel with your name. It doesn't matter what the situation is, we have promised you peace where there usually is no peace—peace over things that have no seeming solution. Peace that allows you to stand among all of the turmoil and all of the drama, yet feel the divinity of God, knowing full well who you are. Yes, that's the work of the Higher-Self.

Oh, there's more: We have discussed the link to God, self-worth, and divine peace. The fourth one would be what we would call *miracles*—consciousness over matter—divine healing—life extension, and putting the body back together when nothing else could. I want to stop right here and tell you something: We cannot discuss these things, dear ones, without weeping in front of you, with the potentials that sit in the chairs before us pretending to be Humans, for we know why you've come. Reader, know this: You are included in this audience. Do you not understand that in the "now" we include you, also? Do you think that you are reading something that happened? No! You are reading about an energy that *is* happening!

We know of the situations in some of your lives, and we say to you, there is nothing incurable on Earth—*nothing incurable.*

It's archaic, your thought system of what might cure you, never understanding the elegance of the divine within. Did you know that you can address certain cells of your body to awaken? Did you know that your intent can bring about miraculous healing? Did you know that you can heal disease—live longer? You want to know how? It comes within the discussion of the third piece, which I'm about to tell you about in a moment. But the sparks—the Higher-Self—is where it actually physically happens.

Here is something for the transcription, something we have said before but which has never been made public. This is the year of discovery. Within Human cellular structure, you are going to find things that you never thought were there. There are those who study biology who have told you that you have a finite number of certain kinds of cells in your body, specifically within the brain. They tell you that you are born with a certain number of nerve cells, and they start dying immediately. [Chuckle] What a thought! How's that for rejuvenation, Human Being? Does that make sense to you? Well, if you're one of those who doubted it, you're right. There is a mechanism in the Human body that gives an allowance for new embryonic-type growth of cells throughout your life . . . all through your life. Your DNA is programmed for this growth to exist in the body, an attribute that you have not yet discovered but which there is potential for this year [the discovery of, that is].

These are cells with no purpose—they're waiting for purpose. You have indicated in the past that they are embryonic, and they are what you have called *stem cells*. From them come stem cells of whatever purpose, whether they are to become part of your heart cells, brain cells (nerve), muscles, bones, immune system, or even thymus. There they sit, pristine, undeveloped, and hiding. What we are telling you is this: I'm explaining to you how miracles occur. There are parts and pieces of your body that are waiting for intent. They are waiting for an energy called compassion to awaken them and to grow into cells that you designed to be there. Science will look for chemistry to activate them, but the real catalyst is intent (consciousness).

Can you create brain cells? Oh, yes, you can. Can you create bone cells? Oh, yes, you can. Do you want to know about miraculous healings on Earth, congenital defects that somehow changed, bone tissue that grew that *never should have*, nerves that reconnected themselves, and things you never thought possible? That is the stem cell that is responding to the intent of the Human Being. You have called it the divine. That is the mechanism. Your science will discover it, potentially, this year— *adult* stem cells that are alive and ready to develop. For each stem cell that develops, there is another one that will become a stem cell. You cannot use them up. To some of you, this will sound foreign, and we are telling you to look to your science, for this will be validated shortly. I give you this because it is so. And it is good news, is it not?

There is a strong metaphor for what is happening to your biology and consciousness. You are moving from a paradigm that involves your *immune* system to a paradigm that now involves the *thymus*. What did I just say? I'll tell you: The immune system identifies the enemy and *fights* it. The thymus identifies the enemy and *harmonizes* with it. From fight to harmony, that is the theme of this next 12-year period. It involves consciousness, biology, politics, and even physics. Watch for harmony in all fields of science—things that will start making sense and dovetailing one with another.

The Child

We have waited to give you the last of the three. We are going to give you up to six attributes of this one. It is not the most important one, for they are all important, and they all must be balanced even within themselves. This one, however, is the least understood—the child. Not physically—we're not talking about the children here. We're talking about the child energy within the Human—one of the trilogy items, the Son, inside. That's what we're talking about.

I'd like to tell you where some of the most amazing power of your life resides. Many would not ever have attributed some of these things to the child energy. The water in the pail can go anywhere. It wants to get out, doesn't it? If the pail has a leak, the water absolutely will pour out and be wasted, so it must be structured and surrounded by a solid.

It is the fluid child, however, that has the *imagination*. The adult is structured. The adult has the authority, but it is the child with the imagination. The Angel, as part of the Higher-Self, has the sparks. It has its own job, and it has the miracles. It doesn't have the imagination that the child does. That belongs to you, the Human Being. It is part of the balance between the Father, the Son, and the Spirit—all of which are God and that's *you*. Imagination—anything is possible to the child within you. It is when the structure of bucket and the pail says, "You have to stay inside," that the imagination of the child says, "But I don't want to! I don't want to!"

It is the child in you that is responsible for *joy*. You thought maybe that came from the angel? I'll tell you something: These two of the trilogy are intertwined, but it is the child within that has to give intent for joy to happen. Then the divinity rushes in to complement it. It's the child inside you that asks for joy. It's the child in you that wants to laugh. That's all part of playing.

Dear Lightworker: If you walk around with a sour face, you don't know about this attribute. If you want to know the catalyst to divinity, I'm giving you a secret now. If you want to activate some of those parts of the sparks, the child has it! Get to know the child, for the child has the joy, and the child has the humor. It's the child part of you that makes the lighthouse smile ... and there are so many serious lighthouses! [Laughter] We weep with the potentials of those in front of us, those family members who can leave from this place different from how they came in. We weep in joy!

Here's the third one: *suspension of belief.* The child doesn't have a belief system. Fantasy is rampant. Anything is possible— boundless possibilities—go anywhere, do anything. This is the catalyst to a miracle. It is the unstructured and innocent child within that asks, "Why not?" When you talk about healing and getting rid of the things in your body that are aging you, it's the child inside that asks, "Sure, why not?" The adult that carries the pail is the one who says, "You don't know how things work, that's why." And it's the balance between the two, which allows for the child's energy of the *why not,* to rise to the surface and create the activity that the sparks of the Higher-Self can give you.

Here's the fourth one: *dependency.* Without the pail and without the structure, the child would be nothing. It would run all over the ground without coherence. There would be no substance in the pail. It would simply run away, evaporate, and become nothing. The adult is there to contain it in love and perfection. The child reaches its hands up to the adult willingly, because it knows that the adult has the structure and safety. That's where the love comes from; that's where internal parenting comes from. It is the balance between the child and the adult, where they both ask for one another. Did you know that? It's not where the adult beats the child into submission. It's not when the adult tells the child to be quiet, since they can't understand serious things. The pail does not rule the substance . . . it takes care of it! The adult takes the child in and hugs it and nourishes it. It is the child who accepts this and says, "I need this structure." It is a marriage for life. How many of you really have married the child?

I'll give you a surprising attribute: The child features *intuition* and *wisdom*. Did you think those would be attributes of the child? Wouldn't they be attributes of the adult? No. Adult is structure, but the wisdom comes from the flexible child inside, and I'll tell you why. Because it is the child who has the emotions! It is the child who will let the emotions become part of you and part of the compassion that we have talked about—that interdimensional trigger that causes miracles.

It is the child within you that develops the emotions of joy that turn into compassion. Maybe you didn't think of that when you were on your knees in trouble. Maybe you didn't think of that when things got real serious—when you needed help—when you didn't know what to do. Maybe you didn't think of the inner child during those times. Perhaps you didn't feel joyful? Of course you didn't! Let me tell you: That's why we're here tonight—to remind you that this child part is there, and it's the catalyst to the sparks. The quickest way to the Higher-Self is through the child. We have told you many times to try and celebrate the challenge! Why? To lift yourselves into the joy that only the child can bring, in order to start the communication to the *sparks!*

Adults, listen to this: You're providing structure and love for an energy of substance [the child], which is the catalyst for the Higher-Self's activation. They marry, they're together, and they've got to be balanced. Did you ever think you'd know that the wisdom would come from the child energy? It does. And so whereas the adult has the awakening energy that we described, it is the child with the substance to do something about it.

So, this might now explain to you, why some of the most serious Lightworkers have so little to show for their efforts. They often go into victim mode, as so little is manifested in their lives. They become those whom God pushes and pulls around, and they endure great spiritual drama. We celebrate them, too, but we ache for them to find the joy they deserve. We ache for them to discover the next item.

And the sixth one? Oh, it may sound like some of the others, but for the child there are *no fences*. Everything is possible. More than a suspension of belief, when the child looks over the landscape of his mind, he sees nothing fencing him in. There has never been a greater spiritual catalyst than this, for this is responsible for your ability to visualize a time, a place, and an energy that will change your reality. These are all related. Do you want to know how to get to the sparks, dear ones? Do you wish to know how to change your reality? Access the fluid, flexible child with no fences. Do you want to know which energy can visualize a time when you were young? I've just told you! It's also the secret to changing the actual reality of your biological clock! The body churns along all by itself. It's an immaculate engine and will carry you through life in a preset paradigm . . . but an old one. It's the child energy that activates the intent and power to change it! When the water boils, the hand that holds the pail has to react, and it can't drop it. It has to run with it.

"Without fences" means that all things are possible. Dear ones, if you have disease in your body right now, or if there is an anomaly within—if there is a problem with your cellular structure, I'll give you an exercise. I want you to take that child without fences and visualize a time in your life before it ever happened. I want you to see your cellular structure when it was fresh and perfect and young. I want you to hold that visualization of no fences, because the catalyst of the child is at work right now connecting to the energy of the Higher-Self. It is starting the process. I told you I'd tell you how it worked. This is it. The joy and imagination of the child starts the process for the sparks to happen for the healing. For what you *visualize*, you can *have*.

The stronger your visualization, the stronger the wisdom is of your belief system, right into your own cellular structure, and you'll feel it. You'll know it. You'll own it! Pretty soon the cells will revert—actually in time, chasing out what does not belong there, remembering a time when they were a certain way, and yes, even awakening the stem cells. This is the cure. This is the miracle. It happens daily to the lighthouses.

There are lighthouses here. There are Lightworkers here. There are healers here who practice this daily and help others along. Healers don't heal; healers balance! You know that. But when they balance another Human Being in a certain way, the body responds. This balance helps another in accessing the inner child's joy, complete with the removal of all the fences, and the suspension of the four-dimensional structure.

That's the end of the teaching. It's not the end of the energy, you know, but it's the end of the teaching for now. How many of you would like to go there in that bucket and visit the child's substance? How many of you would like to look at your lives and say, *There are no fences?* How many of you would like to suspend belief? Well, I'll tell you, accessing the child will activate the Higher-Self in you, the angel in you, and the miracles may begin. This is when the balance really starts to occur.

Dear family member, the hardest thing we do is to leave. We can't do that until we are sure that you are clear on what has been said. The avatars on the planet have no miraculous secrets that you do not. Do you want to know what the attribute of the avatar is? It's a fully developed and balanced child energy. That's where the substance is, because that's the fast track to the Higher-Self. It's suspension of belief. Can you create energy from your hands? Can you change physics? Can you manipulate time? Yes. All of you can. Every single one who sits here. That's what this lesson is about, and in the process, we would like you to apply it to your individual lives. Look into the faces of the past and current avatars on the planet. Notice first the smile, the humor, and the joy. Notice second, the miracles!

Couples who are here, how would you like a stronger bond between you? Let your children come out and play together! Put away the structure for a while. That action energizes the Higher-Self and fills you with love, understanding, and a balanced perception of what is important. Some of the barriers that you have created for yourselves, couples, will drop away, and you will see each other in a fresh light again.

Worker, when you go to work and you again see the one who is the weekday "sand in your oyster," and they are always there [laughter], what do you do? Your vocations are wonderful places. It's a wonderful cauldron of karma, is it not—to be thrown together with people you never would have asked to be with? [Laughter] You think that's an accident, do you? What are you going to do with it? It's the child that gives you the Higher-Self attribute to have peace with that. Things that irritate you will float away, and let me again remind you about karma: When you take away one side of that game, the other side goes with it. Wait till you see the reaction of those who are part of your drama, when you start to love them. They'll push the same old buttons, but nothing will happen with you anymore. All of this is part of going to work. It's all part of going home and living life day-by-day. Human Being, we wouldn't be here giving you this information if it were not common to humanity. It applies to you, all within the energy and love of God.

The entourage retreats from the room, having given you information this evening that you needed to hear. The entourage retreats from the room, but it doesn't want to. It wants to stay and play with all the children here!

Some of you have felt profound energy this night and have felt the love of God in your life. Some of you felt the love of family pressing upon you. You can go home and create the same feeling anytime you wish. You are a piece of the whole!

Let the healing begin! Let the child within you activate the Higher-Self within the structure of the adult. Let joy overcome the drama.

And so it is.

Kryon

*P.S. from Lee: Yes, indeed there was one woman who was newly pregnant in the audience. She came up later and introduced herself.

Live Channelling

"The Unseen Energy Around You"

Channelled in
Santa Fe, New Mexico
July 2000
Kryon Summer Light Conference®

Chapter Two

"The Unseen Energy Around You"

Live Channelling
Santa Fe, New Mexico

This live channelling has been edited with additional words and thoughts to allow clarification and better understanding of the written word.

Greetings, dear ones. I am Kryon of Magnetic Service. This is very different [speaking of the energy of the moment]. You've asked us, in this moment, to come into your presence and deliver words of wisdom, plus whatever else you believe might take place as you sit in the chair, hearing or reading this. Yet, we are overwhelmed as we flood into this room and take our places behind you, around you, and next to you. It is as though the room has been a

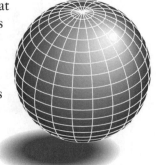

sanctuary for days—as though a great truth has been spoken already—as though the indigenous have been here and blessed each of you and warmed you with their wise energy. It is as though your hearts were softened for the messages that may cut through the Human duality today. Yes, this is very different.

We are constantly amazed by the interdimensional information being received by you, and how much work is being done here (on Earth). This is a family reunion—a precious time—when the Kryon entourage meets the Human family member.

And what we all have in common, despite the veil, despite the duality, is that we are from the same source, whether brother or sister. On my side of the veil, which is the side that you call "home" when you are not there, there is no gender. Yet in your language, we must use the words *he* and *she*. But *we* come to you, genderless in love. You may call it the female energy. You may call it the male energy. But it is a meld of energy called God!

The angels who are speaking to you now are using what we call The Third Language, something we have spoken of continually for the past few months. This language is thick, and it's potent—dripping with love as we take our places in this room. We fill this area from the back and the sides first, moving toward the front. Some of you during this time will feel the presence of "home."

Before we go any further, there are those here and reading this who need an exercise in order to benefit from what is to come. We ask you to suspend your reality for a moment and go to a place where everything is well and good. Use your experiences in what you call your past. Go to the most joyful time in your life, and pull it into your heart. Now hold it there for the time we are here visiting with you. Do not let the duality of humanism grip your heart in a worrisome way. Do not think of the things of the past, or items that are bothering you now. Suspend them in another place. Give yourself a gift today, and be absorbed into the angel-energy that you really are. Suspend all your Earthly cares for this brief time, and let yourself feel joy as you read and listen.

Do you remember the time before the onset of the problems you now have? Remember, we know who is *here*. We know who has chosen to read this! All of this may not be for all of you, dear ones, but the listener and the reader whose eyes are on these pages are included *here* as well.

Listener, we ask you to do an interdimensional thing—something we've asked in the past, also. We want you to join the family that is *not* in your time frame—but rather, one whose eyes are on these pages. We also ask you to join with the family who has decided to play this tape, in what you call your *future*, but what they are calling their *past*. Realize that the energy created right now isn't linear. It's interdimensional, and it exists in the center of your time . . . a place we call the "now." We wish you to greet this extended family that is not in your time. Greet them at the cellular level, and recognize who they are and the potentials that exist within their challenges. Recognize them as belonging to your family!

Reader, can you also place yourself at this meeting, seemingly in your past? Can you join with the listener? Dear ones, they are having the same experience that you are. We invite *all* of you to suspend all Earthly things and listen to the message that follows.

Much talk has been devoted to letting you know that your doom-and-gloom prophecies didn't happen.

Oh, you were given generalizations about this time, but you are not recognizing it, since it's not in a time frame anyone expected. Some prophecies spoke of a "New Jerusalem." They spoke of heaven on Earth. They spoke of an energy shift on the planet and the metaphor of a "white light" coming to the planet. They spoke of Humans finding interdimensionality. They spoke of wonderful science that would extend life! I would like you to know, dear ones, that you sit right within that prophecy! That was a prophecy for 1,000 years from now! Did you know that? Go take a look! But here you are now, sitting in that energy . . . with all the potentials before you to create what was foretold.

In the past, we told you about the interdimensional Human Being. In review, we wish to briefly tell you what we said then, so that this teaching today will be something that will fit into the previous teachings.

We spoke to you of the interdimensional gifts that the Human Being has. We spoke to you about the fact that the gifts are coming to you strongly. We told you of one gift where you could compress time. By the time this channelling is published, these things will also have been published and documented. We asked for this so you would be able to refer to them as some of you read this.

We also told you about the compression of sleep—that the individual Human Being has control of his/her energy to a point that was never thought possible. We gave you hints for compressing time, for there are many of you who are about to have more to do than you ever did before. [Laughter] We broached something that we had never talked about before, which some of you have called "an eye-roller": We've talked about interdimensional life on the planet—about life in the atmosphere that you have not seen, and may never see.

We talked about interdimensional life in water, which responds to magnetism, and changes the very attributes of what you have molecularly identified as H_2O. We talked to you about this new life, changing the very scope of the healing attributes of water on the planet. We told you to look for healing waters of multiple kinds that are going to present themselves on Earth in these years within the beginning of the new energy. We also told you that there are three places on the planet where water flows from the earth, already positioned and magnetized in a way that will assist in longer life for the Human. If that sounds like a myth to you, it is not. We broached subjects that may not be provable, but which are real. We now can also tell you that the three places are New Zealand, Eastern Canada, and Europe.

There is yet another kind of life on the planet, and we speak of this now . . . and so many of you know about it. It's an interdimensional life form within the dirt of the earth. And there's not just one kind, but many kinds. Oh, indigenous ones and shamans, do you remember The Guardians of the Canyons? They are here still. You have covered the dirt with cement and buildings and called it *modern*, but they are still here. Many of the main devas of the forest are still here as well. Interdimensional life on this planet has one purpose, and that is to *balance* this Earth for you. You have heard this often from the indigenous, and you will hear it again from me. We both speak of the consciousness in the dirt of the planet, for it's still here.

Many entities left Earth on what we have identified as the 12:12 energy [April 1994]. But the balancing entities remained. It was the "residue of the Masters" that left, and their absence was felt by many. But the balancing energy of nature remained. This is difficult to explain, so in the channelling session next month, we will enlighten you further about the essence of the guides, angels, and others who are your helpers on Earth.

We're going to discuss interdimensional communication during this teaching session. Some will wish to title this teaching, "The Invisible Energy Around You," or "The Unseen Energy Around You."

There is a universe of invisibility around you, and we can talk of it now because it inspires less *eye-rolling* than it did a few months ago. Some of what we speak about will be called "questionable science." There will be those who will call this "voodoo science" because it's not provable. When we speak of these things, we turn to the core of discernment within the divine inside of the Human and say, *Listen to the information*. Does it *ring* true or does it not? For the things we teach you today are spiritually unseen, yet we speak of them during a time when much of your science is admitting (finally) that not all that is *real* is seen, but is there anyway. Your mainstream science is therefore broaching interdimensional things, and giving credibility to energy that exists but is not available to be viewed in 4D. Therefore, it's a good time for us to do the same.

There are many things that are unseen that you use every day. One of them is interdimensional and not truly understood by your science, yet it is all around you, and it's also the core of our work. We told you about it when we first arrived. You call it *magnetism*. We have other names for this force, but magnetism, although not understood, is seen and used daily by you. You see the results of magnetism all around you. You have learned to create it and use it, but if you ask scientists about the real scientific workings of magnetism, they will scratch their heads and say, "No Human really knows what it is." Yet it is the largest force in the Universe! It carries your DNA instructions for health and longevity. It is also present in the DNA strands that are not biologically oriented—carrying contracts of your life now, your former life contracts, your past and present karma, and the imprints of magnetism given to you at birth, called astrology.

All of those things are magnetic. They are interdimensional and part of your cellular structure. More common to you is your technical use of magnetics. It's in all of your electric circuits on the planet! Chances are, magnetics is in every piece of equipment that you personally own, including the item you used to smooth the clothes you are wearing, the devices you used to cook the food of your day, and the vehicles you will drive home in. Your broadcasting is all magnetic—did you know that? Thousands of pictures—and sound and data—are passing through you right now where you sit, but you can't see them unless you have the device that receives and interprets the magnetics. The computers you use in everyday life depend on magnetic storage of information as well. It's all around you!

Indeed, you've learned to harness it, but you don't understand it because it's interdimensional and invisible. We mention this because there's more to come that is invisible, and since you've already had results and experience with this invisible thing called magnetics, then let the other items we will speak of be just as real to you.

What is gravity, dear ones? It's another invisible force that is unseen. Science does not understand gravity. Even though they have theories that it has to do with mass, and they can see the result of it, they don't know the *why* of it. I'm here to tell you that it does not have to do with mass in particular. Mass is always present for gravity to exist, but it has to do more with what we have called "action and balance." The physicists will scratch their heads even as we say this: It's about matter balancing itself. It is not that much different from what you call *osmosis*, which is defined as "the passage of water through a semipermeable membrane from one density to another." Gravity is the result of physical matter wishing to balance itself within the presence of other matter. It is about compaction imbalance . . . and a *desire* for balance in the *soup* of space energy. This is very difficult for you to see, for it also involves The Cosmic Lattice, which is filled with invisible energy, but it is all around, and is affecting mass.

Think of it as part of what the Universe wishes to do—a grand rule that no one has even labeled yet, called the "propensity of universal balance." That's gravity. You are so used to it that you don't think about it anymore unless it involves you in an accident of falling. Everything you do is controlled by gravity. All your living is built around it, yet you don't think about it because it's invisible. What a grand force it is—this invisible thing that controls your lives! Did you ever think of it in that way?

Air is invisible to you, yet it is thick. When wind blows over a building, did you ever wonder how something so invisible could be so powerful? You take giant aircraft and throw them into the sky . . . and they fly! They constitute tons of weight, but they smoothly glide about. It's about balance. Armies of air molecules rush in to fill a void that is artificially created by your aircraft's underwing. This creates lift, as the invisible power of air actually pushes and lifts the craft into the sky. The "propensity of universal balance" therefore allows flight! It's about compaction, density, and speed (although you don't have the speed part in the formula yet). It's also related to time, but that is for another discussion. For now, think of this universal law as creating invisible force—one you can see around you daily—especially in gravity, water, and air.

The universe abhors any kind of imbalance, and will create forces to balance itself. We'd like to tell you that this is an attribute that your body has as well. The universe is self-balancing, biology is self-balancing, and consciousness is self-balancing. That is why "intent" works, dear ones! When you give intent for something, although it's invisible, you create an energy. This energy wants to flow somewhere. Between the flowing and ebbing, you get synchronicity and action. That's why intent works. It is the catalyst for balance. At a different time, if you should allow it, we will bring you more about the energy of intent, and especially about *why and how* your cellular structure responds to it.

Oh, shaman, are you listening? We're going to tell you some things about balancing that are interdimensional, and also give you information this day about something powerful, yet invisible. Dear ones, there is something happening to many of you. We have spoken in the past of this and have given it a term called The Third Language. Now we are going to take a moment in time to teach you about this. We will communicate five attributes of The Third Language to you (although there are many more than five).

We would like to explain what is taking place in some of your lives that you are not understanding. The new energy is upon you. It floods on to the earth and exists simultaneously with the old. Many of you are feeling it. Time is literally speeding up, and you are feeling the train of humanity moving faster. Many of you are aware of time speeding up even though your watches read the same as they always did. This is a kind of interdimensional speed-up, and it is sensed rather than seen.

Others of you are feeling a *buzz* around you—that is, there is simply too much going on around you all at once. It is spiritual in nature, but to some it feels biological—and some of you have asked for this to stop. Some of you don't understand why it's there. In some cases, you are blocking it so entirely that there's no buzz at all. In fact, there's nothing at all—and for an enlightened person, that is irritating, too!

We're going to tell you why. It's because there is an unseen "broadcast station" called The Third Language, which is giving messages to something you have called your "Higher-Self." The angelic, divine part of you (that is in the now) is trying to receive a broadcast—a tremendous amount of invisible personal spiritual information being sent all at once, called The Third Language! That's the way it works. It is not a linear message stream, so it's a kind of communication that might be new—requiring you to sort it out. Using a metaphor for explanation: It's asking you to *tune in to* the broadcast parts . . . like selecting the stations within many choices. And when you understand that all of the information is being given together at once, you will have a better idea of how to sort it out.

The question, of course, is always, *How?* I'm going to give you five of the most common "stations" that some of you are beginning to receive all at once. I'm also going to remind you of the energy of intent. Once you understand what is happening, your spiritual intent will help sort out the information. It's kind of like your intent is suddenly seen as the device that will allow for the selection. Remember? I told you about the invisible power of intent. It's real, and here is just one way in which it manifests.

Guide Talk

The first of the five "stations" is what we call "guide talk." Many of you have called this *intuition*. Some of you have seemingly lost your intuition, and you might say to yourself: *"What a time to lose this—in the new energy! I always knew what was right and wrong and felt led. Now it just isn't working for me."* Yes, it is! It's just that it's "in there" with all the other information.

"What can I do?" you might ask. Tune in to the intuition and tune out the others. For now, say: *"I am linear, dear spirit, and I give permission to only tune in to the intuition channel and tune out the others for right now."* You're going to ask for the kind of energy that matches what you wish to receive. This has to do with the use of intent, and your ability to specify what you wish to have.

Watch your intuition come back! For those of you who have never had it, watch it develop. For those of you who want to know how to test it, it's a reaction to the first thing you think of (trusting first reactions). Give it a try. If you've never tried it before, tune in to intuition within any kind of a situation. Some of you have used the pendulum. This works through your own personal guide talk. Test it. Get used to what it feels like when it is correct or not correct for the energy of the situation in your life. That's called guidance, and it's the "guide-talk station."

We wish to let you know what is happening here. Why, all of a sudden, do you have this barrage of information all at once? Why not the old way, where it was given to you in a linear fashion? It has to do with your enablement in a new energy. In the past, you sat in meditation and received whatever was given. Now you have a choice of what is to be received. It's all part of your expansion and interdimensionality. Therefore, this is a lesson on how to take the new communication, separate it, and use what you wish.

The Hugs

We're going to call the second one the "hug" communication. Have you been hugged lately? You probably have, but you didn't recognize it for what it was. Let me tell you what we call the hug station. We call it *validation*. This will explain why so many of you are caught at just the right moment, and your eyes are steered to the clock that reads 11:11! [Laughter] It doesn't say 11:10 or 11:12, does it? Why did you look at just that moment? What does it mean? It means that you've just been hugged! How else are we going to bring your attention to us? It's something you can see with your eyes and then remember that we love you and hug you. Why did you look at the clock at that moment? Because an angel tapped you on the shoulder and whispered, "Look now! Look now for proof we're here with you!" It's the hug station. It's validation of the existence of The Third Language. The next time it happens, why don't you stop a moment and celebrate the event? If you do, then we get the hug back! Try it next time.

Construction Angels

The third is construction energy. You've called it synchronicity and co-creation. This is the big one! It's the area you feel is the most important, for this is where you get answers to the big questions. The construction angels (or guides) represent the group that helps you with the big picture, fulfilling synchronicity and facilitating co-creation. This is the place where lives change and the work is accomplished. How do you find it? It's time to give intent to "tune in to" the "construction station." Some of you sit in that place asking all those life questions, but instead of answers, all you get is buzzing or silence. How do you tune it? Again, say, *"Dear Spirit, I know that you're there, and I ask to be tuned in to the energy of this group."* Ask for the energy of solution in a linear fashion, one at a time . . . and that's what you'll get.

Think about it. Isn't it better to have a selection rather than just receiving what is given? Isn't it more enabling to be able to create a situation where you tune in to a specific energy? The answer is yes! Now it's time for you to understand the interdimensionality of this process called The Third Language.

Communication Feedback

The fourth is called "communication feedback." There was a time in the old energy when you might have knelt before Spirit and simply felt loved. Communication feedback was the energy given back to you that verified that you were "in touch." You got used to a certain spiritual or physical feeling, and many of you are now reporting that it's gone or greatly reduced, and you miss it. Well, it's not gone. It's only that you must now learn to select it. The Third Language is a 100 percent always-on language for you to tune in to at any time. Now we are saying that you may have communication feedback no matter what you're doing— eating, driving, or meditating.

You don't need to create a space in front of an altar, since this sacred space is already created by your simple intent. The sacredness? It's the interdimensional Human Being, loved without measure—walking the earth, pretending to be Human. You can have this energy anytime you want to. Say to Spirit, *"Tune me in to this station or that station."* [Laughter]

Tune in to *communication feedback* and you'll know that we're next to you. You will again have the feeling you desire that reminds you that we're here. It's the age of discernment. It's up to you which energy you need to tune in to and how long you stay there. It's going to require a wisdom factor of the angel inside of you that lets you skip around this interdimensional dial, to tune in to any energy you need when you need it. This is new, and this is The Third Language's attributes. If you haven't recognized it, you're going to be barraged with noise, and you won't know what to do.

Hand-Holding

The fifth one may sound like the second (hugs), but it isn't. It is called *hand-holding*. Some of you need that right now, and you may wish to tune to that station! Some of you might wish to tune to several of them at once. *Is that possible?* you might ask. Let me tell you something. Yes, it is! You are going to have to get used to what it's like to receive them one at a time (in an old linear fashion), and then you may move to the new interdimensional way of receiving two, three, four, or even five at once! This is all part of the expanded Human consciousness learning in this New Age.

Hand-holding—what is it? It's what happens in your closet when you think you're alone. No messages are given. No energy is transmitted except for one: The love of Spirit for a family member. It's simple, yet it's often the most profound energy you can summon. Sit in the dark, and have your hand held through the veil by the greatest energy in the Universe—a family member with a name just like yours. There's nothing like it! I would like to tell you, family, it has also become our favorite, because in the new energy, we feel the squeeze of your hand returned! Indeed, it has become the one we enjoy the most.

Those are five of many—five that you needed to hear about today. These are the five that can change the hearts, minds, and lives of so many of you here wondering what's going on.

We have something new today—something never presented before. We have a new parable of Wo, the first one in the new energy. This is Wo in the New Age! Now, we preface every Wo parable to remind you that the character "Wo" has no gender. Wo is a WO-MAN, you see. [Laughter] But for this example, as in the past, we will call Wo a "he." In your language, calling Wo an "it" would be improper.

Parable: Wo and the Great Ship

Wo was on a grand ship—one we will call the ocean liner of humanity. He was enjoying life along with the billions of others on the ship. The ship was immense and grand. It represented humanity, lineage, history, and the energy of Earth. It represented all things that were ever in regard to Humans on the planet.

The ocean liner was majestic, and Wo loved it. He didn't have to do much regarding the ship. It steered and powered itself, and it took Wo and the other Humans sailing on it where they wanted to go. It took him many places. Wo really didn't have to think much about it—he just enjoyed it. There also didn't seem to be much danger involved as long as Wo worked a certain way within the energy of this ship, stayed on his own deck, and relaxed on this great vessel named *Humanity*.

This particular ship was uniquely different from regular ships, for it was very safe. It had a lifeboat for every man, woman, and child on the ship! Think of that—one for every single person! If anything ever happened, the lifeboats were there—stocked and ready.

Everything was fine. Wo's entire life had been spent on this ship, and he had grown used to it. All was well . . . until the millennium shift. In January 2000, the ship named *Humanity* sailed into new waters. Wo had never seen anything like it before, and the ship got into trouble. The iron that the ship was made of was beginning to be corroded by the energy of the new millennium water it had entered. The ship lost integrity—leaking badly—listing to one side and then the other. It was slowly sinking!

Many were afraid and didn't know what to do. It became obvious over time that the ship was not going to survive. Wo had never heard anything about this from the scriptures or prophecies that foretold many things about the great ship in the past. He didn't know what to expect. No prophet had ever spoken of the ship sinking! They had told of it perhaps needing help, or even stopping momentarily while it was repaired and changed . . . but this ship of the old energy was sinking!

All of the comforts Wo had known and the paradigms of how things worked in life were also going to go down with this ship. It was unbelievable! Was humanity going to perish along with the ship? Somehow Wo felt not.

Slowly, each Human Being was encouraged to climb into his lifeboat. Some of them abandoned the ship well in advance, saying that somehow they had expected this. The lifeboats slowly pulled away from the sinking ship, and what a spectacle it was! Wo waited until the last moment, thinking perhaps that there was a way the big ship would come back to life. He couldn't believe it was really sinking.

In the process of remaining on board, Wo saw some amazing things. He saw people angrily yelling at one another. They wouldn't get into the lifeboats! They were going to go down with the ship because they were angry. The sinking didn't make any sense at all to them, and they were lashing out at God, or whoever had steered the great vessel into turbulent waters. Some of them were so torn by what was happening that they said they could never exist on any other kind of ship, and they would not even try. After all, this was the only ship they had ever known, and there was no other around. Therefore (they thought), if they took to the lifeboats, they would die anyway.

Wo climbed into his lifeboat, lowered it into the seemingly dangerous waters, and pushed away from the sinking ship. Others took their chances with Wo and also entered their lifeboats at the last moment, lowering them with the safety ropes into the water. In horror, Wo and many others watched the angry ones go down with the ship. The great, comfortable ship of *humanity* slipped almost without sound into the deep waters of a vast ocean that could no longer lift it up or keep it afloat. To many, that was the end of everything. But to those who had risked going to the lifeboats, there were more surprises ahead.

Wo was adrift all by himself in his tiny boat. He, like the others, had oars and provisions for only one day. He looked around him and saw all of the other little white boats dotting the water all the way to the horizon. There had to be millions! The metal of the old ship had not survived the new-energy waters. The boats that Wo and the others were now in were wooden, safe for now—safe for at least one day until the provisions were gone. Wo wondered what was going to happen then. The lifeboats slowly drifted apart over the vast ocean. Each new lifeboat passenger could go anywhere he wanted—each Human Being deciding for himself which direction might be best as he took up his oars and rowed.

There was something apparent to Wo right away. The lifeboat was not what he expected. He thought it was one thing, but it was becoming another! The boat was made of wood. It was small, oar-powered, and had provisions in the food/water locker for one day only. There was no protection from storms; it was vulnerable to weather, and he knew as well as the others that they could be dashed to bits if the weather got bad, whereas on the great ship of *humanity*, if the weather got bad, everyone would simply go inside. It was very different having this much responsibility, and also a bit frightening.

On the second day, Wo realized something was different. As he opened the provisions locker, the one he had opened three times in the last day, the locker was again filled with food! He remembered eating all of it the day before, yet the food some- how had replenished itself. "Provisions for one day," the in- structions had said? Yes, that's what they said. He began to realize that his lifeboat was giving Wo provisions for the *one day* he was in!

Each day, as he opened the provisions locker, there was sustenance for one day—no more, no less. Wo thanked the boat, for he realized that somehow it was magic, and he celebrated each morning in the boat as he ate and drank. "Thank you, Spirit," Wo said. "It looks like I'll live a little longer." Wo worked the tiller to steer the boat. He would row and steer, and row and steer. Although he didn't know where he was going, he took a course that seemed somehow intuitive. The more he celebrated within the boat, the more it responded to him. The more he loved it, the better it performed!

Something amazing happened in the second week of being on his own. Wo went to the back of the boat where the tiller was, and much to his shock, he saw something that was never there before—an engine! There, lying at the rear of the craft, was an outboard engine. Next to it was fuel for one day in a can. Wo positioned the engine where he felt it should be, bolted it easily to the back of the lifeboat with the supply kit next to it, and fueled and started it. With a roar, it came to life, and chills ran up and down Wo's body. This indeed was magic! Who had supplied the engine and fuel? Was it an angel? God? Perhaps it was Wo's interaction with the boat? He didn't know. But he blessed the engine and the boat and the food/water locker, and in the next hours, he began to learn to use the engine to both steer and power the boat.

After a day of travel, the engine sputtered to a stop, and Wo looked at the fuel can that he had emptied the day before. He lifted it, and somehow was not surprised to find fuel for one day! He filled the engine's tank and laughed. "God bless this boat!" Wo cried out loud to anyone who could hear. He was filled with awe and joy.

Wo was now able to steer a course in a direction he felt intuitively would be a good one. He noticed that a few others were following the same path. Although not in communication directly, he felt a feeling of family with the few other boats he could see. He also noticed that some of them also had engines! Wo wondered for a moment who was following who—and if they might all be deceived . . . going nowhere, or around in circles, but it seemed that they were all pointed in a good, intuitive direction.

[Dear ones, when the indigenous of this Earth gather to celebrate the four directions, did you know that they are celebrating magnetism? Indeed! Like the ancient indigenous, Wo had some inner guidance showing him the way . . . navigating without a compass.]

Within another week, a squall came along. Wo said to the boat, "This is what I and the others have feared the most. Show me what to do!" He thought he heard the boat reply, "Celebrate the fear, Wo." So Wo knelt, and instead of praying for help, he celebrated the storm. Suddenly, another amazing thing happened. Wo's eyes widened as he watched. He had somehow expected the magic power of the boat to stop the storm. Instead, the boat *grew* a covering! As the storm intensified, the boat sealed itself in such a way that it rode the storm with no damage, and Wo didn't even get wet!

Wo now realized that the more he celebrated the boat, the better it got. He realized that somehow he was an extension of the boat itself. It had many attributes that he began to recognize. When he was depressed or in fear, the boat seemed to be weak. He even thought once that he saw some leaks. But when he was joyful, a lot of things happened—miraculous things. Wo even felt that the color of the boat changed somehow!

No wonder there was one boat for every single Human Being on the great ship. Now Wo understood. Each lifeboat was somehow filled with the energy of the Human whom it belonged to. It had sat unused all his life, since the big boat disguised any real use for it. In actuality, Wo could have left the big ship anytime he had wished to, but why do it when the big ship did everything for him . . . or did it? Wo now began to realize that although he didn't know what tomorrow was going to bring, he was free to steer his own craft into the uncertainty. He also realized that his vessel was a good one, growing with him as he grew with knowledge. He began to feel empowered and joyful about the change that was forced on him. He began to feel sorry for those who didn't get off the big ship. How could they have known about the magic lifeboats?

In time, Wo began to examine some of the other distant boats that were like his. He looked around and saw that some of them also had covers. Many also had engines, and the oars were being thrown away, or stowed. It also wasn't long before he realized that they were all headed to a central point, and he could see it in the far distance . . . an island shrouded with fog.

One by one, the boats steered closer to the island shrouded with fog. Many hovered at the limit of the fog bank, choosing not to go in. Through the fog, they heard commotion—much noise and clanging. You could sense the indecision. Most didn't know what to expect or what lay beyond the invisible, thick fog. Slowly, however, they all realized that to stay on the outside of the fog was to deny discovery. One by one, the small white magic boats disappeared into the fog toward the island they knew was within it. Wo also decided to take the risk of moving into the unknown, and although invisible, he trusted himself and his craft as he sailed into the fog.

For about an hour, Wo and the others made their way slowly toward the noise, uncertain and apprehensive—not knowing if they were approaching doom or salvation. What met their eyes was astonishing! Indeed, there was an island, but one they realized was not yet to be landed upon. Almost as one, they stopped and held their distance—staring at what they beheld.

On the island, there was the most immense interdimensional ship under construction that they had ever seen! It wasn't shaped correctly, as the pointy end wasn't in the front! The engines weren't where they belonged, either. Every cabin where a Human Being was supposed to reside had a wheelhouse, and somehow they were all going to steer the ship together by consensus. It was an interdimensional craft taking shape before his eyes. It was very much like his lifeboat; however, he could see no entity or entities doing the building. Seemingly, the ship was taking shape on its own, and the more lifeboats came to surround the island, the faster the ship was being built.

And so Wo and the others, with *one day* of provisions and *one day* of fuel, began to circle the island in ceremony, saying to themselves, *"We will land on the island when it's time, and board the ship when it's finished—a miracle ship that is amazingly built as no other ship we have ever seen. It's one that will work in the new-energy waters, and when it's ready, we will know it and we will all board together. Then together, we will name this great craft. We will name it something that honors those who sail the waters of the new millennium."*

———————--

Now, dear ones, how many of you are in that lifeboat? The old ship has gone down, dear ones, and the way of life some of you knew and even spiritually trusted is seemingly gone. In some of your situations, the leaving of the old has even been purified by fire—and you know whom I'm talking to, don't you? I want you to remember something. Do you think you're alone in that boat? You're not, any more than you are alone in that closet we often speak of.

We want you to circle the island for a while and trust that the new ship is under construction. We want you to know that the love of God is shining its beautiful rays of sun on your life. We don't want you to trust any other person but yourself. We don't want you to go to any other Human and ask what you're supposed to be doing. We want you to go inside of yourself, tune in to the station that is the most meaningful for you, and bask in the energy of a lifeboat that responds to you in so many ways. Let us hold your hand, create synchronicity, and provide co-creation. We'd like to hug you if you would let us. Let us give you the sustenance of one day's provisions—over and over again. This may give you a different definition of *abundance!*

What's going to happen with the new ship? When is it going to float itself? This entity does not know. For the lifeboats will grow using their own miracles, and when it's an appropriate time, they will land all together and celebrate. Human consciousness will shift even more, and the ship will be christened with the name *Humanity II—The New Jerusalem!* This ship brings the promise of a peaceful Earth, and a wise humanity who sails upon its powerful waters!

This sanctuary where you listen and hear will remain a sanctuary as long as you give intent for it. Create a solitude of peace, and think about what has been said this day. When you finish this communication, be still for a few more moments before rising. This is indeed a precious time!

We're not in a vacuum, you know. We know of your life, your challenges, and your trials. If you haven't felt the love of God this day in your life, perhaps it's time you opened your heart a little more to the reality of the interdimensional spiritual beings around you! They are filled with love and gifts for the Human who wishes to tune in to them.

Indeed, dear ones, you are dearly loved!

Kryon

Live Channelling

"A New Beginning"

Channelled in
Tel Aviv, Israel
October 2000

Chapter Three

"A New Beginning"
Live Channelling
Tel Aviv, Israel

This live channelling has been edited with additional words and thoughts to allow clarification and better understanding of the written word.

On October 27, 2000, amid the violence and turmoil of what the Israelis call "The Situation," a Kryon seminar was held in the middle of Tel Aviv. Attracting a sell-out crowd of more than 1,000 people, many put aside the fear of terrorism associated with large spiritual meetings, and showed their courage as they anxiously awaited the channelling that follows. What Lee reminded these attendees during the all-day session is what Kryon channelled in March 2000—that in the new energy, things may appear to move backwards.

In March of 2000, Kryon channelled the following information, published in September of this year in *Kryon Book Eight, Passing the Marker:*

"Dear ones, in these next few years, you are going to see some reversals. You may look at these reversals and say, 'You know, our Earth seemed to be doing pretty well until we got to this place. Now it seems hat there are some reversals of the good things that were happening.' How many promising peace agreements on this planet are suddenly now stalled? How many issues politically and tribally have simply reached a stalemate? Have you seen any agreements simply fall apart lately? What's happening here? Isn't this the new energy?

"Also, there will be action one way or the other within some issues that have simply been stalled for a very long time. Things that have seemed stuck will unstick themselves, and some will appear to move backwards in chaos!"

Now, the people of this volatile region are indeed facing this very same thing.

Our hearts were touched greatly by the warmth that these people emanated. Although mostly Jews, we were also aware of those of many faiths and cultures, all desiring to finally find a solution to one of the world's most perplexing and long-standing cultural problems. As Jan and I received hugs from so many before we departed a week later, we were aware of how much appreciation there was for those who visit from the outside, those who try to understand a difficult situation—if only for a few hours.

As you read the following, put yourself in the place of these Lightworkers, many from a lineage of great masters— ones who walked the very earth where we were speaking. Many are in fear and would love to know that before you retire each night, perhaps you might send energy their way. Visualize peace. Don't tell Spirit how to do it; just visualize the Middle East finally healing itself in a slow but positive manner. See the children unafraid on all sides. See love doing the work that diplomats could not. See a miracle!

Kryon in Israel

(Simultaneously translated into Hebrew for the crowd)

Greetings, dear ones, I am Kryon of Magnetic Energy. [Note that Kryon changed from the normal greeting of "Magnetic Service." This is because of the difficulty translating this term into Hebrew.]

The voice that you hear now is the one that you have been hearing all day long [speaking of Lee's lecture earlier]. But for those of you who have come to sense the energy of Spirit, you know the energy of who is visiting you. So we say to you in these opening moments of discussion that this is the sister, the brother, the family member called Kryon—the one who has no more power than you do. This is the one who comes before you for the first time in this area, and who greets the family as we have never done before.

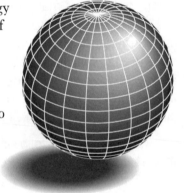

We proclaim this a reunion of the highest order! We proclaim this a time when energy can be combined in a way that it never has before in this great land. Let the entourage, which has come in through the crack of the veil, spill into this place and cover it with the thickness of love. Feel those entities, if you wish, between the seats—between the aisles—some of them behind you—some in front, taking their places before you as the love pours into this space.

Hold your own energy, the one of the divine angels that you are, and prepare to greet those who come into this space by your intent. Some of them who may visit you this evening in love may surprise you. Some of you felt that you were coming to sit in this energy, having no idea whom you might really meet, for when the angel says, "I will," miracles happen. In a space where more than 1,000 of you sit, you may manifest whatever you choose—one voice. One consciousness may change the reality of all that is.

Greet the readers of this information, who may live in a different land. For they are joining with you in the "now" energy of this timeless event. Long after the lights are out here in this building, the energy of this moment will be lived again and again. In some ways, each time these words are revisited, the event is again "live."

Many of you thought you came here this day to feel the energy of Kryon—to sit and bask in the love of Spirit. Perhaps you had no idea the way this works, for you have the transcribed words of the Kryon messages [all the Kryon books have been translated into Hebrew]. But that's different from being visited in person. For when you sit in this space and the entourage surrounds you and begins to wash the feet of the angels who sit in the chairs, something different happens, which words on a page cannot convey. You have given intent for the area around you to change, and it is doing so now.

Let us tell you this: You have no idea who came to see whom! We are in awe of those who sit here. We know of the lineage of each of you. We speak now of those who are from the area and those who have traveled long distances. Yet there is no difference in our eyes, for we know who you are. We know of your spiritual names. We know of your lives. We are aware of the fears and the uncertainties. We have surrounded you for so long with the entourage of love, if you have asked for it. Now perhaps you will get a chance to feel what it's like to have the thickness of love swirl around you, to be touched on the back, the shoulders—and to be loved without measure. For this is what happens when you get together and combine an intent to allow the love of God to be felt. You get to "feel" it. There is no organization or religion around this. Although your organizations and ceremonies are honored before God, since they embody the search for the divine, it is the essence of the Human Being that speaks to you—the love of God that is in every pore of your body, where the real divinity hides.

Someday, when all is gone and the body is finished carrying you within the Earth lesson, the angel inside you returns to the spiritual place called "home." When that occurs, you will find no organization or religion there—only the love of family, one for another. We have seen you there, at *home*, over and over and over and over. We know your face, and not the one you think you have now. We are aware of you when you sing your name in light to us—and you wonder who came to see whom?

We look around now and we say, "We expected you." We know who you are. The moment you gave intent to sit in the chair, we knew who would be here, and we expected you. The energy began to increase in this place, and those who planned to visit you from my side of the veil started to line up. Don't be surprised if some of you experience a feeling of lineage this afternoon. Perhaps those Humans who have passed over in your lives are here? Well, they are! Within the spiritual entourage that floods over this place, there is so much family!

Before we can begin the teaching, we must remind you how interdimensional you are. None of you come into this earth alone. You do not work through your problems alone, and you do not leave alone. There is never a time on this planet when you are alone. We remind you of this so that you will know that as we speak today of what is necessary to move to the next level, you will not feel that we have asked you to make bricks without straw. Instead, you will understand that you have the hand of the divine at your side. You will understand that you are empowered to do what is asked—that around you is an interdimensional energy that is ready to be called upon—one that has changed and increased even in these last months.

Oh, dear ones [chuckle], some of you pretend to be alone. We have told you this before. You climb into the closet and you shut the door and you turn off the light. In your sorrow—perhaps within your deepest fear, you feel you are alone, never knowing even for a moment that in there with you is an entire entourage having a party! You can't be alone. It's spiritually impossible. Oh, you can deceive yourself and pretend all you wish, but while you're pretending, the entourage is there. We tell you this to bolster your peace, and give you solace over what you are enduring even as we visit you now.

Human Interdimensionality

There are aspects of things around you that you may be unaware of. One of the biggest is this: I am here to tell you that the entity that has your name, called Human, may seem to be complete, but it isn't. Part of you is not here! You have heard the expression, the *Higher-Self*. This is accurate. Part of this *Higher-Self* of you is in a planning session, co-creating with the other Higher-Selves of the rest of you in order to create synchronicity—to co-create a new reality with you.

I know this may sound confusing, and we will again channel on this subject. Understand that we must speak of interdimensional things using metaphors in this teaching session, and we will present the following information with a reminder that much of what is to follow is interdimensional and therefore often metaphoric.

Listen carefully, for there will be concepts presented that perhaps you will not understand the first time around. Part of you is not here. Part of you is within what some of you have called the "guides and angels" around you. We call it *energy*. They cannot be numbered, for they are one, yet they are infinite. You have the very essence of Spirit around you constantly, and this essence is a loving essence, ready to be activated with compassion.

Your Extended Family

Here is the second attribute: Again, we will expand upon this even within the next channelling. Dear ones, have you ever wondered whether those Humans who have "passed over" are watching? What happens to a soul? I have just given you information that says you have many pieces, and that they do not reside all in one place. It's difficult to imagine, interdimensional that it is, and hard to explain in four dimensions [that you sit within]. We are telling you that as you are in many pieces, so too are the ones who lived with you and who departed—even some who were ancestors. What we are saying at this moment is that part of you, dear ones, whom you call the guides, whom you call the angels, are those Human beings whom you have known as Human family, but who have passed on. So we give you this information: When you think you feel them, and you wonder if they're able to see you and what you're going through, they *can* see you. It's intuitive information, and not just your imagination. This is not a metaphor. Indeed, they are with you, or what we call a portion of them.

If you call upon the names of your fathers, you might be interested to know that a piece of them is with you. This goes for any Human who has been with you as friend or family and has passed over. Part of their karmic attributes are to be with you in this way. It is the same with you when you leave the earth. The difficult part of this is the realization that you, or part of you, is still active as someone else's guide!

Perhaps this energy of past family is an energy you would like to draw upon this very night? How many of you are aware that you are your own ancestors? How many of you have walked in the desert before? How many of you are aware of just how long you have owned this land? [Kryon chuckle] I speak to shamans. I speak to what we have termed the medicine men and women and the ancient priests. I speak to those who have awakened before, and we will talk about that in a moment. For these are the ones who can change the reality of a land. The ones who have awakened before are the ones, who by their very thoughts and actions and calling upon the interdimensional parts of their own divinity, can change the reality of the land under their feet. For the energy of it, and what happens to it, belongs to their co-creative powers.

The Changing Energy of the Planet

There are paradigms of existence on Earth that are changing. Again, we speak of metaphors of energy, since it is the only way we can speak of interdimensional things. Your biology is beginning to shift. Some of you are aware of the ability to live longer. We have spoken of this in the past. Science will enhance this for you, and an old energy paradigm, which has Humans living and dying in short life spans, is beginning to end. A new energy, which allows a different kind of biology, is now available. Slow as it may be, you will start to see it in your very bodies if you wish to. For those who call upon the divine inside will have answers because of the intent they show.

You are moving away from the paradigm of the *immune system* to the paradigm of the *thymus*. The immune system has worked well for years, and indeed, it's about to work even better. But it is a system that intercepts and fights the enemy. It is the immune system's paradigm of biology, and it's also the way Humans have handled strife between nations since nations started forming. Although it's an old paradigm, it has been married into Human consciousness since the beginning. Even the old scriptures speak of it, as when "the eye offends you, pluck it out!" It is important for you to remember the parable we gave you about the old scriptures, and how many of them described a Human who was sleeping. When the Human who is sleeping awakens, there has to be a new book of wisdom. How many of you carry around the books you used as children? Understand the metaphor here, and you will understand the place of old scriptural teachings in respect to the new Human Being. God never meant for instructions given in an energy of yesterday to be carried around today, or used forever. In fact, this is why channelling occurs at all. Does it make sense to you that Humans would have great spiritual change, yet their spiritual manuals would remain static?

The shift is now to the paradigm of the thymus—something that will awaken within and create harmony instead of confrontation and fighting. The way things work, therefore, is shifting from interception and fighting to that of harmony. Think about the elegance of this: Harmony does not ask for destruction. Instead, it uses energy and wisdom to create something that is a catalyst to bring the former invader to a place of existing with common purpose.

Within the Indigo Children, you will be able to see developments in biology as they become adults, as another generation takes their place that is different from your own. Part of this seeming metaphor will actually have substance within your four dimensions. This is not a prediction; it is a fact, which is happening now. Already, they [the Indigo Children] are developing some organs in their bodies that are more sophisticated than those you have in yours. The new breed has arrived, and we will speak of them later in this very channelling. Here is an important metaphor: You are moving from the paradigm of the *two* in energy to the paradigm of the *three* in energy. This is not dimensional talk. We are not speaking of a second and a third dimension. Instead, we are speaking of the energy around the *two* in numerology and in language; and the *three*, which is coming into your new way of life. The *three* in numerological ways speaks of a catalyst. The *three*, therefore, has the energy to create something else. It is the age of the *three*, and some of you know what I'm speaking of.

The First Three

The first *three* is what we have described as The Third Language. This is an interdimensional spiritual language that some have called *new intuition*. It is a language that sits above you and is divine. When you face another Human Being, you may speak the same language, but The Third Language, the energy of the *three*, is a catalyst for full understanding at a level much higher than you are used to. It is one that Humans will use between Humans, and they will know of the true feelings of others. They will know of the energy of others. It is the ability of this Third Language to hook humanity together in a way that has never been hooked together before. It's an interdimensional way that is new, one that needs to be studied and practiced—one that can be drawn to you with your intent.

One of the attributes of The Third Language is that you cannot deceive, cannot lie, and cannot escape your true feelings. The Third Language, therefore, is one of wisdom and spiritual purpose. Look for it in the Indigos, for they are developing it now.

Call it a new gift with a changing grid if you wish. Eleven years ago, I told you of this, the new abilities and the new gifts of the changing grid, and by the year 2002, it will start to be obvious that there is indeed another way of communicating. It's The Third Language.

The Second Three

We speak now in metaphoric terms regarding the third exodus—the first one being out of Egypt, the second one being an exodus from all parts of Earth into this area, and the third being the exodus of an old energy of slavery, of oppression and fear, into one of wisdom and hope. It's an exodus away from concentrating on the land, and instead, is connected and enhanced with spiritual energy that will flood in and push the old things away. Included in the old things will be former assumptions about what should happen here—former assumptions even about what those around you expect from you. Profound it will be, and Earth will see it if you allow it.

This is the promise that is here: Cloaked in "the situation," there is a jewel. Cloaked in "the situation," there is promise, and like so many times before, we say to you that the reasoning and elegance of the energy being developed hides so completely that you cannot see it. In linear time, perhaps it will take longer than you wish, and we're going to give you some things to think about regarding that. But here is another three, one that may surprise you—but not all of you.

The Third Three

Now don't get excited or anxious, but we wish to speak of the third temple. [This is a reference to the Temple Mount, where the first two Jewish temples were built and destroyed in history. It is in the Old City in Jerusalem.] There are those who say that for the earth to ascend, the third temple must be rebuilt where the other two were. Well, I'm here to tell you something: It's being built right now! It's interdimensional, not built with mortar or bricks—not with the stones of the area as before, but with the *intent* of those Lightworkers in this room and around your area. It may shock and surprise you to know that there are Lightworkers working on this temple inside themselves—even on the other side of the borders that are part of the situation. They are ones whom you would never think of as doing this, but they are.

For it's going to take *two* agreeing consciousnesses to remedy the situation, bringing in agreement, consensus, and therefore creating the *three*. We know this sounds mysterious, but you will understand in time how the two together can create the *three*. The temple is being rebuilt metaphorically, and it is this third one that represents wisdom in the hearts of those who occupy this land. It is a profound step. It is strong in its potential. It has a wonderful foundation. It gleams with gold and hope, and it is part of your lineage. This is what scripture has referred to, and this is what it has always meant. That is why it was so elusive, and even those who are not religious here will understand what the old faith has said. The old energy would never allow the third temple. Look at the root word of *Jerusalem* in Hebrew, for it sounds out the *two* energy. The third temple is in progress— different from all the others. It's the one that lets you worship inside with a family that you didn't expect to be there. That's where the angel belongs—the one who uses The Third Language. This, indeed, is part of the new Jerusalem, the beginning of the *three*. Does it not make sense that if the angel of God is inside the Human, and the Human is beginning to realize it . . . that there would be a temple there, too?

The Jews, and the Metaphor of the House

We have referred to the metaphor of the Human house before. Each room is a different culture—a different consciousness of humanity worldwide. The house is complete, and has stood through time. You might ask yourselves, *"Where is our room in this metaphoric house, as Jews? Where would it be? Perhaps it's one with a beautiful view, for we like water a lot."* [Laughter.] *"Perhaps it's the kitchen, for we have wonderful food in our land. Some say it's on top! Yes, that's where it is, on top—the highest one. It has to be there, since Kryon has channelled about the lineage of the Jews being important to Earth."*

It's none of those places. Let me give you a metaphor of where your room is in this house of Earth. *You don't have a room.* Instead, you represent the foundation! Oh, perhaps it's not as glamorous, but let me tell you something: When the foundation cracks, the house crumbles. To give you an idea of the importance of your room, we tell you this again and again: As goes this space you call Israel, so goes the world. They are firmly allied, and as one goes, so goes the other. Call this spiritual accounting, if you wish, but the connection has been known and explained to you many times in the past.

That is the importance of this area. That is why all eyes are upon you now, the entire world knows of the situation, and the highest structures of power on Earth are all trying their best to help. All history has known of this place, and the spiritual significance of it. All history has known the Jews, and many have tried to take the foundation away, to tear down the house, and to become the new foundation. We have told you that at the cellular level, your ancient and present enemies know that no stone can remain of the Jewish foundation for them to gain the power that they wish. You can even see this in the present situation. There is no other situation on the planet like this. It is a play of energy that is beginning to shift, and with shift, there is often anxiety.

You wonder why you chose to be here? You could hardly wait to get back! You could hardly wait to come in again, knowing all of the things that might happen, for you are the foundation. You are the strength. You are the ones who have been here over and over—part of the dirt of the land. You understand the earth. You are *one* with it. Some of you have even tried to live in other places, but you keep "snapping back" like a rubber band, and you don't know why.

The very dirt of the earth calls to you here. This is where you belong! But you knew that, didn't you? We're going to tell you something. We're going to give you four points of advice about what you can do to complement and solve the situation. Some of you will say, *"You know, the situation never would have happened if we had done something different. We had our chances early on. We could have done this or we could have done that. We didn't do things correctly. If we had, this current situation never would have happened. We wouldn't be where we are today in this uncertainty if we had taken care of some things early on."*

I am here to tell you, dear ones, that nothing—nothing would have worked. For what you have now is the setup you designed, the one to have unrest here. You made it yourselves. It was the way you planned it, and now suddenly, a new energy arises—one that no one predicted, where you are now able to finally make things work. Nothing you could have done would have ever changed the situation. It played itself out perfectly to the end . . . but in the last decade, the earth changed its destiny, and you are now ready to redesign the plan. My partner [Lee] mentioned to you before that what you are seeing within the situation are the "rumblings of a solution," odd as it may seem.

We are going to give you four things you can do, and all of them are going to be difficult. We're not going to tell you what political plan to have. We're not going to tell you what leader to elect. For those items are very three-dimensional. No. We're going to tell you what to do personally to bring about collective change. These are profound exercises, and when you do them, they will not be just words. If you will do these things, dear ones, you will change your area, and those around you will feel it, also. Those on the other side will feel differently. Consciousness will change. In other parts of the world where they've pulled down the walls—that is, forgiven one another and done unexpected things to create harmony, they created the slow miracles of impossible cultural shift. It can also happen here. People change when consciousness is focused on the divine portion of the Human Being.

Celebrate

Here is the first of the four: Look at the situation. Look at it hard. See it in all its ugliness. Feel the fear and then celebrate it. Celebrate it! Can you do that? Did I say this would be hard? Can you celebrate a challenge? In the *now* you can. This is the catalyst. It is the *three*. It puts upon the area a compassionate blanket that says, "We know better. What we are seeing is not the final energy. We celebrate the change of solution. Our hearts cry for the death, but at the level of the divine, we celebrate the new solutions being created." This is hard. It must transform fear into creation. It must take you from a *two* to a *three*.

Visualize

The second one: Visualize in your mind the perfect solution without knowing what it is. [Audience laughter]. How do you do that? Here's how: Visualize yourself peaceful, as if it was finally over... not just suppressed, but over. Take the *now* out of linear. Make time advance to a place in the future where you say, *"Oh, we got through this."* Feel the peace without worrying about future events. Feel the peace of something happening, which indeed is finally working and has wisdom. You don't have to remember how it happened—just feel it!

Again, you are creating compassion—the catalyst of change. You are filling empty energy spaces with an energy of solution, one you can't even comprehend. It won't be the first time the Jews did that! Your lineage is filled with this: surviving the unsurvivable—having trust, faith—holding the hand of those who spiritually know more than you—connecting to God and being lifted up. And here it is again. It does not have to be "religious" to be worthy of your looking into it. For the divine is inside, and we have said it before. Personally, you are as spiritual as any temple. The essence of God sits before me.

Responsibility

Here is the third one—perhaps the hardest of all: Look at the situation and remember—remember that you created it. As sure as you sit in these chairs, in the planning sessions on the other side of the veil, you created it! This was the plan. *"Oh, I don't know, Kryon, that's a tough one. Why would I ever do that to myself, to my family?"* Let me give you an expression we have given before: *Iron sharpens iron.* You are the ones between the hammer and the rock being sharpened—divinely sharpened. Each time the hammer comes down, it's not easy. The challenges seem to increase, but what emerges is a fine tool—one that is so sharp in its wisdom and in its solution that it is entirely new in concept. *Iron sharpens iron.* And so at a level that you don't even know you have, you chose to come back and be sharpened in the wisdom of God. It isn't the first time you have made this kind of choice.

Your Vows (a Revisited Concept)

The fourth one is perhaps not as hard as the others, but it is still profound. Listen, shamans, we have told others around this earth something you need to hear, also. You've been here before. You have *awakened* before. You have picked up the pen and scribed the scriptures before. You are your own ancestors! This is not the first time you have felt the love of God in your midst. This is not the first time you've felt the entourage around you. But in this whole energy, so many of you gave vows to God. Some of you even married God so that you could focus completely on spiritual things, and you spent your lives as ancient priests on your knees and in the sackcloth. Some of you did that right here.

Maybe you didn't know this, but we are here to tell you that vows to God carry over from lifetime to lifetime. Did you know that? Now, let me ask you, shamans: How many of you have vowed poverty? How many of you vowed to be alone? You want to know why relationships between people don't work? Because you feel guilty every time they do! There is a vow inside you that reminds you that you must stay celibate in order to worship God! But those ancient vows stick as residuals within you, and you fight them every day, even in the new energy.

Perhaps it's time to drop them. We give you this information so that silently, in your chair or at home, later, if you wish, you might consider dropping those old energy vows. Here is what you might say: *"Dear Spirit, I drop the vows of the old energies. I deserve to be abundant, to be loved, to be with those who love me. I deserve to have a new beginning. I deserve to be part of a new energy of solution that helps change the land."* Remember the spiritual axiom: First take care of yourself . . . then the things around you will change.

For some of you, these four things simply sound like words in the air. But they'll create more energy than any sword ever could. They will shake the land with their profundity. They will shine light into dark places. They will build a temple in you that will heal the land around you. And in the process, you will conquer no one . . . and the others will conquer no one. In the process, together you will eventually discover family and conquer differences.

Ownership of Holy Places?

Let me discuss another thing: No one owns God! This is one family, one Earth, one humanity, each with different tasks. No tribe owns the essence of God. We tell you this because this is also part of the solution. Finally, there is a potential of a recognition, perhaps, that the holy of holies can never be owned by anyone, ever. Perhaps they should be stewarded, and not owned? But for this to happen will require the ownership of responsibility for honoring the integrity of the family . . . a respect of things important to each other. No one can ever, or will ever, own the holy places. In the old energy way of "the immune system," there was always a fight for the what was considered sacred. Now we are inviting an energy of "the thymus" to create harmony, instead of fighting for the same sacred things.

The Opening

There is more, oh, there is more: We're going to do something that is necessary, now that you know you have the tools. It's something that some of you expected because you knew a change would have to happen in this place. We're going to give you energy, but at the same time, we draw upon your permission—the humanity in this space, and those who are praying at this moment all over the world, to do this. Many of you expected what follows at a cellular level.

In the name of Spirit, in the name of family, we open a spiritual portal in this great land right here and now. [Pause] And now we are going to define what that means: A portal in this new energy is not an opening where God flows in with splendor. Instead, a portal is a spiritual energy door—an opening that allows the Human to connect to wisdom. Each Human Being, on their own, with intent, may access this portal, and walk through the new door. And through the portal is an advancement, a catalyst, a *three* of wisdom, solution, inner peace, and yes, even joy. The portal acknowledges the wisdom of the Humans and the enablement of the humanity. With the opening of this portal, we are going to give you information we have never given you before, for this is the time. This information is global about the new energy. This information will be transcribed and given to thousands in these next few weeks. It's time.

Return of the Ascended Masters

We speak now also to the readers who are casting their eyes on the page. We speak now to those who are of many ancient and powerful spiritual beliefs. This is the year of the beginning of the return of the energy of the ascended masters worldwide.

You may say this is metaphoric, but listen: Most of the ancient belief systems on this Earth had ascended prophets, and so many believers are expecting them to return. Well, the return is imminent, but not in the way you expected. Like the temple, we tell you this: The essence of the ascended master is about to enter the Human heart and mind if you choose. For those here [speaking to the Jews], we say that the one whose chair you leave empty within your ceremony, is about to sit down and have dinner with you! It's about time, is it not?

This ascension energy will happen one Human at a time in many cultures. We speak to the other cultures that have expected a second coming, a first coming, or even a third coming. We say the same is true for you. For the joy you feel in the worship of your ancient masters will manifest itself in this new energy, within *you!* For if you look at the core of all belief systems, you will find the love of God. And if you wonder about that, we say if it looks different from love to you, that's because of what Humans did to it, not God.

Let us make ourselves clear. The energy of *the return* is at hand, worldwide. There is protocol here for this. Some have said *"I don't think you can take the profound divine energy of an ascended master and pass it to a Human Being."* Let me remind you of the old faith of your own history [again speaking to the Jews]. Elijah had a partner, Elisha. And if you recall, Elisha, after being informed about the upcoming ascension, asked the prophet this: "Dear Master, may I have your mantle when you ascend?" And the answer was "Yes, Elisha, if you can see me ascend, you may have my mantel." It was a test of vibrational shift—a test of enlightenment, was it not? If you will read the ancient history that you have, you will find out that not only did Elisha see and report it, but he also received the mantle of Elijah that was passed to him. And he took the spiritual mantel of the prophet and did great works. And where he walked the Earth, Humans felt the love of God.

The mantle of the master, the ascended one, was passed to the Human Being who was still alive. Now, is it such a stretch of your minds in an interdimensional way to understand that this event is happening again? This is what they meant when the prophets of Earth spoke of their return. Again, we say that this is not a religious proclamation. This is about family! It is about the way things work in an interdimensional way. It was always this way, dear ones, but how could interdimensional spiritual concepts be given within an old energy? Each ascended master knew of the potential of this time on Earth. It's contained in many scriptures, and the return of those masters was foretold for this, the time where you are now hearing these words.

The Ones Coming

That's not all. There is a group of Human beings coming whom you will not be able to control. They're going to think differently than you do. You're not going to like some of the things they do, and you're not going to be able to do anything about it... for they are your children! These are children all over the area, not just in Israel. They're on all borders, in all tribes, in all lands and communities. Don't be shocked if the children get together and teach the adults a thing or two about peace in this next span of time. When the children have more power, things will change. We are telling you this because it is so. It is part of the promise. It is part of the solution. There is a different kind of Human Being coming who will shake hands with the divinity of God on both sides, a Human who understands that the heart is the center—a Human who understands the difference between the immune system and the thymus.

Some of you will leave differently than you came in. You will carry intent for the mantle, knowing full well that you can leave this place and take on the mantle of the ascended master—to walk differently among those you work and play with—to feel an inner peace about yourself and your land and those who are part of *the situation*. But there has been much more going on here than teaching.

Did you feel the touch of those whom you knew before, but whom are no longer living? They are here, you know, for this is an important reunion. We told you this when we started. We don't want to leave. The entire time we have been here, each one of you has had your feet washed. Some of you have felt the pressure of Spirit upon your shoulders. Some of you have seen the colors that are on the stage. Some of you will leave here knowing that Spirit talked to you today as a family member. And some of you will wonder if any of this could be so.

Each is loved equally. It's not what you do, dear ones—it's not about the works. It's about the journey! You are a family member, and we're going to see you again as we've seen you in the past, over and over.

There will come a day when you and I will see each other open-eyed, and when we do, you will sing your name in light to me in the Hall of Honor. You did it before, you know. And when I see you, we will discuss the time when the Humans came together in Tel Aviv, pretending not to know each other on this day. And then we'll have another reunion . . . one that is spectacular beyond words.

If you could see what I see, you would see the potential of what we have described on this planet before. For 11 years, we have given a label to the potential that you now have before you.

For the Jew and the Gentile, we have called this energy the beginning of *The New Jerusalem.*

The New Jerusalem is not a place in Israel. It's the description of a city of peace called *The Earth.* How appropriate! Is this truly the center? On this, the only planet of free choice in the Universe, is this the center? Yes, it is. But somehow you knew that, too, didn't you?

So it is, dear ones, the entourage now pulls away from this group, back through the crack in the veil. What an honor to have been able to be around you for this short amount of time. What an honor to visit the foundation in the center of the Universe.

And so it is.

Kryon

Ask the readers right now, the ones who are seemingly not in your time frame, if they are actually seeing this "nonexistent" page! Of course they are! Can you join them in your love, even though you perceive them in your future? Reader, can you join those here [in the room] NOW? The answer is yes. Therefore, you have just participated in an interdimensional time event.

Kryon

(New Hampshire, November 2000)

Live Channelling

"The Interdimensional Human" Part II

Channelled in
New Hampshire
November 2000

Chapter Four

"The Interdimensional Human" Part II
Live Channelling
New Hampshire

This live channelling has been edited with additional words and thoughts to allow clarification and better understanding of the written word.

From the writer . . .

Okay . . . some of you are asking, "What about Part I? Where is it?" The live channelling of "The Interdimensional Human, Part I" is Chapter 12 of *Kryon Book Eight, Passing the Marker.*

Greetings, dear ones! I am Kryon of Magnetic Service. We have said it so many times—that there is an entourage pouring into this place through the veil—one that is going to make itself known to you this day.

Dear Human Being, there is an attribute you may not be aware of fully, which we have mentioned before: Beyond the intellect—beyond that part of your brain that wonders whether this communication is real, there is an energy that we can only call divine. There is an energy of family. There is an inter-dimensional piece of you, which you have no concept of, within the duality that you walk around in. And here you are, seated in these chairs, sitting in the energy of the divine. Some of you this night will not be disappointed,

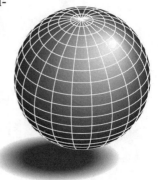

because flowing in here now is an awesome energy of those whom you have known in the past as family—those you've known on the other side as friends. What is flowing in here is what we have called a "soup of energy," flowing into this place and around every chair.

There is so much to tell you—so much knowledge to impart to you in this moment, which we call precious. Instead, we would like to celebrate the divinity of the family for a moment. We would like to celebrate *you!* Some of you have said, *"Well, Kryon, I don't feel real divine right now."* Well maybe it's time you did! For a moment, suspend the belief of the intellect. For a moment, we invite you to feel the family as it pours in here with its loving arms that say, "We expected you."

Time after time, we have sat in this energy [speaking of New Hampshire]. Time after time, we have greeted family in this area. Let this be the best reunion yet. Let this be the most profound one because of what is to come. This is the first time we have addressed you in the new energy within this area. We have something we want to say about that. Dear Human Being—dear angel disguised as a Human Being—listen to me: This family member [Kryon, speaking of himself] knows what you've done! The entourage that comes in and surrounds you sees the perfectness of the divinity inside each of you! We know that it is *you* on this planet right now who is responsible for the new reality and the new situation.

The family that is here celebrates the Human who is here! The family announces something profound to you and wishes to let it ring out all through this hall: We are looking at those who have decided collectively to create what is going to be known eventually as the potential of the New Jerusalem. It had to start somewhere, and I'm here to tell you that it started with the shamans of the earth . . . those awakening who sit here hearing and reading this!

For those who sit here and read this are those who have awakened before. These are the ones who have been searching for the divine pieces inside. These are the ones sitting in the chairs reading and listening, who so often will come to a meeting such as this. And so it is splendorous intent that separates the energies of what you could have done from what you instead chose to do. It's all about choice, is it not? There is so much to say—so many stories—and we know them all, dear ones. We know who you are by name, and although some have heard it before, we're going to tell you this: There comes a time when we will again see you on the other side of the veil. When we do, we'll recognize one another, and you will sing your name in light to me! And we'll wink at one another because of this day when you were disguised as a Human Being and we met. Metaphorically, that "energetic wink" between us will say, "I remember it, too—the time we met on Earth when you didn't remember what you looked like—when you didn't remember your purpose on Earth—when you had no idea what *home* was really like." We will remind you that you played out the role perfectly, and how much we loved you throughout all of it.

Some of you might be asking, *"Why am I here? What brings me to the planet?"* Some of you may say, *"I'm unhappy right now."* We say this to you: There is an entourage around you that moves with you daily, that knows everything about you. Did you know that? Pretend to be alone, but you can't be. We've told you this before. There is so much activity around each and every Human Being that it would stagger your interdimensional imagination. [Kryon chuckle] Much is hidden, but about to be revealed.

Some of you have elected to feel the energy of the divine around you and have taken some small steps to allow you to feel this. But this is the year where it could begin in a larger way. We sit in an energy now that we never could have told you about before the energy actually began. And it began shortly after we saw you last time. Dear ones, there was no entity on the planet who could have told you what could have happened at the millennium shift. Would it be the beginning, perhaps, of a change of consciousness? For you are the planet of free choice. You could have done anything, and what we saw was intent—a celebration of the new.

The old energy could not get through that celebration—could not exist during it—and the event was grand indeed. This may sound unbelievable, like the string of many unbelievable things we're going to give you tonight [Kryon chuckle], but that millennium shift was celebrated throughout the Universe by family members from the Great Central Sun. All over the Universe, they knew what had happened here. We are not necessarily talking about the other life forms that may be on other planets. We are talking about family! We're talking about those who are like you. We're talking about those on the other side of the veil. A universal celebration went from one end of the Universe to the other, and it was [is] grand indeed. You might say, *"The earth is only a speck of illumination in the midst of an infinite beach of light. How could it be grand?"* Although that is your perception, the earth is the only planet where this test is being performed.

Listen to this: This is the only planet where angels disguise themselves in flesh and blood and show up with a design of not knowing who they are. And in this new energy, you have allowed a family to come in from the other side of the veil tonight, and some of you will feel the hugs to prove it.

Surrounding your chairs right now is the thickness of love, if you choose to feel it. Reader, are you getting this? Within the energy of this message, we invite the seers who are here to witness the colors on the stage. We invite the seers in here to witness the colors on the floor [the audience]. We are going to talk to those of you who came with secrets. Oh, we know what they are, dear ones, for we live with you! We say that in the most loving way. Dear ones, you think you have a secret? It is known by God; it is known by family; it is known by Spirit. Some of you have secrets you have not told others because you felt they would not react well to them. Some of you carry secrets regarding your biology. Don't you think we know about that? Some of you have situations you have brought into this place as you sit in the chair listening and reading, and you say, *"I'll do my best to sustain myself, but when I leave this place, I'm still going to be anxious."* Indeed! If that is your choice, you can have that. But let me give you another alternative, oh one of divine choice: What if you were to leave this place without it—changed? What if you visualized taking the situation and leaving it on the chair when you get up? How about that one? It is your choice, but you may say, *"Well, Kryon, those are only words."* Oh, no. No. When words get transformed into intent, intent manifests reality. The co-creative Human Being who is the angel makes the difference, and you can't even fathom that you have that power. Only words? If that is the case, then why did the words of the vows you took in past lives become such a powerful player in your reality now? And the answer is this: Words of angels have power!

We're going to give you interdimensional aspects tonight. We're going to tell you things we've never shared before, as well as things we have given you previously. But it is the first time that any of this information is going to be transcribed for all to share.

We are not going to leave the subject of love just yet. It's a celebration. Humanity has indeed shown its divinity in the year 2000. As you look around the earth, there are trouble spots. As you look around your community, there is anger. Perhaps there is violence; perhaps there is fear. Dear ones, that tells you a lot about the Human processes. It tells you a lot about the end of certain energies—about things being torn apart because there can be no more fence-sitting. We told you that. We have also told you about an opening chasm between the old and the new, which will create profound changes on the planet. We told you about an energy "drawing to zero," where many things must restart themselves into a wiser frame of perspective.

The ETs and the Year 2000

Some of you have asked the question, *"What about the ETs? What do they think about all this?"* The answer? They're astonished! Did you know that every time you show your power to move your reality, it frightens them? Did you know that many of them have left in dismay? Do you know that some of them have left in great fear? It's because the Human Being has started to change reality. You know that the ETs visit this Earth. The universe is teeming with life. How could it be otherwise? No ET may touch you without your permission. We have told you that for years. Did you know that they're starting to see you do something that has confused them? Some of them have been in a space they thought was safe, for it was somewhat interdimensional. The Human Being they know is 4D.* They have a 5D presence, perhaps even 6. In physics, this means they can do things that you cannot. This is not an enlightenment measure . . . only a physical one. Their time frame is different, and their reality is physically different. Suddenly they are finding that you can see them, whereas you could not before! Suddenly they are discovering that you are becoming more like them in your physics, and that does not work for them. Did you know that? Let me ask you this: Why is it that they are so dedicated . . . often risking their own existence, to discover what makes the Human work? Suddenly they are finding that in 60 years here, the rules have changed, and they are no longer able to "work in the dark."

[*Kryon's use of 4D refers to our common four dimensions: (a) height; (b) width; (c) depth; and (d) time. It is also now understood by science that there are at least 11 dimensions in atomic structure.]

We seldom speak of these things, for the information is often dramatic, and not about the love of God, which is the message of Kryon. But this information is about the appropriateness of the angels on Earth [you] moving into another dimension while pretending to be Human. We tell you that because all things have changed. All of the energies around you have changed. Even some of the most steadfast of all principles of physics are beginning to move because you have given permission to expose them.

Interdimensional Commonality

Let me tell you who you are. It's time to reveal a bit more about the interdimensionality of the Human Being. This is an extension of the teaching that we gave some months ago [July 2000] when we revealed information about guide energy. Now it's time to reveal information about Human energy.

We're going to give you information that is difficult to absorb. How do you tell a 4D creature about double-digit D? How do you tell a linear creature that what they do *now* can change their past? What they have done already seems to be set in cement . . . but it isn't. How does that compute, dear linear one? Yet it is so. The answer is that it computes with The Third Language—what we have previously called "the catalyst of divine communication." Many of you here, and reading this, will receive the pictures and the concepts at the cellular level—the divine level of what we are giving you as best we can in a linear fashion, one word at a time.

Dear ones in this room, in this great space where you sit and listen, you are joined by tens of thousands of other Human Beings at this instant as they read these words. We know who the readers are because they have given intent to cast their eyes upon this page—a page you might say "does not exist yet," because you are in linear time. We ask you to put yourself in the *circle* of time, understanding that the past has manifested into the *now* for you, which eventually co-creates the manifestation of your future—something you think you have not yet created, but you have. All the potentials for manifestation are there, waiting for you to come upon them and manifest the appropriate energies. This may seem like backward talk to many of you. You better get used to it, for what we are doing is bringing you into a *now* time frame of interdimensional things. These are the things about which we must speak.

Ask the readers right now, the ones who are seemingly not in your time frame, if they are actually seeing this "nonexistent" page! Of course they are! Can you join them in your love, even though you perceive them in your future? Reader, can you join these here *now?* The answer is yes. Therefore, you have just participated in an interdimensional time event.

We have told you before that many things that are going to be brought to you in an interdimensional fashion may look odd, weird, and spooky because you have not seen them before. But we remind you that it is only because you are unfamiliar with what is common that makes you feel this way. Just because you have never experienced it, it does not mean it doesn't exist.

We have given the parable before of the sheltered, primitive native who lives on the tropical island. He is happy, and he has always lived in the tropics and always will. This native, who loves where he lives, enjoys wonderful weather—always warm and humid. Suddenly he is exposed to a block of ice. He has never seen ice before. He has no concept of what this could be. He doesn't understand that it is common water—something that surrounds his own island, and which is very familiar to him. But he is seeing it in another physical form, one that is common on Earth, but which he has never experienced. Naturally, ice has existed all along in physics, but he's never seen it in his reality, you see. One of the first things the Human Being does with information of this nature is to fear it! So it is, therefore, that the things that we bring you even tonight might be feared, for they are radically different for you, yet they are common in the grand scheme, much like ice was to the native.

The Interdimensional Human

It is time to tell you about how some things work, and we're going to start with the Human Being. Then we're going to move into some biological areas and present information that we have never discussed for transcription before.

Human Being, you are not all here! [Laughter] Now you suspected that, didn't you? Listen: There are pieces and parts of you that are missing from what you consider to be the complete Human Being. In a four-dimensional space called "your reality," you have put skin on a creature, had it born into the Earth plane, given it a name, and called it the complete Human. But it isn't complete. It doesn't even begin to be complete within multiple dimensionality.

Here is information that some of you have always suspected. This explains how many things work, and it explains the tendrils and the strings that are magnetic between the pieces and the parts of who you are individually. Individually, you are not all here! There is a portion of every single Human Being in this room that is spread out into interdimensional space . . . and the parts have many purposes.

(1) Let us speak of the first interdimensional one that inhabits your body. The divinity that you call the Higher-Self is not the end-all of the spiritual part of you. It's simply the one that stays with you in your body that you can sense. That Higher-Self is the part that you cling to. It's the magic; it's the spiritual part; it's the part you try to talk to and communicate with. But it's only a part of the name you call "yourself."

I want to give you the other parts, and I want to tell you where they are. I wish to tell you what they are doing, also. If, at the end of this, you say, *"This is unbelievable,"* I will have accomplished my goal. It is the love of God that has allowed such communication at The Third Language, and some will "see" it. Eventually many will understand that all that is being spoken tonight from this stage is true—that you are so much larger, spiritually, than you think you are.

(2) There is a part and a piece of you that is on the other side of the veil right now as your guide. *"What? You mean to tell me, Kryon, I'm my own guide?"* Yes, a piece of you is. And we have described the guides before, and we're going to review this again. There is a piece of "you" that is part of the energy, which is what we call the "guide soup." Again, we tell you regarding guides and angels: You want to put numbers on them, give them skin and wings, name them, and say, *"There's three, there's four, there's eight."* Actually, they're infinite, yet they're one, like an ocean that is one ocean, but filled with millions of parts of water. Your guides and angels are forms of energy, not pieces of your 4D existence. We have told you this before: Part of you is in your own guide-set! What better advice could you have than a piece and a part of the angel that you are, sitting on the other side of the veil as a guide? It's a guide that is cemented to you wherever you walk on this planet, but one who knows you intimately— who knows why you are here—knows the contracts, and knows the predispositions that you have. What better energy could there be for you, than *you?* Get used to it. That's the second part of you. Do you ever talk to yourself? Enough said. Long ago we even described a possibility where your guides might retreat temporarily from you. When this happens, it's devastating for a moment! For *you* have left . . . *you!*

(3) Let's talk about the third part of you. There is a part of you that is on the other of the veil, which is in a planning session

with all the rest of you! Now how could that not be? Think about it. Human Being, have you ever wondered how co-creation works? Have you ever wondered how synchronicity works? Are you aware that you cannot have synchronicity by yourself? It has to be in regard to those around you. Are you aware that you are also someone else's synchronicity? It has to be part of complex planning.

Co-creation is not done in a closet. It involves moving through life, giving intent, and an interface of energy with everyone you touch—everyone you come in contact with—those you shine your light around. What kind of planning do you think that takes? It's on a scale that has no time and yet all time. There is a planning part of you and also every other Human Being on the Earth, on the other side of the veil. Perhaps you had this idea that there was a planning session before you got here and now you're on your own? No. How does that make you feel, Human Being—angel—divine one? There is a piece and part of you on the other side of the veil that is coordinating with others for synchronicity, for co-creation, and for your intent. Did you think you were in a vacuum, and things around you just "happened"? No. There is guidance and planning still going on, and it's you, and the others around you that are doing it—all of it—waiting for your search to take you to the place where you realize that the *ice* is not strange at all. [Laughter]

We have told you about the challenge in your life being testing. We have told you that there is a golden plate that has your solutions as well as your challenges. We have told you that all is in balance, and in the past we have told you that you create your solutions at the same moment you create your challenges . . . way before you got here. Now you know that the challenges are 4D, but the solutions are multiple D!

Now, how do you think that's facilitated for yourselves while you're here? What about the other Human Beings? Some of you feature 4D prayer: You get on your knees before Spirit and say, *"Please, God, make them change. Make the ones around me do this; make them do that."* Let me give you the interdimensional way: Instead of pleading with God to change others, start with yourself! Change yourself as much as you are asking the others to change. If you will show your light in this way, it begins a planning session for the others, too! I'll tell you what happens. Although it's through individual choice of the other Human Beings around you, your change creates energy. There are those in the planning sessions that see this and bring choice of intent to those around you. For you are creating a reality of your own through your divinity, the Higher-Self, the Guide-Selves, the Planning-Self, and every interdimensional Human Being around you is potentially affected. They are not changed, but rather they are given the energy of new choice, sometimes a challenge . . . just because you changed yourself. This often creates search, compassion, and the beginning of real differences in all your lives.

And you want to put skin on the Human and give it a name and have it walk around the earth alone? Hardly! That's not the way it works, dear ones. I haven't finished telling you the rest.

(3) This is going to sound odd, unbelievable, and very strange. Part of your contract here, as best as can be described in your linear fashion, is to be with those in your last Human family on Earth, which you departed from before you incarnated in the body you have now. Did you know that? Simply put, you are part of the guide-sets of those you left in the last lifetime! You might say, *"Well now, Kryon, that does not make sense in timing."* You're right. Get used to it. It does not make sense. In the NOW, all of these things are possible. *"Do you mean that I can be in two places at the same time in different time frames? I can be in the past and the future at the same time?"* Yes. And you will never understand that as long as you are a Human Being. At the level of The Third Language, however, it is the love of God that supplies this gift

of understanding, and in a moment, you'll understand more of what the gift really is.

So, Human, you are busy someplace else helping family that existed in your past! Think of how profound that is! There will be those listening and reading who say, *"I still don't understand a thing he's saying."* But the language of the *three* presents to you what we are saying in an interdimensional way: You are doing work while you sit here, and you thought you were doing nothing. Perhaps you wondered when you were going to get on with what you came here for? You've been doing it all along in another place, in another time. Some of you have had dreams that showed you what you were doing. You cast them off as just so much fantasy, but now you know they were real. So often the dream state is an interdimensional place where your brain disengages and free-floats. The energies of the *now* may come in, and you see them and feel them. That is why so many of the dreams that you have make no linear sense, do they? They are out of time, out of place, jerking around from costume to costume—have you noticed? You are closer to your actual reality when you're dreaming than when you're awake.

The "Longing for Connection"

I will give you another attribute. Here is an attribute that many of you have not thought of, and it's time it got presented. We have just told you that the Human Being's structure is not all in the physical body—that part of it is on the other side of the veil, part in the guide-set, and part of it even in the past. Now, if you are that segmented—if you are truly that spread out, wouldn't you feel something? Yes. I would like to give you an attribute that Lightworkers are starting to hear and recognize and understand. Some of you have been watching, looking, and hoping that someday your "twin flame" would walk in. Some-day the soulmate whom you know is *out there* will "come back."

Oh, if you only knew what that meant! Here is the truth: You're not expecting another Human Being, dear ones; instead, you're asking for the return of those interdimensional parts and pieces of you to combine with the 4D self. You feel the longing and the love, and you want this so badly! We're here telling you that that's the longing for the pieces of *you* to come together!

Now . . . what does that tell you about our teachings over the last 11 years? We have hold you to discover self—that's where the magic is—that's where the love is! And now you are in the energy that promotes this reunion. It's a reunion that is so grand that those pieces can touch one another in an interdimensional way. They can greet one another and say, "It's about time we found our self-worth. It's about time we fell in love with ourselves. It's about time we walked the earth tall, sufficient, abundant, and proud that we are together." That's what that feeling is about. That's what it's always been about, and now in this energy we can give you this information. The longing for the love of your life is often the longing to connect with all the *you* parts that are spread out. Blessed is the Human Being who discovers self, for that Human will have internal love—not dependent, no longer longing, content in his/her life, and a grand lighthouse of energy.

More about Guides and Angels

A few months ago, we told you that the guides were an "energy soup." There were never only two or three, you know. Eleven years ago, we gave you metaphors, just like scripture has done for eons. The *three* information of the guide-set is a *three* energy. It does not represent three guides with three names with skin and wings. What is the *three* energy? It is the energy of the catalyst. It's the situation where one energy creates another, meets its promise, its manifestation, and its creation. We indicated back then that the energy shifts of Earth, and you, personally, would move from the *two* energy to the *three*. Now you know the metaphor of what we were speaking of. The guides are infinite, yet one. It's difficult to explain to you how such energy could surround you in the closet when you turn off the light, pretend to be alone, and cry in private. But we're all there—we're all there.

Every Human Being comes in to the planet with an entourage. You may try to list them one at a time and give them names in your meditations if you choose. That's a very linear thing, and we understand it. But let me tell you, your guide-set is infinite, yet it is one. *"Exactly how many guides are there, Kryon?"* The answer is yes. [Laughter] When you plug in something electrical, do you ask *how many electricity* are coming through the wire? How could you "tap in to" Source [Spirit] with questions like that? Yet in 4D, that is exactly what you do!

We've described this before, how such a thing could be, but let me give you some insight also as to *who* is there. Maybe out of time, out of space—but we want you to understand and celebrate *who* is there. When we opened this evening, we told you that there was an entourage that was going to pour in here and surround the chairs. We told you that some of you would feel hugs this very night. Reader, we included you, too, remember? Some of you will feel pressure on the shoulders, on the knees, and perhaps the head. Let me tell you who's facilitating part of that: Dear ones, if it is true that you are in some interdimensional space and are fragmented—that a part of you is helping those in the past that used to be your family before you reincarnated, then you might project right now those *who* are part of your own guide-set as well.

The ones whom you knew on this planet as family, who have passed over, are currently sitting on your shoulder. This is truth, dear ones. A piece and a part of them, whether they've reincarnated or not, is with you right now. "Out of space, out of time," you might say . . . yet they are here. There is the mother, the father, the sister, the brother, and the child. They are all here. Do you ever wonder if the ones who departed that you loved so much, that you anguished so much over, could ever "look down from above" and see you? Well, they don't have to "look down." All they have to do is glance to the right! There is a piece and part of all of them with you now.

We invite some of you to feel this and understand what we're saying. It's part of the love of God that gives you this, so that you will not be alone . . . ever. It's a part of the promise of family that we have never discussed with you before. It's never been transcribed before—part of the energy that you carry around with you are those who passed on in your own lifetime.

Now, whom do you think taps you on the shoulder to see the 11:11 and the 12:12 on the clocks? Why did you look at that particular moment? Why not when the clock was displaying 11:10? It's because you were tapped on the shoulder by those who love you and surround you, who wanted to say, "I want to show you something very unique and interesting. Look at the clock now!" The next time it happens to you, rather than feeling a wash of "What is this about?" or "Oh, isn't this interesting or odd?" we challenge you instead to say, "I love you, too . . . I love you, too." For that's what's going on. It's a tap on the shoulder. Your own loved ones are saying to you, "We're really here! Look at the clock—look at the clock! We're here, and if you don't believe it, we're going to have you do it again and again and again until you understand that these things are not coincidental. We want you to know that we are proud, and that we love you."

The Hiding Light

There are those in this room and reading this right *now*, who would like to hear this. Do you want to know what you're doing in life? Waiting, are you not, for something special? [Kryon chuckle] *"Dear God, when am I going to find out what I'm supposed to do?"* How many times has Spirit heard that in your secret times?

I'd like to tell you about a very dark place. It's the bottom of the ocean. There's an anchor there imbedded in the mud, doing its job. At the bottom, there isn't much light, so it's very dark and cold. Encrusted with mud and barnacles, the anchor is connected to a dirty chain. The chain goes up hundreds of feet, and on the surface, there is an ocean liner with literally thousands of Human Beings. Now, if you were to interview the anchor, the conversation would go like this: *"Woe is me; I'm in the dark. I'm not going anywhere. I'm encrusted with mud and barnacles. I am not pretty. Dear Spirit, when am I going to get on with what I'm supposed to do?"* [Laughter]

Can I talk to the anchors in the room, please? Can I tell you how beautiful you are? Can I tell you that there is a chain connected to every Human Being in your life? Do you wonder what you're doing, and do you wonder when you're going to get on with your purpose, or your spiritual work? Well, you're right in the heat of it, and you don't even know it! Mom, Dad, what are you doing in the family? Worker, what are you doing in the workplace? You walk from place to place, and you hold your light. That lighthouse shines light in spaces that were dark before you ever got there ... and you wonder when you're going to get on with it. Anchor, let me tell you that you have chains connected to many people. You don't see them—you don't know it. You're asking to get on with things, but we're here celebrating your lives because you're there as a great anchor, unmoving, holding that boat from dashing itself into the rocks. You don't have all the facts, and so we are here to say that you are dearly loved. You may be right in the middle of your contract, but on your knees before Spirit begging for your contract! [Laughter] Think about it. Do you really wish to be removed from that place? When you leave and shut the door, the room will again be dark. We didn't say it would be easy . . . dear anchor. That's why we call you Light*workers*. Many of you are in places that would be very dark indeed without the light you bring. So . . . why not instead pray the interdimensional prayer: *"Dear God, tell me what it is I should know."*

New Information about Human Biology

We cannot come to this area [New Hampshire] without giving you science. Some have asked, *"Why is that, Kryon? Is this area different from other areas?"* Oh, yes. Each area has its own individual attitudes of energy. This has been the one that has been selected over and over for revelation in what you have called science, and what we call "the way things work." We're going to reveal to you, in simplicity, something that has been revealed to one of the researchers in the room. But now it can be transcribed for all to hear and see.

[For the listeners in the room]: There will be energy developed from within the potential of eyes on the page right now. We are speaking of now. We are also speaking of what *you* have called your future, but we see the reader even as we speak. This has nothing to do with fortune-telling or predestination. What we see are the intents of those, even now in your time frame, who have brought themselves to read these words on the page before them, which is also, in a way, the page before you. Remember, in our thinking, they are also in the room with you now.

Magnetics has never been understood by your science. The reason it has been unfathomable is because it is interdimensional . . . that is, only partially in 4D. You have two items on Earth that you live with daily but which you cannot see or understand—magnetics and gravity. If you knew the inner workings of magnetics, you would understand that it is an interdimensional force that presents itself. You have worked with the *results* of magnetics, for you know how physics will react, to some degree, within magnetic fields. And you have made good use of what you have studied as the effects of the use of magnetics, but there is not one Human who totally understands what it is, or knows truly how it works. The magnetic field of the planet literally imprints information in a communication to the cellular structure of the body, and we have told you this many times. You will have the ability to understand and see how this operates soon. Then, finally, there will be understanding. The fact that you will not be able to travel from planet to planet without carrying your own magnetic field with you will also be realized, for the magnetic field of the earth supports life. It is part of the picture, and it is part of your biology.

This year (2000), your science has acknowledged that what they have looked at for years has now revealed itself as being interdimensional. My partner has spoken of this even in the lecture today. But you might notice something: They have chosen 11 as the number of dimensions inside the heart of the atom. They are wrong. They missed it by one. For those involved in the mathematics of those decisions of what you have called the strings, I give you this: You forgot to count the zero as a dimension! For when you do, there are 12. For those involved in that study, they will know what I mean. There are 12 dimensions at the heart of all matter on the planet. There are 12 dimensions at the core level of all physics—all through the Universe—12. We have revisited the 12 over and over for you, to make you aware of these things. Magnetics involves the 12's. It is base-12, and we remind you in magnetics and in biology, which we are now going to discuss, to look for the 3's and the 4's and the 6's, which all modify into the 12's. You can still use base-10 math to solve base-10 and -12 problems, but you simply are not using the elegance and speed of the 12 system when you do so.

Listen: How many meridians of the body are there? Twelve. The ancients told you that. Now there are some healers in this interdimensional new energy who are discovering more. Even those of you who use the science of the 12 meridians of the body have discovered other meridians *above* the ones on the surface of the skin. Now we tell you that these new energies are going to present themselves to you in groups of 3's. It is not an accident that you have discovered some of these, dear ones. They are apart from the body, and now you're starting to treat the whole Human, including the interdimensional parts.

There is more to this than you think. Some may say, *"Kryon, you talk in circles."* Yes. [Laughter] Your DNA consists of 3's and 4's. Take a look. We have told you this before; look for the 12's. They are everywhere. And now we tell you this: There is symmetry in the twisting of the DNA that yells base-12.

The Human genome has been exposed this year for its elegance, and the map has been laid out for you to see. This is also the beginning of the discovery of the 12's, but it has not yet been coded or decoded. There are three steps to the discovery and the unveiling of the Human genome—the mapping, the coding, and the singing, and we're going to tell you about that "singing" now. Listen to this: We are going to speak of cellular vibrational attributes in a way that we have never discussed before. We wish to finally present what we're going to call *The Cellular Choir*. It's wrapped around "magnetics singing to magnetics," all in this interdimensional soup you thought was just biology. We're going to explain as much as we can to you about what this means.

When the Human genome is finally decoded, there is the potential of discovering The Cellular Choir—the discovery that Human cellular structure "sings" a certain tune, and it does it very well. Although somewhat metaphoric and simplified for this presentation, that tune is Human health. It keeps the body alive, but what is missing from the genome study will be "the tune master." For there will be revelations within this metaphor that the Human body could probably "sing" many tunes, but only one set is being sung, and it's an inefficient one! Who wrote the tunes? Who programmed the codes? Who is responsible for the "words"? This is metaphoric, and yet it is not.

There is a biological cellular choir. The Human body, at the cellular level, actually sings. These "tunes" that it sings are complex, and they harmonize in complex ways. You have probably heard about those healers in the past who tried to find certain frequencies that would resonate with certain parts of the body—certain systems of the body where the healers would have some positive results by the application of those frequencies? It is so, but what they have is not complete, so the success of the single frequency method is difficult to repeat.

Human bodies sing like a choir. Cellular structure vibrates at hundreds of thousands of vibrations per second, and we use the *second* as part of a 60-base. It's in 12's, too, and so is your clock. The body has a clock, also—a profound one, and it is 12-based. The *choir* sings to other cells in complex ways, and the other cells, literally, at levels that you cannot comprehend yet, understand what the choir is singing, and they respond as though they had instructions. *"Kryon, do you mean to tell me that if we had some way of measuring this, we could actually 'hear' it?"* It's out of your hearing range, of course, but it can be revealed. Yes, this is part of the discovery that is potentially in your backyard. The Human body resonates at complex frequencies well above 100,000 vibrations per second. Not one tone, not one per organ or per system, but in multiples. They sing in a harmony, which is complex, but specific to each organ and system. They also sing in certain ways to the body's clock, synchronizing with the magnetics of the moon, and creating signals that age your structure. By the way . . . this metaphor to music is sometimes more than a metaphor. How many notes are there in standard Western music between, but not including, the duplicated octave note? The answer? Twelve.

Some Can Hear It

Let me tell you something that no one has ever been told. It has to do with the breakdown of the Human body—regarding the aging of the Human body and the choir. Your aging body will often start to break down the ability of the Human ears to block out the lower-frequency portions of The Cellular Choir. Some of you have ringing in your ears, don't you? Scientists don't understand why that is either, so I'm here to tell you what it is. Although you are hearing only a few of the very low tones (compared to the tones of the cellular structure), The Cellular Choir is what is getting through to be heard to some degree by an aging ear system. Do you understand what I'm saying? You're actually starting to hear a portion the choir. This is due to the breakdown of a system within the inner ear that has the ability to filter it, but not in an aging ear. The next time some of you are hearing the ringing and find it distressing, I want you to start understanding what it is. Then perhaps you will not be distressed, since you understand it's part of health. You're just now starting to hear something that was blocked totally when you were younger.

It is well within your interdimensional tool set, the one you are now beginning to create, to measure the harmony of the choir, and to start building tools that will complement them. *"Do you mean, Kryon, that we're able to sing to the cells?"* Yes, you are. You can do it right now in an interdimensional way, which we call "discovering your divinity." This is the essence of all miracles. It's when the Human Being gives intent and says, *"I can change my bodily structure. I can put bone where there was no bone. I can chase out disease. What I'm going to do is have my divine parts interdimensionally sing to my cells, and I'm going to get miracles."* And you do! It's not new; it's been with you for a very long time, and you can call it whatever you want to, but that's the angel inside singing the correct "tunes" to the cells.

Now, there is the potential for you to develop devices within your science, if you choose to go there. There will be a tendency for some to be afraid. We have said this before. This elegant science that can heal the Human body, that understands how The Cellular Choir works, is also one that could be devastating if used improperly. Again, it will be your choice. I will tell you this: There are certain choir notes in certain dramatic structures, and we're being metaphoric now in some ways that could be disruptive to Human cellular structure to the degree where DNA would simply unwind itself, and the Human body would die almost instantly—all by singing the wrong tunes.

What are you going to do with this? Are you going to fear it if it starts to come your way? Are there those who are going to use the information improperly? That's up to you, dear ones. But you have opened this bag of interdimensionality, and it can't be closed. It's the love of Spirit that says there can be peace with this; there can be integrity with this. You don't have to worry about it being sequestered and used against you if it comes out into the open and everyone knows about it. When you took the step of changing your future those years ago, you gave permission to stay! You gave permission to void the prophecies and to create an earth that will have another scientific revolution similar to the one you have experienced in the last 100 years—only this one will only take 24. With this permission you created comes still another level of responsibility and integrity regarding what you will discover. Many will fear the technology that your very divinity has given permission for . . . a technology that will double your life span as a starter.

Grand healing can take place, the same kind of healing that took place in the temple of rejuvenation in Atlantis. You've probably already figured out that the first "tune" you might try to discover is the one that is sung to the body's clock. This is for the researcher in the room, information that has not been given to him: Would you like to discover some of the notes and some of the chords? You can do this in your *real time*. For there will come a time when you can present these *chords* in an interdimensional way to the Human cellular structure. When you do, look for and observe the sympathetic vibrations when you present the right chord. In real time, the cellular structure will react a certain way that is obvious, and you will know you've found the correct frequency grouping. This also goes for every kind of disease known to the Human. They will also react both positively and negatively to the frequencies. Real-time exposure. It will cut all the hit-and-miss experimenting and save time.

"Kryon, are you telling us that all we have to do is to have certain kinds of sound machinery present multiple frequencies to the body, and we're going to have healing?" Yes, but there is one thing I haven't told you: The instrument that does it, that records it, that plays it—the instrument that *sings*, has got to be a at least a seven-dimensional player! [Kryon chuckle] Nothing you have on the planet now will do it, but it's the understanding of what it's going to take that will help you create the science of it.

For those of you who don't want to wait for the machinery, let me remind you that this power is within you now. It's the divine part of you, which is interdimensional. You've got a seven-dimensional player in your body. It's higher than that, but we use the word *seven* as number-energy. It doesn't even fit into the 12, does it? It is the number of divinity that we are quoting. It's divine numerology that can *sing* the choir notes of healing.

Some of you will say, *"Well, I didn't understand anything today!"* [Laughter] In The Third Language, we tell you this: The love of God has given you information today that researchers on their own, without ever hearing this, have the potential to discover. We have a tendency to tell you in advance, so that when science discovers it and it gets published and validated, you will remember where you first heard it! Then you will understand that this communication was real. Our time together isn't about science. It's the time when family gets together. These things would never be given to you, ever, unless you were searching for the divine and you came to sit and hear or read in the energy with a family member: the sister, the brother, Kryon.

Before we leave, we're going to give you a reminder that we have given to so many others. Lightworker, we ask you again to examine who you are. Now that you know there are multiple pieces, we invite you to activate all of them, and in the process, how would you like to drop the vows? Why wait? It is the universal attribute of the shaman and the medicine man who sits here listening and reading. If you're interested in these kinds of things, even if you were dragged here by a friend, I'm telling you that there is a reason you sit in the chair. You can drop those old vows, those that carry over into the DNA that help keep you alone, poor—that keep you in anxiousness and in guilt, and especially the big one—the one that keeps you from loving yourself. Do you know what the common attribute of the *anchors* are here? They don't love themselves. How many of you stood before God in a past life and said, *"In order to focus on God, I'm going to be lonely. I'm going to grovel in the dirt. I'm going to put my head lower than anybody's head. I'm going to wear sandals; I'll never have anything good because I don't deserve it. I'll focus on God by doing these things."* How many of you have said that? I'm going to tell you: Almost everyone in the room and everyone who was led to read this document down to this conclusion is in that category.

There is a precious soul in the room who only has eight weeks of life on this planet—has only been here eight weeks [speaking of the infant in the room]. This child doesn't have any of the vow attributes at all. The Indigo Children—they come in with the vows dismissed. It's part of the divinity change in the evolution of humanity. But you still have them, and they don't. What are you going to do? Perhaps in these seconds when the family hugs you and holds you, you might say, *"I feel those who have passed on, and they are around my chair. In the name of Spirit, I drop those vows. They are no longer appropriate in this new energy. I vow instead to find those pieces of the ascended self, to bring them together to find self-worth; to find or develop partners in my life who also have self-worth, who have found their pieces and put their parts together, also. I vow to Spirit, in all appropriateness, for sustenance and sufficiency in my life—not to worry about money. I vow before Spirit to find my divinity and to find the love of self."* And then, dear ones, that *anchor in the mud* will be revealed in all its divineness—in all of its beauty.

A big difference, is it not? This all has to do with realization of self, of recognized divinity, of all the things we have talked about. And then I say to you the thing my partner does not want me to say: You never have to come back here, ever. You never have to sit in a Kryon meeting. For all of this energy and communication is possible in that closet where you're pretending to be alone. Creating this energy is not dependent on any kind of ritual. It does not require that you join anything at all, for the core issue is the prophet inside—complete and total . . . and we would not say that if it were not so.

As goes the Humans in this room, so goes the earth. Can you spread the love of God by walking and saying nothing? You can—anchors and lights that you are. I hope that there are those of you who have felt those past entities around you. Did you ever wonder if they are proud of you? Yes, they are, because you're the ones who did it. You are the ones who sit within an earth that no prophet ever described or predicted—ones that have a potential like no other future ever seen.

The last time we were here [November 1999], it was uncertain what you would do. Now we sit in a brand-new energy, one that is moving into the next level. The next step is the year of the *three*. You thought there were changes in 2000? Just wait! The year 2001 is the next step, and it represents the movement into the *three* energy . . . the catalyst.

And so it is that we say good-bye, but not for the final time, for there is no final time. We will see each of you again in the Hall of Honor, where we will call you by name. We will wink at one another and remember the day we met in the area you call New Hampshire, where you all gathered together, pretending to be something else.

And so it is that we have a hard time retreating from you. It has gotten harder and harder to close these communications, the closer you get to finding who you are. The visits from family on this side of the veil are something we look forward to in a way you'd never imagine. Again we say, you have no concept of who came to see whom here today. We knew you'd come, and you did. And in your intent, you've allowed the energy of Spirit to surround you—the loved ones to surround you. And in that energy of love, we have all basked, and we have loved you and washed your feet this night.

And so it is.

Kryon

Live Channelling

"The Return"

Channelled in
Buena Park, California
December 2000

Chapter Five

"The Return"
Live Channelling
Buena Park, California

This live channelling has been edited with additional words and thoughts to allow clarification and better understanding of the written word.

The 2000 Review – "The Return"

This meeting represents the annual "Home Room" meeting of Kryon in Southern California, Lee Carroll and Jan Tober's home base. It takes place in December of each year.

Greetings, dear ones, I am Kryon of Magnetic Service. With this voice, an energy comes rushing into this place, which this entourage of Lemurians has chosen to create [speaking of the audience]. There is no magic here this afternoon. There is nothing here that is out of the ordinary. For this is what happens when this many angels get together! And we have to say, as we have each time we have been before this assemblage, that there is great honor here. Into this room pours energies that you know. Into this room pours what you have called the helpers and the guides. Into this room pours family this afternoon.

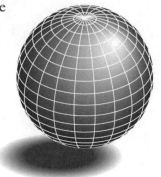

Let me tell you, reader, you don't have to sit in that chair alone. You think you're alone, and you pretend to be alone as your eyes scan this page. But I wish to tell you that there is an assemblage sitting in front of me in *now* time that welcomes you here. Whereas you may think that linear time would prohibit such a meeting, we are telling you that this is the difference between the old and the new.

Reader, you have one pair of eyes, along with the pair of ears of those with you who are hearing this. There are two pairs of organs right now that are doing the work of one: those hearing and those reading. And we say to you that these all are in the same spiritual time frame. So we welcome you, reader, right now. All of those who sit in front of me know of your existence. Even though you are not "here" at this meeting, we invite you to be greeted as though you were, by this family who is sitting here with the energy and the love of Spirit. For that is what this is about.

Dear ones, sitting in this assemblage, we invite you this night to drop the barriers of disbelief and say to yourselves, *"Could this truly be real? Is there a moment where the same voice that came from the burning bush would also be able to talk to me? Is it possible that the essence that spoke to the prophets of the past is the same essence that would come to me now and speak?"* It's not just probable; it is so.

Let the proof be in the energy that is developed around your chair. Let the proof be in the colors that are seen by many of you before this time between us is over. Let the proof, if you need such, be in the pressure that some of you will feel—the touching in certain places of your body that some of you will feel—this very evening before we are finished.

The questions have been asked this very day about what the earth is all about. The question has been asked, *"What's the next step? Where are we going from here?"* And even the questions that haven't been asked are so often on the tongues and in the minds of those who would also say, *"And what's my part in it?"* Some of the unanswered questions this night have never been asked out loud. They go like this, *"What am I supposed to do? What's my part in this? When am I going to understand what's next for me? I seem to have been marking time all this year. What happens next?"*

Oh, dear ones, let me give you a message. It's a message that bears repeating and one that you should hear as well. You have no idea of your part in this—your interdimensional part. You sit in the chair in this room and give up your day for the purpose of enlightenment training. Reader, you sit in the chair and take up your time, as well as the listener in front of me, and you both search for the Higher-Self. That tells us, as family, a great deal about the intent of those who sit in a place like this. But you are really in the dark as to what is going on. You walk around with much hiding from you, even as you facilitate this great planet!

Your intent to be here, reader and listener, is a message that tells us that there are seekers sitting before us—that there are searchers, and that those who are reading and listening are ones who sometimes come to celebrate the energy, and sometimes they come because they are troubled. Many come with questions. There are also those with secrets here ... both reading and hearing. Let me tell you about that: The ones with secrets—some so profound that they have not yet been shared with another Human—really have none. Don't you think the spiritual entourage around you knows what you carry around? God is not in a vacuum, dear ones. Your spiritual family is not ignorant about your life.

All that is said this night, and the metaphor to come, is presented in love—love that is for you, Human Being. You are a family member—a piece of God—an angel disguised as a Human Being. You are here now, just like the time before, and the time before, and the time before, and the time before.

There are only three of you in this room this afternoon who would call this your "first time around," and I think you know who you are. The rest of you are shamans, medicine men and women, monks and nuns, priests, and ones who have awakened before. Some of you have lost your lives in spiritual service, and some of you have given sacrifice while you lived within the vows that you took . . . and we know who you are.

Some of you are your own ancestors! We know who you are, too. You settled the land here! That's why you can't leave it. [Chuckle] Try as you might, you won't be able to leave it. Some of you have tried, but only to keep snapping back like a rubber band. You wonder why that happens? Because you cultivated the land when there was nothing here. When there was no city, you were here. When the animals came into the tribe for you to eat them, you were here. You made the pottery that is in the very museums that you go to visit within your city. Go and take a look! You are you own indigenous ones, so many of you. Over and over you came here, shamans.

Spiritual Year Review—2000

This is a review, with additional comments regarding what has been channelled to you in 2000. It's also a review of many of the things that have happened this year, but we wish to put it together in a way we have not done before, as a reminder of what has taken place and, indeed, where things are headed. At the end of the review, we give, perhaps, a revelation to you and an invitation to create something.

Movement of the Two to the Three

We have spoken all year of the movement of the energy from the *two* to the *three*. Yet, still many do not understand what that means. Are these dimensional references? No, it's a reference to the *energy* of the two—of the old—moving to the energy of the three, which is the new. Not too long ago, we spoke of the rebuilding of the third temple in Jerusalem—something that is to be without mortar or bricks. We spoke of the third Exodus, and we spoke of the New Jerusalem ringing with the *three*. We've spoken of the *third* language, and now you sit on the edge of having completed the first year of the new millennium—the year of the beginning of the realization of the shift.

Some have said, *"Kryon, you are speaking of things for the Jews, are you not?"* No. I'm speaking of things for humanity! We have said this before: As go the Jews, so goes the earth. Therefore, what is good for them is good for you. So, their lessons of bringing themselves together with their former enemies are your lessons as well. If they can create a New Jerusalem out of the darkness of hatred and strife around them, then so it goes for you as well, and so it goes for Earth.

The interdimensional is beginning to become commonplace. That, dear ones, is the difference between the old and the new energy. And that is what we have hinted at for 11 years. Can something called "Human nature" really undergo a profound change without eons of evolution? Not only is the answer *yes*, but it just did.

In 1999, there wasn't any entity that could sit on the other side of the marker [the millennium shift] and tell you what was going to happen. You sailed your ship of humanity into this new energy harbor, and we're going to tell you the difference between where you *were* and where you *are*.

How did you expect to create something on Earth that had never been created before within the same old four dimensions? You couldn't. Now we look at the interdimensional beings here in the room, moving from the *two* to the *three* [you]. The year 2000 is a two; the year 2001 is a three. Did you notice? We told you of moving between the 11/11 and the 12/12. Let me condense the 12/12, if you haven't already done it. It's 3/3. If you haven't thought about that, moving from the *two* to the *three* is becoming interdimensional—starting to think out of the box—

using what we have called The Third Language. This is a metaphor, dear ones, for the energy of the *three* is a spiritual language—a language that some of you even ask about this very day [within the seminar].

"When am I going to be able to speak to the Guides?" you asked. They've been talking to you a long time! The question should be, *"When am I going to be able to hear my Guides?"* And the answer is *right now* if you want to. You can do it at the heart level. This third language is about emotion—about compassion. It's about finding the child inside. It's about reverting to some of the energies of creation itself.

Science

Again, we say that it's difficult to explain to a 4D audience—about 5, 6, and 7, isn't it? We told you about these things that were "on the way," and now they're here. We told you about dimensionality—that there were far more than the four you live in, present in your reality. Years ago, we sat in a town you called Sedona, and we gave you a science channelling. We told you all about the fact that you sit in a multidimensional universe that is constantly creating itself. A few years ago, we told you about The Cosmic Lattice—energy in space you have yet to discover. We told you of the way things work, the speed of consciousness being far grander and greater than the speed of light. Suddenly, this year, your science surrounds you with the validation of things we have been speaking of all these years.

The scientists in 2000 who were able to see the incredible speed-up of light using magnetized gas were indeed seeing what they thought they were seeing. They had discovered that the speed of light is only the speed limit of matter relative to 4D. There is more. Those who sat around in the city you call Salt Lake and put together an experiment that seemed to be the Holy Grail of science—cold fusion, you called it—were laughed at because they could never create it again. Yet, those trained scientists saw what they saw, but they scratched their heads because they could never create the results again, and it was frustrating, since they didn't know why.

These examples have something in common with one of the greatest scientists of all time, the one you call Tesla. He couldn't create identical experiments over again, either. He saw what he saw, and he wrote it down. Every once in a while, he would have a continuity, and the experiment would react the way it did the first time. But he could never create a consistency of results because he was dealing with interdimensional aspects—ones he could not control. He was frustrated to see things work in a marvelous, miraculous way, yet never be certain he would see it again.

We are telling you that all of these things that had been hidden have the potential of showing themselves again in these next years. For this is the year of the beginning of the interdimensional realization. The works of Tesla will come forward and be presented, and will again be reality, if you choose it to be so. The experiments for cold fusion will indeed be repeatable, because there are those who will discover what the missing piece was—a piece the experimenters did not even know was there to begin with, since it was not in observable 4D.

And so it is that you are interdimensional beings and your science has now admitted that they think so, too [referring to the acknowledgment by science of the existence of interdimensionality . . . a year 2000 announcement]. We have to remind you: What do you think that might indicate regarding your DNA? We have told you now for some time that there are 12 strands—2 you can see, and 10 you cannot. That sounds very similar to the message you've now received from your physicists: They say tha there are 11 dimensions at the center of all matter—4 you can see, and 7 you cannot!

Your DNA has always been interdimensional. The interdimensional patterns that appear on your "invisible strands of DNA" are those of karma, karmic residue, life lessons, a print of who you used to be, your spiritual contract, and the energy of the spiritual vows you took in past lives. There's more:

Your astrological magnetic attributes are there, too. The energy of your very birth—the day, the hour, the time, the solar system—all are imprinted onto the parts of the DNA that are not chemical, but magnetic. We have explained before that the mystery of magnetics is that it's not in 4D! It's wrapped around gravity and time, and your science will discover that, and that is why Tesla was unable to make it perform the same way twice. When the math starts to create and explain the unseen . . . the 5th, 6th, and 7th dimensions—all the way to the 12, you'll be able to work in these mysterious multiple-dimensional places that you never even acknowledged before. This is the real opening, the beginning, the revealing of energy work that is remarkable.

With the science comes the realization of the truth behind the Lightworker—that this interdimensional energy is what you have always been working with, but it's now enhanced in this new energy of the *three*. All we're saying is that your science is going to come along with you now. It is finally catching up in theory to what you have been doing in practice.

Interdimensional Life on Earth

We spoke of interdimensional life. It hasn't been seen yet, and it hasn't been proven yet. Oh, but it's there. We disagree with your scientists. There are not 11 dimensions at the center of the atom; there are 12 [from a previous channelling in New Hampshire] if you have 12 dimensions at the center of the atom, and you are made of atoms. Doesn't that make *you* interdimensional? If there is an acknowledgment of multiple dimensionality within all matter by science, does it make sense that *all* the life on the planet would only be in 4D? No. Life and matter are commingled. They shake hands in creation.

You're going to find the rest of it soon—not beings like you, but support life . . . life that is small, in support of you and your environment. Some of this life is magnetizable . . . similar to the core of your own biology (DNA). Some have been waiting for your discovery of them through magnetics—for they react to it! Magnetizing some of this interdimensional life will enhance water; some will even heal. Like the balanced ecosystem on the planet that has the trees giving you oxygen, there is an interdimensional life force that helps posture your very health, and some of it even resides in your DNA.

Wait until they find out about intelligent DNA! Doctor, are you listening? This is for you: We never broached it before, and we never talked about it [speaking of the researcher in the audience Kryon has been working with]. There is a life form ripe with discovery for you to find—more than chemistry—it's consciousness. It's a consciousness that responds like a switch that can be turned with the right magnetic pulsating influences. Interdimensional life is even within you—an intelligence that resides in your DNA that is part of your biology. Your DNA is far more than you ever thought it was, and I'm not talking about the Human genome in 4D that you have just mapped this year, curiously *three* years ahead of time. I'm talking about the rest of the interdimensional DNA complement of the Human Being—one that has within it, living intelligent interdimensional life.

The Interdimensional Human

The last time we were together, we spoke of the multiple parts of *you*. We spoke of how much of *you* is spread around the universe, but you are not aware of it. Not all of *you* is contained in that skin you gave a name for, which you call Human. Pieces and parts of you are on the other side of the veil—ones that you never even knew you had. We explained to you that it had to be that way. Who do you think is "up there" planning all this? [All laugh] It's *you*! What do you think co-creation is about? What do you think synchronicity is about? It's about planning between Human Beings and between the Higher-Selves of Human Beings on an interdimensional plane. You do understand, don't you, that you are someone else's synchronicity? It must be that way.

We spoke of the multiple parts of your guide-set. We spoke about all the pieces and the parts that go to what we call the guide- energy "soup." We told you that you can no longer try to count them—an old energy concept. They are infinite, yet one. It's time to take the names off of them, take the imaginary skin off of them—even the wings. See it for what it is—a grand and glorious energy that belongs to you. Call it a choir of energy that sings your vibration, if you wish. You won't be that far wrong.

Opening the Chasm Between the Old and New

We told you in this year [2000] of potentials of current events that some of you are now seeing. We talked about the chasm opening, and this was indeed the year for it. We spoke of those who were stuck in the "old," and those who are willing to go to the "new," and we told you that some would be pulled "off the fence" and would be filled with spiritual rage . . . and that indeed is with you now. In this spiritual rage there are those right now who feel that it's proper and right—claiming their old belief systems—to kill and maim—to do whatever they choose, in the name of Spirit. And they are in the minority, dear ones.

Know this. You are going to see more things coming to-gether, not apart, because of the opening chasm. The reason why is because as the chasm opens, there is going to be a universal acknowledgment that in order for the earth to exist, Humans everywhere are going to have to agree to tolerate each other. Like the train pulling away from the old station, the old energy is going to be left behind, a thing of the past. There are still many standing on the platform, angry at the ones leaving, and trying their best to stop the train. They cannot, and the result will be turmoil and chaos until they eventually give up. And when they do, the train will have left them.

Religious Division

We spoke about the division of religion, and now it's all around you. Some of you have looked to the Middle East and said that this is obviously the heart of it. "It's between Islam and the Jew," you said. We want to take a moment to remind you of something, something perhaps you had not considered. As a Human Being, we want you to look outside *the box* for a moment and remember and honor both of those systems.

There is no difference, dear ones, between Moses talking to the burning bush and Muhammed talking to the angel in the cave. We wish to remind and inform you of *who* the angel in the cave was. From his own admission, Muhammed knelt and got information—information that was later written down and scribed in what is today the center of the Islam belief system. Who was it? It came from the angel Gabriel. Did you know that?

The message that Muhammed received was filled with love, and it spoke of "the one God." When Moses approached the burning bush, the voice of the same angel spoke the same exact message. Moses, the father of what you call "monotheism," received the same message about God that Muhammed did . . . and from the same angel! So what you see right now in the Middle East is a Human problem, not a God problem. And since it is a Human problem, it can be solved within the purview of the Human Being—one who is becoming interdimensional.

Don't be surprised if it takes a bit longer there in the Middle East than it may in other parts of the earth, because they have been there for eons and eons, in a man-made spiritual energy box that has walls a mile high. It's going to take a while for those walls to be reduced. It's going to take new consciousness—perhaps even a new generation, but eventually this is what the potential of this particular moment is in time. It's also what the intent is of the majority there. Do not be fooled by the few—the ones watching the train leave without them.

Stalemates

In March [2000], we spoke about potential political stalemates [chuckle] and you're sitting in this exact situation [USA election]. You're about to see what that will create in your government, and what that will do to your political system. For those of you who are upset to have something so split and seemingly unmovable—one force against the other—equally strong so that neither can move—we say this: The only way solutions may be created now, is for the two forces to stop pushing at each other and instead learn to join where appropriate. Call it a forced union, if you will, but the paradigm of how politics is performed is about to get a lesson in uniting instead of separating. That's the potential, dear ones, and it's one you created. You may see things you have never seen before even within your own political system, something we gave you predictions about this very year. When there is no majority and no minority, how does a system built around having that, survive? They must actually listen to each other, and some have to compromise! Watch.

Celebrate the Birth

"Kryon, what's this got to do with me?" you might ask. *"Oh, you've told us about the anchor, told us about our place as the lighthouse,*

but what does that really have to do with me? What is truly the biggest issue that is happening right now as we move into 2001?" We'll tell you. Although it may seem to be a review, you should hear it on this side of the ocean.

This culture where you sit as you listen to this is in celebration [December]. Every year about this time, the music changes, the lights go up, and this culture works itself up over the birth of a baby—whom you have called the "Master of Love." You give each other gifts and celebrate with family. Some of you—not of this culture—work around it all, but it's still there, isn't it? I'm going to tell you something and give you an invitation: It's time to celebrate the birth of a baby, and it's not the one you think.

Some of you have suspected or felt something about old prophecy. Profound religious information that had been delivered to humanity in 4D many years ago is really multidimensional. I will call it the "coming together," or even the "final coming together." It's the time when the Higher-Self has permission to meld with biology. It's the time when you pull the pieces of your divinity together. It's the time when dimensionality starts to increase in the Human Being, and it's time for the ascended masters to all return!

One of the things many of your cultures expected in the new millennium energy was the return of their masters. Which ones? That depends upon what you believe about God. What we are saying is that this was not an accident . . . the alignment of many cultures expecting their own masters to return at the same time in Human history—at the recent millennium change. Indeed, the energy of the *now* is ripe for the return of the avatars, the divine masterhood—the shamanship of all those who were expected to return about now from many cultures and beliefs. But it's not quite what you expected in 4D.

Listen: This baby whom we invite you to celebrate is *the returning consciousness of the ascended masters all coming together into the energy of one child*—a child being born and celebrated in the hearts of many Humans right now. *"Which master?"* you might ask. *"After all, they all represent different belief systems."* Really? Take a look at the core information of each one. Take a look at the source of the information they gave you. Take a look at one divinity and one message! The message from the burning bush? In the cave? The Sermon on the Mount? The one given to the Asian masters? It's the same one from the same source, given to Humans of different cultures in different time frames of history. But the message speaks of one God, one divinity, and the ability of Humans to achieve oneness with it all, because they are God! Take a look! Be aware that the doctrines and dogmas that were begot from it were the work of men, not God. Be aware that the separation came from fear, not love. If you could have placed yourself within hearing range of all the greatest prophetic words given to the masters in many languages over the ages, you would have heard the same voice, from the same angel, giving the same message!

Every time this season comes around, I want you to think of the child inside you that now has the essence of the burning bush, of the angel Gabriel sitting in front of Mohammed, of the ascended masters, and the great prophets. There was information that Elijah would return to set the stage for the Messiah. It has happened! Celebrate the child Elijah in your heart. Those of you who would celebrate the Passover, it is time to have that one whom you set the chair for, sit down and join the meal! For he is here, and so is the Messiah whom he was supposed to come before.

The one the Christians have asked for to return, has arrived! Even the ascension on the temple mount of Mohammed now has reversed, and that is also among the energies of the divine baby. It's all about love. It's about return. It's about coming together. This movement of the *two* to the *three* is what you have predicted in all your prophecy. It begins the potential of a thousand-year cycle—a reign of peace—a New Jerusalem. But it's not as you expected, is it? It's about union, not separatism. It's about coming together . . . a return of the divine family. Can you see it that way? Are you able to rise above your cultural bias and accept this divine energy that includes those you were told were not "your" prophets? It is a challenge, is it not . . . just like your new politics . . . just like the train pulling away from the station with the cars all linked together . . . moving into a new energy.

I wouldn't have said this unless it were so. Indeed it is profound in its implications—that the energies—not the persona—not the skin and the flesh—but the consciousness arriving in the Human heart in these new times is filled with the ascended masters of the earth. It's for those who have awakened and given intent for it. It will not be forced onto any Human.

It's a big difference for you, moving from the *two* to the *three*. It's a change that invites you to say, *"I am ready for the birth of a new child—the energy of the ascended masters, all of them—the avatars that promised to come back—coming back together—united hand in hand."*

While many Humans on Earth spiritually fight over who's right and who's wrong, this baby is being born in the consciousness of many, united in the love of God. And that's what's happening, dear ones. That's what's really happening.

Celebrate the child! Celebrate the return! Some of you vibrate with impatience. You came in, knowing this potential was there. You went past the marker [year 2000], and there was no termination. You could hardly wait to go forward and anchor. Some of you are just now starting to awaken. You're starting to remember why you're here.

Dear angel, disguised as a Human, you never have to come back to a meeting like this. You can create this energy at home, and it's not even dangerous. [All laugh] It's a good time right now to see the colors as they pour in to you in an incredible love wash of Spirit [speaking to the seers in the room who are able to "see" the colors of energy around Kryon].

There are those here who have given intent this evening to celebrate the returning child. Let it be known that we know of this. And so we say to you, let the healing begin! It's a good time for it, for by this point in this program you have cast aside a lot of those walls that kept you from saying, *"It can't be true."* Now, here you are, reader and listener, knowing it is. Perhaps by this point you understand that we know your name. Disbeliever? Let me tell you something: You are as loved as every Human Being here. You may leave this place and laugh at everything that happened in this meeting. It does not diminish the fact that you are family! We're going to tell you that the love of God goes out the door with you, just like it goes out with everyone else.

If you never make any kind of decision one way or the other, we'll all get together one day, and we'll celebrate your lives on the planet just like we celebrate the ones who are healers and workers and anchors and lighthouses. For you are all family, every single one—created equal—each of you is a piece of God—no one any greater or grander than the other. Is it any wonder why the entourage loves you as they do? Disbeliever and Lightworker alike, this entourage washes your feet!

One year ago on a weekend just like this, my partner sat in this spot. We said words to you right before we left, and I'll never forget them. It seems like yesterday to me—a moment ago. We told you the potentials of passing the marker, and we said the words, "Thank you, thank you, thank you." Why should Spirit thank Human Beings? It's for what you've done here. You've created something grand, yet you have no concept of it.

The big picture is still missing to most. *"Why?"* Many still ask, *"Why am I here? Why am I going through this? What's it all about?"* When you get to the other side of the veil this next time, there'll be a gleam in your eye and you'll know—I'll know. And you'll sing your name to me in light, and metaphorically we will hug one another. For then, all will be clear.

For now, however, there is still the veil. There is duality. We say this to you: Trust what your heart tells you about how important it is to spiritually take care of yourself. The longer you live on this planet, dear Lightworker, the greater your anchor, the greater your light, the more the earth will change. Claim the parts of the DNA, some of which are alive. Live a long life, and be peaceful within it. In the process, feel loved by the family around you. And next time you see the double numbers—the double letters, why don't you say, *"I love you!"* [Speaking of those that continue to see the 11:11 and 12:12 and 4:44 on the clocks.] It will be an acknowledgment of the interdimensionality of the spirit group that surrounds you—tapping you on the shoulder saying, "Look at the clock! We're here! Look at that sign! We're here!"

There's never been a time in Human history when we, on this side, were this close to that interdimensional group called "millennium humanity." The proof of it is in the consciousness and understanding of the eyes on this page, and the ears hearing this message.

And so, dear ones, this entourage retreats from this place. And so, dear ones, the love of God has been shared with the family today.

And so it is.

Kryon

Live Channelling

"Nine Attributes of Spiritual Growth"

Channelled in
Toronto, Ontario, Canada
March 2001

Chapter Six

"Nine Attributes of Spiritual Growth"
Live Channelling
Toronto, Ontario, Canada

*This live channelling has been edited with additional
words and thoughts to allow clarification and better
understanding of the written word.*

Greetings, dear ones, I am Kryon of Magnetic Service. As we enter the room, there are many here who have never felt the energy of the family member called Kryon. There are some of you who have read the words, heard the voice in their own heads and minds, but have not experienced the energy. Perhaps what you are hearing does not fit what you thought it would be? If that is the case, we ask you to put the voice that you choose in your ears instead of this one. For this is a family member named Kryon, saying that at this moment there is an entourage that comes in here, which is specific in unity to this group. This is a saying that means that it is "unique in unity to this group." Not only do they know you, but the entourage, which pours in here and sits between the chairs—the ones who walk between the aisles and stand next to the ones they select—knew of your coming. It is a designed group, if you will—one who knew of the energy of the individual who walked into the room.

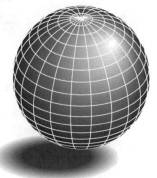

Every single Human who sits in the seat hearing and reading this is an angel disguised as a Human Being, for the duration of a life on this planet. It's an entity unique to the energy of the earth—connected to the earth—walking a path that only that Human Being can. The entourage pours in here and takes its place next to you—a unique, eternal creature of the Universe.

You might ask, *"Well, who is here, Kryon?"* Some of you will know before this energy retreats from this room, from this area, who is here. Some of you will smell them—a smell that only you will know. Some of you will have other senses activated, which will tap you on the shoulder and seem to say, *"Yes, Spirit was here."* Some of you will have the validation of the fact that we are here by way of the "thickness of love" that permeates the area, the bubble of energy that often pushes upon the individuals in the chairs. We call it "the bubble of love," for we have no other words for it. The Human is being honored. That's what is happening.

The entourage that is here has visited this room previously, and we have told many of you how this works, yet there are some who have yet to put it together. We know of the intent of the visitor. There was a time when you gave intent to come here, whether it was weeks ago or hours, and we know when it was. We have told you the mechanics of this in the past. We told you about the activation of the energy you call "the guide-set," when you made certain kinds of decisions and gave intents. When you chose to come and you gave the commitment to be here and sit in the chair, to sit on the floor, to open the page and be in this energy—we knew it. When you did that, there was a specific energy that was assigned to come into this room for you. This is not a generic spiritual group that flows in here every time there's a meeting such as this. This is a unique group designed for you . . . designed to honor you with specific energy.

They have taken their places next to the chairs where you sit. Reader, feel the energy of the one who knows that you gave intent to open this book. These are the ones who are supposed to be here; some whose faces you even know have now taken their place. Some of you will walk from this place changed because you knew they were here. My partner told you that these things are in a spiritual *now* time frame, one that does not match the Human time frame very well. Things happen all at once in a time frame on the other side of the veil, and although the future is unknown, the potentials are solidly there waiting to manifest. It's difficult to explain how the future, past, and present can be so combined, but perhaps it will give you insight as to how we see your lives.

Some believe that God knows everything in the future, but this is not so. God is *you*, the family that sits before me—a family that creates the reality of time as it goes forward in your perspective and as it co-creates. The power of God resides in the room where you sit. It always has. Three days ago, this entourage, which is here now beside you, rehearsed. It rehearsed! This is a strange thing for Spirit to do, is it not? Have you ever heard of such a thing? Why would we do such a thing? When this room was dark, we were here. In the wee hours of your last morning, we were here. We contemplated where you might sit. Metaphoric as this may be to you, there is the core of truth here. We rehearsed! Why would this be? The answer should be obvious, and perhaps now you are going to cue into this phenomenon. Would you rehearse a meeting of a lifetime? Would you rehearse for meeting a hero? We rehearsed because it was an important reunion.

Now, here we are. We "look around" and say, "Look who's here! Look who decided to come! Look who decided to sit and endure the hours in this place because they wanted to know more about themselves, their families, and their children. Look who's discovering their divinity! Look who's having a spiritual awakening in their lives." That's why it was important for us to sit for a very long time and rehearse the energy that's before you right now.

Now, to some this may seem to be a fable, yet the seed of truth is this: That's how important this energy is right now. All that has gone before today has postured this energy right now. Perhaps some of you are feeling those who rehearsed in this place? They've found you where you sit, and are now beginning to wash your feet in preparation for the teaching. And so we say, let the teaching begin.

There will be a time to see the colors on the stage, and there will be a time to see the colors in the group [speaking of those who are able to discern colors etherically and physically during the channelling]. But for now, we start the teaching.

This is a time when we wish to give you information regarding spiritual growth. We have never given information in a linear stream that was all about spiritual growth. There are nine elements we wish to present to you during this time, and some of them will be new to you and some of them will not. You may hear about some and say, *"I knew that."* However, some of you may also say, *"This is indeed something that I needed to hear."* Some of you will say, *"Of course. That's why I sat in the chair!"* In that case, you will hear us say, "That's why we rehearsed!"

Spiritual Growth

In order for us to give you the nine elements, we have to start with the first. Although that's obvious to you, we had to rehearse this, since this kind of presentation does not make sense to interdimensional beings. In this linear game, the first one we present is always the review.

Why are you here? Why is it necessary that the Human Being be disguised? As we have said, the Human is actually a *piece of God.* Briefly we will remind you that your life is not a test of the Human Being. Instead, what you're going through is a test of *energy*, a test of energy that the Universe could not do by itself. You, as pieces of God, collectively are biased in love to the degree that this particular test had to be done on a voluntary basis. The volunteers were the pieces of divinity who agreed to come to the planet disguised as Humans, unaware of who they were. An energy veil would prevent them from seeing the reality of their own selves, of the past selves, and of other Human lives they had also been. Indeed! Here you sit, still in that spiritually manufactured reality, even with its own time frame.

Earth is a unique place in the Universe—which we call the center—Earth. It is a metaphoric center of potential for something else. Why? So that here on this planet, dear ones, what you do with your free choice, what you do on a neutral playing field of energy, will indeed enlighten other parts of the Universe. It will create a balance between dark and light in some areas that you have no concept of. It won't be realized until you again reach the other side of the veil, when we see you again. Then all will be remembered. It's a beautiful cycle, but one that is hidden from you by the veil.

For now, the word *veil* is a good one, for indeed it veils the truth of who you are. As many of you know, you are here, therefore, to see what you're going to do with the challenge of what you call this lifetime. Adding to this puzzle you can't see is the fact that there have been multiple lifetimes for everyone here. Even more puzzling to your Human mind is that in "real time," we tell you this: Some of you are still enjoying the last one! How could such a thing be? It is, however. We have given you this interdimensional information even this year—that is, how you can be in two places at the same time and how one place affects the other. It explains much about your intent, your co-creation, and your ability to change reality.

There is much here that you do not and cannot understand. Yet you have volunteered to come with the veil in place, to have a duality that is so strong that when you look at yourselves in the mirror, you only see the Human, never the angel. Yet as this entourage poured into this place and took its place next to you, it sat with angels! You see, the duality is only one-way: yours. We are sitting next to family members we have known eternally in both directions [Kryon's way of saying that Humans are eternal—both past and future]. So, indeed, the "why" is discussed first because it reminds you of the test of energy on the planet and the role of the Human who comes to potentially awaken to the divinity within, or not.

The main attribute of this test is this: There is no judgment around you or what you do. It is completely and totally free choice. We gave you this information many times: that when you return to the other side of the veil, there is only a celebration. It does not matter what you did. It is not about your works, contrary to what some of you may have been taught. It is about the journey! And just as on Earth, when the play is over, no matter who had the knife stuck in their chest when the curtain came down, the cast all gets up and they have a party! And so it is on the other side of the veil. It's *what you do* with the energy while you're here that matters. It's about planetary measurement of where the energy goes after the Human Beings are done with it. That's the test. And that's the "why" in synopsis.

(1) When Does Spiritual Growth Begin?

Here is the first attribute of spiritual growth. Where or how does it start? How does spiritual growth begin in the Human, and how is it maintained? What are the mechanics of this? We now give you information, some of which is known, some of which is new. Listen to this. You have always known that a spiritual quest has to start within the Human Being asking the question *Why?* or *Is there more?* It is, therefore, an awakening to a portion of the Higher-Self, we say. Some have said the Inner-Self; some have said the Other-Self. It becomes a realization, a part of the Human Being—biology is asking questions regarding divinity.

It doesn't mean that a person is becoming a Lightworker. It doesn't even mean they are becoming a spiritual person. This search has to do with questions about the *why* of humanity on a personal level. There are many who are asking about the Other-Selves who would never be in a meeting such as this, or reading the page you are. They are honored, and they are beautiful, just as you are. Some of them may surprise you as far as where they are on Earth and what they claim as their *religion*. It may surpass your biases, or perhaps it may not even get past your bias! This is also part of the energy test for you . . . whom you allow in your mind to also be spiritual, for it tests what you have been *told*, opposed to what you *feel*.

Anyone who searches for the divine, no matter what they call it, is an awakening Human Being. That's the start. It's with intent to wonder if there is more. How many of you are reading this, or have come to this meeting because of that very attribute? Many of you have only just started this growth process in the last few years. It follows exactly what we told you about the potential of humanity to change the veil—the reality of this time of your new millennium. Literally thousands are beginning to ask, *Is there more?*

Now, here is information about this search process, about the actual nature of the process of spiritual growth. We have never broached some of these subjects in channelling before.

(2) How Permanent Is Spiritual Growth?

There is an axiom in spirituality and also in Human consciousness, which is this: You can never return to a *less* aware state. In other words, it's impossible for the Human to *un-know* something. Have you ever thought about that? When it's in your consciousness, it's there forever. You may suppress it, but it's there in the memory engrams, the neural pathways of your existence. Everything is there that you ever saw, felt, or learned. You cannot, with your own desire, undo it. The magnetics of the circuitry has operated within your brain, and you cannot unlearn it. It's impossible.

Now, what is true for Human consciousness is also the axiom of spirituality, and it goes like this: Healers in the room, have you ever wondered about the next time around? Enlightened soul, happy in the love of God, basking in the spiritual energy, have you ever wondered about the next time around? Some of you very wise souls, who have been through much, ask this: *"Dear God, will I have to start over when I return?"* Have you ever asked that question in the dark, when you thought even God wasn't listening? Have you? Some of you angels who sit here in Human form have actually decided not to come back because you don't want to go through it again! This is actually very funny.

We have news for you, and now it's time for you to remember: Lifetime after lifetime after lifetime, you can *never return to this planet in a less aware state.* Here is what we mean. Everything you have gleaned and learned this time around is available to be *picked up* and continued the next time around. It is so, and that means that sitting here, there are monks and shamans. It means that sitting here, there are indigenous medicine men and women. Sitting here are those who have nurtured this land since the first time Humans saw dirt! You know it, too; you belong here. Shaman, are you listening?

Some of you were so aware of this that when you arrived on the planet it was only a matter of growing up, and within a few years you picked up the gauntlet, pasted on the mantle of your old spiritual growth, and continued your work . . . and you know who you are. *"Now, Kryon,"* you might say, *"that doesn't make spiritual sense, because we have free choice! When we come back into the planet as another Human Being, perhaps we have the same soul, but don't we have free choice about this? Do we have to be a Lightworker? Is it predestined that we will continue what we started the lifetime before?"*

Ah, here is an attribute that we have never discussed before: the *closet Lightworker*. The answer to your question is *no*. Of course there is no predestination, as we have told you before. But let me put it in perspective for your culture [that of Canada]. Imagine the man or the woman who lives in a house. In that house, in the closet, there is a pair of skates and a uniform. The person who lives there is a fine athlete, part of the greatest hockey team in the country. There he/she lives, but it doesn't do any good for the team unless the skates and the uniform get put on. The closet, therefore, must be opened with intent.

What kind of person is this? This person is one who, when they embrace the concept of their talent, will pick up the mantle, recognize it, and paste it on with glee. But there are many who don't want this because they're afraid of it. Some of them are even here. Some have just read it. Do you know other Human Beings, dear ones, whom you look at and say, *"This is a precious soul! If they could only know what I know, they'd have more peace in their lives. They wouldn't worry, they wouldn't be angry all the time, and they wouldn't be so filled with drama. I wish I could impart to them what I know about creating a safe place—about finding divinity. I see a healer 'in there,' but they're not coming out."* Maybe it's a mate, maybe it's a brother, maybe it's a sister. As we've already told you, there is nothing you can do besides taking care of your own space and holding your own light, lighthouses.

If you know a person like that, I would love to tell you what the attribute of that person is. You're looking at a giant spiritual athlete. There is a shaman there, just like you. This time around, however, he or she has chosen not to look in the closet, to recognize the skates or the uniform and put them on. This is the *closet Lightworker*. All that they worked through the last time around simply awaits the putting on of the skates, but that requires the first attribute, intent. Many of you know this kind of person, and some of them sit here, reading and listening. Oh ... if you only knew how well you could skate! That was number two.

(3) How Do I Know If I'm Growing Spiritually?

How does a person know if they have spiritual growth? How can you know if you're growing spiritually? That's easy. Now we review things that we've already told you. Constantly you ask the same questions, and the same answers are delivered. Now, however, there is an interdimensional atmosphere. Much will be revealed within what you have seemed to already know. Let me ask you this: How do you view your past? You see, *we* see it in the *now*. Therefore, the energy of the past is *now*. How are you dealing with that past *now* energy? Think about the events that shaped who you are. Are you carrying some energies that perhaps shouldn't be there? Perhaps it's not appropriate for you to be angry with someone in your past. Perhaps it's not appropriate to hate them, yet some of you do. Perhaps you don't ever discuss it, yet God knows. How are you dealing with the past? Your past is not past at all. It's happening *now*. That's why you carry it around with you *now*. When you think about certain things that have happened to you in your past, dear Human Being, situations you helped set up, how do you feel? Does it make your heart beat faster, make you mad, get a reaction from your biology? I have to ask you, therefore, when is this happening? Is your heart beating faster yesterday? No! It is manifesting *now* in your cellular structure. Therefore, the Lightworker who has spiritual growth has indeed dealt with the energy of what we call the *now* of the past. How do you see the past?

Here's another one: If things happen in your life that are about *you*, do you buy into the potential drama? Can you involve yourself in a situation where there is indeed drama—and your name is there with it—and yet you divorce that name and that dramatic energy from the situation? Some of you are having plenty of practice at it. How are you doing in the *now*? How are you doing with fear?

Fear has many faces. Fear always comes from a lower *chakra*, did you notice? Fear is something you have a chance to thwart, understand, void, and neutralize before it ascends to the higher chakras of intellect and emotional shutdown. It does not have to control you. It was never meant to. Fear is always an invitation—an invitation for you to surpass it. How are you doing with that? How are you doing with worry? Now we're getting down to it, are we not? Where is the spiritual growth factor? Those are some of the measurements, and only you can answer how you do with them. That was number three.

(4) Spiritual Growth—Always Negative?

Number four is what we would call "the hard one." There are those of you who always equate spiritual growth with unfortunate challenge, something you would call a negative aspect of your life. Some have said, *"Dear Kryon, does it mean if I go to the next level, if I give intent for spiritual growth, if I give intent to find my divinity, does that mean that I'm going to catch a disease? Is that going to be my challenge? I've heard the phrase, 'no pain, no gain.' I don't want that."* It goes on. *"Dear Kryon, if I give intent for a higher dimensionality in my life, does that mean I'm going to lose a family member? Does it mean this type of horrible challenge is going to visit me?"* No, it does not. Yet there is such a feeling that it *should*, that many create it anyway in order to feel that they have grown!

With this feeling, no wonder the Human Being has such a "seed fear" of enlightenment. No wonder Human Beings—when they search for divinity—in the back of their minds say, *"Yes, I want it, but then again, maybe I don't."* It's in the minds of many, you know . . . that they must suffer to help God.

What does it mean? I'll tell you. I've never said this before, and you should *all* hear it now. All of you *take turns* with the difficult challenges in your many lives. Some of you carry imprints of incredible sorrow and grief from your past lives. In a residual way, the feelings are still there, since it's always the *now.* You're clearing them this time around, but this time around for you, there's no plan to again visit what you actually have already experienced. You already did it! You take turns. How do you know whether it's your turn? You don't. That, of course, is part of what makes the veil, the veil. But just so you know, there's no axiom that says Lightworkers who take on a load of spiritual growth will have miserable challenges! Hardly!

Not all the tests are what you would call *negative challenge.* There are many kinds of tests given to you in this room. Oh, dear Lightworker, we know who you are. How do you handle joy? When the friends show up and say, *"We're going to go dancing; we want to go out and have a good time; we want to laugh; we want to tell jokes and be together; we're going to go dancing!"*—what do you do? Perhaps this is metaphoric, yet actual for some of you: Some of you will actually say, *"No, I'm spiritual, you know—can't do that. Better go without me."* [Laughter]

The ones who are spiritual are often very serious, and they wish to be "staid on God." If that's you, you just failed that particular joy test! Oh, it will come around again; it always does, for these are the mechanics of challenge. When joy is presented to you, how many of you chase it away? How many of you say *"I'm not good enough"?* When an energy starts to visit your life that looks promising and wonderful, how many of you knowingly or covertly chase it away? You failed that joy test! Not all the challenges are what you would call negative. This is an example. It's a big one, too. How many of you have smiles as your natural facial expression? Do you smile when alone? Is joy your native state of being? If not, why? This is a profound spiritual test of growth.

Let's again speak of the abundance test. We approached this issue before, Lightworker. How many of you healers will not charge for what you do? Do you not understand that money is energy? That is all it is; it is your cultural energy of sustenance. It is the method that allows you to exist in your culture. There is nothing about it that is evil. There is nothing about it that is dirty. It only has to do with how you use it, dear ones. It is your responsibility—a test—yet it is not seen that way.

Some will say that it says in scripture, *"We read about the Master chasing the money changers out of the temple, and it clearly showed us that money was not to be part of God . . . that money was bad."* That was not what was shown at all. That was an example about the consciousness in the temple. It showed that activities in the temple should be about keeping the temple pure, and not commingling it with anything else. It was not about money. It was a metaphor of the Human body. Did you ever realize that? Most of the profound happenings of scripture you read about today have hidden meanings to help you with your spiritual wisdom. Few are there to be emulated literally.

How many of you healers who would not take money, would instead trade your craft for being warm at night? You might say, *"I'll do some healing work, and I'll trade it for wood."* If you say yes to this, but not to accepting money, it shows you that you have failed the abundance test . . . another profound challenge related to the fear of money! It has been said that money is the root of all evil. Take a look! It actually seems that way, since so many deal with the energy of money in a way that does not suit their spiritual growth. Doesn't that prove the point that the abundance test is a great one? Even your wise Human sayings reflect the challenge.

You are in a system that uses the energy of money, and here is the irony: You are energy workers, and yet you won't work with the energy called money! Some of you feel that to barter is better than taking money. For your culture, it isn't. The truth, which is not easy for spiritual Humans to accept, is that this is a dodge of the entire issue. You can't return to the old ways when you were monks and expect that to validate your spirituality in a modern society. Deal with your culture as it is. The advice? Take the energy called money, and work with it as you do the energy of healing, joy, and spiritual growth!

There is nothing wrong with this. If you are one who will not charge for what you do, you have just told the Universe what your talent is worth. You sent a signal all the way through to the other side of the veil. When those signals come in, the family of guides and spiritual energies do their best to honor everything you've said. Think about what signals you send. Too spiritual to go to the party? Too spiritual to accept energy for what you do? God will enhance your life with what you create. That's our promise.

Not all tests are what you think. How about the peace test? How many times have you had in front of you the ability to solve the drama in your life but instead you wallowed in it? Perhaps you didn't think we knew who was reading these words? These are the mechanics of spiritual growth. How do they fit for you?

(5) How Does It Work?

So, what are the mechanics—the attributes of spiritual growth? This is number five. The first is this: The process goes in stair steps. It is not one smooth, continuous journey. It's stair steps. It has to be. Have you ever thought about this? There is a period of study, of growth, then there is often a period of rest—a period where growth stops. Some Humans in their linear growth track say: *"I am going to be an enlightened Human Being; I'm on my path to ascension; I'm going to give intent; and there's going to be a long slope of learning until I get there."* But that's not the way it works.

First of all, let me ask you this: In school, do you remember the first test that you ever took as a child? When you finished the test, did the school let you pass through all the grades? The answer is, "Of course not." When you finished the first test, you simply moved to the next level and received another test. It is so with spiritual growth. This will explain to some of you why there is a time when you feel there is no growth, a disconnection. Many of you sit in frustration and beg Spirit to "come back" and help you complete the process!

We so often hear, *"Why is nothing happening? Why is Spirit not fulfilling what I am trying to co-create?"* We see all of the worry and anxiety, yet the guides are sitting there saying: "Why don't you accept the rest period? You deserved it and earned it. Why are you not resting?"

It's about balance, is it not? Growth is about resting and growing, resting and growing. Yet the balance of this has rarely been seen. So many of you are in constant growth, and that's what feeds you spiritually. We're telling you that it's time to learn spiritually, to enjoy a recess!

(6) Can You Grow Too Fast?

Here's number six. Can you grow too fast? Can spiritual growth be something that comes faster than you can absorb? The answer is yes. Maybe it's time, Lightworker, for you to look at that. Many are anxious to receive everything. *"Give me every-thing you can!"* Oh, we've heard this message before.

Sometimes you're asked, "Are you ready to go to the next level"? You reply, *"Oh, yes, give me everything. I accept it."* Then the headaches begin—the sleepless nights are there. Then you wonder why that is, and say, *"How can Spirit do this to me? I need to work in the morning. I can't sleep but three or four hours a night. What's going on?"* We're fulfilling your request, and everything you give intent for is honored. Only you, angel, know how much you can take in—what is comfortable. Are you one of those? Perhaps you should ask for your growth to be slowed down.

What can you do? You are in control, so perhaps this ought to be your message: *"Dear Spirit, feed me the food of spiritual growth that my biology appropriately can accept in the state that it is right now."* How about that? There is no reason for any Human Being to ever be physically uncomfortable with spiritual growth. If you feel that this is happening to you, maybe it's time you had a talk with yourselves, with your divinity, and with Spirit. In your quiet time, in front of the mantle of your altar, say *"Slow it down; slow it down; there is time; there is time."*

(7) Why Is It So Hard?

Number seven. Why is it so hard? You know what we hear from you, dear angels? Constantly we hear you cry, *"Why is this so hard?!"* And I'll tell you our answer—and we've never said this in these words: "Because it hides!" All the work you do, hides. The lovely Human who asked the question today [in the Kryon seminar]: "Should I move?" was given the answer "You are a point of light, an anchor in your area, a lightness-of-being in the process of lightening up areas that are dense around you." If you leave the room, you take the light with you when you leave. In other words, the light that you carry hides from you, and you are not aware that you are leaving others in the dark. Is that what you really want?" Of course not. Your spiritual growth and your effect on others hides from you.

Seldom are you able to see how you touch another person's life when they're around you. They may not even know your name, but it's how you treat another Human Being. It's how your love shines through in situations, how your wisdom works, and how you give it. It's not about works you might do . . . ones you can see. Sometimes just holding your personal truth around a person, one Human to another, will cause that Human to ask, *"Who am I?"* Speaking to themselves about you, they might say, *"In this other person I see a safe spot. I see some joy. This other person has something I don't have, and I want to know more about what it is."* Perhaps then, that person will move on and you'll never see them again. Profound energy has been exchanged at a divine level, and you didn't even know it.

How many situations do you face in life that you feel are temporary? *"I'll never see those people again,"* you might say. What do you do in those situations? Do you create your joy, or do you use it as a time when "nobody is looking"? It's another test, because there are Humans around you who are watching for the light, and you are it! Family member, are you listening to this? You think you've got one in the family who will never "come around," never wonder to themselves if there's something more meaningful in life? Let me tell you something you may not have realized: What you do from day to day, how you treat that person, how you treat the others around you is "seen" by an invisible energy within each person. Because of what they have seen in you, maybe that person someday might ask the question, *"I wonder if I have skates in my closet?"* There are seeds of magnificence in you as you touch every single person. It hides so completely, however, that you don't realize it.

We've given you solutions for this situation. We've said in the past to "celebrate the unseen." You might say, *"Dear Spirit, I don't understand what's happening to me. It would seem like things are turning bad, but I celebrate the badness! I don't know what Spirit knows; I just know that I'm going to carry my light right through this time."* Remember, there is a balance. For every test, there is a solution. The test for the Human Being is in front of you; the solution is in back. It's a balance, you know, like the scales of justice. Blessed is the Human Being who turns around to look at their past to find the solution to the *now*, which is their future. That was number seven.

(8) A New Set of Growth Attributes in the New Energy

Number eight is a brand new set of spiritual growth attributes, which we've been talking to you about for months. All through the last year we spoke to you about the interdimensionality of the Human Being. We told you about moving from the "two to the three," broaching the new dimensionality. We've given you information about The Third Language. We've told you about "talking to your DNA." We've told you that spiritual growth is no longer what it used to be. Spiritual growth now requires *talking to the cells*. Spiritual growth is now altering the magnetic resonance between the parts of the DNA that talk to one another, which decide whether or not you're going to have the disease or not, whether the contract is going to be fulfilled or not.

Are you getting this? It's so promising! Every single Human Being is capable of this. Young person, senior, your age is an illusion—you're all the same age—*we're* all the same age! The family is eternal. You've moved into the potential of the New Jerusalem, but you're never going to achieve it until you learn that your power is good enough and grand enough to change the very cellular structure of your own bodies.

Processes have been given to you, chemistry has been given to you, inventions are on the back tables ready to be brought forward. It's all there to support you. These things would never have been presented to humanity if you had chosen not to move into this new energy! It's a good time for you to see the colors on the stage, for there are some healings that are about to take place. Some of you are really starting to understand what all of this means. Perhaps you're feeling your feet being washed? Now you know why.

(9) What Are the Results of Spiritual Growth?

Number nine, the results. What are the results? We'll list it this way. In a Human life of potential turmoil, seeming inappropriateness and worry, the tests often seem to be negative ones. The result of spiritual growth? You have a safe place—a sanctuary, a place where you can be and claim: *"I am divine."* A place where you can feel the family hug you. It's a place like this, in this room right now where you read or listen. What did you carry in here? What are your thoughts right now? Are they about a sanctuary? Are you celebrating the reunion that's taking place here? That's the invitation.

Some of you have come this very evening to this page, this meeting, to be healed. So we say to you: Let the healing begin! For in this posturing of energy, there's a divine catalyst that would allow for such a thing. It's not sequestered to certain preset scenarios on the earth, where you have to go certain places or do certain things. It could happen here and now. All it takes is the mechanics that you know so well—the intent—the appropriateness—the co-creation. Let the healing begin, and let it start with your past, which is in the now, which will then alter the biology of your eternal being.

We spoke last time about an attribute of the Human Being. Do you know what has happened within spiritual growth to humanity? All of you together, the ones with the skates in the closet, the ones who are skating, and the ones who don't know how—all of you participated in something remarkable.

Last time we were together, we spoke of the mythology of Camelot. The last time we sat in front of Lightworkers, we explained Camelot to you. We gave it another name—the New Jerusalem. We explained the mythology and the profundity of the message of the boy-who-would-be-king. It represents the spiritual growth of all humanity. It's about the evolution of a spiritual divinity that raises the veil, which changes the magnetic grid, which allows for awakening for thousands who would never have been interested in their own divinity.

In the mythology, there existed a rock that was fused with the sword—welded together, never to be separated. The hilt of the sword projected out of the rock. The two might as well have been made of the same material, they were so solidly melded. Yet when the timing was ready, along came the boy-who-would-be-king, and he performed alchemy upon the physics of the rock and the sword. The rock separated because of the energy that was present in the boy, and he withdrew the sword and said, "Behold Excalibur, the sword of truth!" Excalibur was alive, and sang the F-note of the heart chakra—love. It is a sword in the allegory because it begins the battle with the old energy. And so it is that the boy-who-would-be-king created the wisdom of the Round Table, and the peace that was Camelot. We have told you that this was a myth, perhaps. But now on this planet, it has been manifested and is a metaphor of the Human Being in this year of 2001. For the *boy-who-would-be-king* represents *you*.

You have the alchemy. You have the magic. You will see in these next years things you never thought you would see, spiritually and scientifically. It will indeed be a new kind of world. In the process of your spiritual growth, you will have the ability to look at the past and create the solutions of the future. You will be able to generate the integrity needed to make the decisions of what is appropriate and not appropriate; of what should be done and what should not be done—a new responsibility, a new dimensionality for the boy-who-would-be-king. The skates in the closet? They represent the catalyst to alchemy. They represent the potential intent and the ability to pull the sword from the rock.

Angel, the hardest thing we do is to leave a room like this, especially with healings in progress. There will be some of you who do not sleep this night. There will be some of you who will leave this meeting, vibrating at a level that you didn't expect. Some of you who have come in doubting will go away wondering whether indeed the skates are in that closet! Listen: You don't ever have to come back to listen to, or to read, another Kryon channelling. For all the spiritual growth that we have talked about—that we have discussed this night—all the attributes are available to you in the smallest space that you can fit into. It's about you and God. It's about your spiritual awakening, and discovering self-divinity. It's about the Inner-Self that resides within. It's about the joy of the child that some of you have buried and are giving intent to rediscover.

So much is here, so much revelation, so much love. There has never been a better time in the history of humanity for you to look in that closet! Perhaps that team uniform is there with your name on it? There are healers in the room who don't know it yet. There are potentials unrecognized, but it's up to you.

And so it is that the family has visited you tonight. As they retreat from the room, they pick up their bowls filled with their tears of joy. We say to you that all of what you may have felt this night is available anytime you come before Spirit. Take a moment to look into the eyes of those who leave the room tonight. You're looking at family! The joke is that you've known them. The joke is, they exist in lifetimes that are parallel to yours right now, in the *now* that appears to be in your past—past relationships: mother, father, sister, brother, cousin, and mate.

A tremendous ancient and ongoing karma exists between many of you, but because Humanity has pulled the sword from the rock, it need never be manifested. Because it's not necessary anymore. You have changed even the reality of the test. Yet the joke is that with all this energy around, you do not recognize one another. There will never be a group like this. Its uniqueness is special.

And so it is, dear family, that we leave this place. And so it is that there has been a thickness of love and energy brought into this meeting, some of which is *not* being picked up and withdrawn. Some very special energy has been picked up by the reader and the listener. Some of what was bought here will go home with you. That is the promise, and it's because some have decided to pick up the mantle and find the divinity within. Perhaps one day, the Human Being will get out of bed, stumble into the small room with the mirror, and the first thing you will see is the angel! Then you'll know Earth has changed. That is the potential of the New Jerusalem.

And so it is.

Kryon

[About the United States]: Things cannot remain the same. Honored are those who understand that important changes are afoot. The biggest changes in all of these places will be the old vs. the new. We're here to tell you that the Human Being who sits here and who reads these words is the one who can change this. It cannot stand as it is. The potential for the most profound creative changes come in the year of the three [2001].

Kryon

(Vancouver, BC, Canada)

August 2001

Live Channelling

"The Unity of Humankind"

Channelled in
Vancouver, BC, Canada
August 2001

Chapter Seven

"The Unity of Humankind"
Live Channelling
Vancouver, BC, Canada

*This live channelling has been edited with additional
words and thoughts to allow clarification and better
understanding of the written word.*

This channelling was transcribed from the last Kryon event *before* the September 11, 2001 tragedy. Presented within it are profound hints of the importance of certain items. Kryon has seldom mentioned the religious leaders of Earth, but here he chose to do it . . . even focusing on Muhammad. He also never speaks about politics or identifies countries, yet here he did it as well, giving information about the crossroads that the United States was facing. At the time it was channelled, it was good information. After the 9-11, it is startling! One month later, our lives changed forever.

Greetings, dear ones, I am Kryon of Magnetic Service. Dear Human Beings, angels each one, we tell you this: There is a presence in this place that is the presence of home. We flow in here gently, quietly, and with reverence for the angels who sit in these chairs. I am speaking to two ears, and my communication is being read by two eyes. We invite the readers at this moment to join all of those who are listening. Readers, we understand who you are and when you picked up this material to begin to read. There is no accident that finds your eyes on this page. We are all here together, listeners and readers.

We have said this so often, but we must emphasize this to you: Listener, does it feel like *now* to you? Most of you would say yes. Reader, does it feel like the *now* to you, also? Those who are reading will say yes. Then who is right? Which *now* is it? We point out that we're all here together, and it has always been this way. If you can understand this concept, it is not that much more trouble to understand that next to you are all of the energies of those who have ever lived!

Perhaps you think that when you put those visualizations into seeming space, nobody is listening? Everyone is listening! When you cry from your heart with pain or frustration and you wonder, *"Is anyone listening?"* Everyone is listening! That is why the now is so-profound-filled with potential and waiting for creative energy to come out of the body of the Human Being, who is the only one who can change the very fabric of reality in this lifetime, in the next one, and also the one that used to be!

All that you ever were is wrapped into who you are now. All of the energy of what you call your past lives is still with you. You are still living them. Is it any wonder that we say to you, "Isn't it about time you dropped the vows? Isn't it about time that you changed the reality you feel is unchangeable?" A new paradigm has arisen. It's about changing. The last time we met with you, we told you that the grid change was going to be finished soon. We gave you some time frames of when these things might occur. We told you that it's not going to be that far away in your linear time when things will begin to be manifested for you.

Let me ask you this: Are there potential projects of yours that have seemed to last forever? Perhaps you cannot complete them. Have there been blockages in the way? Has it been frustrating for you? Have you tried to reach out but have been unable to touch those things that you were intuitively promised from God? Our time is not your time. We use this phrase now and we've used it before: There will come a time when things will quicken for you and the manifestation of what you've asked for, expected, and been told are yours will begin to take shape as you create them—all in an atmosphere of spiritual stability and appropriateness. You will get used to the new energy; The Third Language will come upon you, and you'll know what it is like to have an interdimensional connection with Spirit all of the time, not just in meditation.

These things will stay cemented in your reality and you will build upon them. It is difficult to build a house on moving ground, and we have told you this now for ten years. The grid change will come to fruition and will stabilize. So what is frustrating to you and blocks your way are what we call spiritual stalling tactics, keeping you from building too quickly—keeping you from building on shaky ground, building on the wrong ground—all given in love. We hear your cries of frustration. We do not mean to trivialize any of this, but we say enjoy the rest, dear ones, for there will come a time when the future becomes now. The reader is different from the listener, the eyes are different from the ears, yet you are one family.

Unity

We give you information this day, but underlying all this information is the love that Spirit has for the family—the one who has gathered here listening and reading. We give you information about unity. This is information that you need to hear, understand, and pass on. Some have asked, *"Dear Kryon, you have indicated that we are entering a period of unity, but all around us is chaos. What can we do about unity? Where is it?"* Let me give you some answers. I'm going to give them to you in the order of the least important to the most important. We must start with the definition of *The New Jerusalem*. Here's a phrase that we've used again and again. Naturally it's a metaphor, but one with meaning that will become clearer for you as you think about it. For, literally, it is at the center of the end of your time frame, and represents the lineage of the Jews.

Quite often we have used their lineage in our messages and have used what has happened in their history as the metaphor for a beginning of the New Earth. We have done this because theirs is the lineage that decided to be part of the end, and of the beginning. It does not make them more special than anyone else. It is simply their task in the overview of the earth's energy, and how we measure the energy of the planet.

We have told you this before: The New Jerusalem metaphor is not about a city. We have spoken of the rebuilding of the third temple. This is not about a building. These are metaphors about the earth. The New Jerusalem is a metaphor about the potential for this earth to draw itself to the completion of the old energy— emphasizing that all of the old paradigms of struggle and hatred are in vain. Whereas for eons, the way of things was conquering and war, this energy has the potential of having that old paradigm draw to a close. The New Jerusalem is the final Jerusalem. We've spoken of the third rebuilding of the temple and the metaphor of the lineage of the Jews, but let it be known that it is also a metaphor of humanity—information that you are not truly understanding yet. Lemuria and Atlantis were involved in the metaphor of the energy of "temple number one." They were destroyed. Some have felt that these were a myth. Others felt that perhaps they were real, and were destroyed in the great flood.

Indeed, the latter is so. Continents moved around. There were shifts, and it took years. Societies and cultures more than 10,000 years old were lost. The first temple of consciousness was torn down. This is a metaphoric first temple, not the real one. Not so obvious, but every bit as potent in the history of consciousness within humanity, is that in the early 1900s you had another chance for shift . . . another chance to rebuild. Consciousness actually began to raise, and the earth felt that it had a chance to move forward in other ways that it never had before. But free choice prevailed as it should, and this did not happen. The choice of a few affected the many, and instead, there was famine and war, mass destruction and death. The temple was torn down. That was number two.

An empowered humanity could have changed this, but you were not in that position yet. The few had power, and the many were changed. Now, here you are at the millennium shift. Let me tell you what is different from what it was in the early 1900s. You have already shifted the energy of this planet greatly. It is not about shifting the energy now; it is about solutions. At the 11:11, you gave permission to shift, and now the energy is shifing. Suddenly, there is a mass consciousness of this planet that actually desires to rebuild that temple. The third temple being rebuilt, therefore, is a new consciousness—the last temple. This is the potential, and this is why we were excited 12 years ago. We responded by moving the grid. We knew it would take 12 years and told you so. Now you sit in the 11th year of the 12th. Do the math. Does anyone understand the phrase "moving from the 2 to the 3"? It's part of this new scenario. And when this new consciousness has been rebuilt, the grid will respond, and the metaphors will start to be explained.

What a time in humanity! And as you move to rebuild the third temple, there will be great opposition . . . just as we have told you. But this time, the few cannot enslave you as before, due to your new paradigm.

Religion—The Biggest Hurdle to Unity?

"Kryon, you speak of unity. What are we going to do about religion? There have been those who have said that this is the biggest stumbling block for peace, for it is religion that has caused so many of the wars, the dissension between those who believe in God in different ways. There's

no tolerance!" Really? This subject is the least important of all of them! Let me give you some concepts. In the beginning, Abraham, the father of monotheism, knew about one God. He was given the information very early on. He built the tribes around one God, worshipped the one God, understood about the creation, and gave honor to the one God. Out of the grids of the Indus Valley came the great Hindu religion. It was about everything being one. They honored the soul of the oneness with everything. There are those who would say, "Yes, but look what has happened. Now they have many, many gods."

We say this to you: All of the Gods of the Hindus are reminders of the one. In their process, the many become the one, and the one are the many. It's much like what Abraham believed about God creating all things. Out of the same great energy arose Lord Buddha, and he proclaimed that there is a oneness of all things—the dirt you walk on, the sun—everything you see and feel is one. It is God, and it is you. And then he said something before he passed on that many don't remember. He said, "We never want you to worship any Human Being. I appoint no successor, for we are all one."

It's just like the Hindus and just like Abraham. Buddha knew about Human nature and was asking for those who followed the teachings to find their own center, not one in some other Human. The master of love came along and said, "God is love." The Christ gave the message of the oneness of the love of God. He enabled Human Beings and gave them new information of how honored they were. He gave the beatitudes. "Blessed are the meek, for they will inherit the earth," he said. And here you sit, meek warriors! Perhaps it is prophecy? He also showed how to manifest healing, and even abundance, while in the Human body. He taught that the unity of God was in the power of love.

Muhammad spoke to an angel in a cave, and that angel was Gabriel. It is the same angel who spoke to Moses in the burning bush—the angel of communication. I know this, for I was there. He gave Muhammad information that helped him create the great nation of Islam, and the message was: "There is only one God." And what did Muhammad do with this message? He united the tribes of the Arabs. His purpose? To give them the joy and peace of the one God of Israel!

Muhammad honored Abraham. Did you know that? Go back and read his words. Did you know that the rugs of prayer originally faced toward Jerusalem? Did you know that on his ascension, he consulted Abraham and the Christ? It is written in his book! And so it is that the nations of Islam joined together with Abraham's vision, and with the Master of Love. And that is the truth. That is how it all began. Muhammad was about unity. He died young in his vision, killed in his hometown by the very tribal family whom he was trying to unify.

We tell you this: Religion is not the issue, for the core is all the same as given by the creators of every major religion on Earth. The core is unity. The core is wisdom and the love for God. It is what Humans have done with all of this that is the issue.

Politics—Is Unity Possible?

[The country being channelled in, is Canada. The country right below, is the United States.]

"Kryon, what are we going to do about countries and politics? We'll never get around that! If we are going to have unity on Earth, how are we ever going to get around that?" Let me tell you this. You are all in training! Did you notice? The country right below the one we channel in just had an unusual election [USA]. It is a country founded on "majority rule," but it now has no real majority! Did

you notice? In order for it to do anything in its Congress, many more than ever before must cross the bridge of differences—the aisle, as they call it—and join the others who do not believe as they do. And they must do this on a daily basis, even for the small decisions of governmental business. Tolerance is the key, and they have produced a situation where they must do this. Did you notice? Therefore, the United States is currently in its greatest learning period. This country is going through something right now that is "old energy awareness." Will it work, or will it not work? An issue that is very old will be tested. Call it the last gasp of testing, if you will. Below you, in that country, is the old energy concept of isolationism. Is it proper or not proper? How much can the United States join the world, and how much can it remain separate? It is a profound issue in its scope.

When was the last time you saw rioting and death and destruction over trading with one another? Part of the old earth is reacting to new concepts, and they are reacting in fear! Now, what you face in your country [Canada] are decisions over another fearful issue called "separatism." It is also a last-gasp scenario that will either work for you or not. You must make up your minds, for it is an old energy that cannot carry into the new millennium very far. There must be a decision. It cannot exist in the form that it is in now. It represents an entire attitude based around fear—the fear of losing a culture, fear that this or that will happen. It is not commensurate with the energy of co-creation, or wisdom, or even peaceful coexistence.

[For the United States]: Watch for this, for there must be decisions. Things cannot remain the same. Honored are those who understand that important changes are afoot. The biggest changes in all of these places will be the old vs. the new. We're here to tell you that the Human Being who sits here and who reads these words is the one who can change this. It cannot stand as it is. The potential for the

most profound creative changes come in the year of the three [2001].

The Biggest Solution

"So, Kryon, that's the biggest unity problem, right? Politics?" No, it is not. The biggest issue doesn't have anything to do with politics or religion. Then what is the biggest issue regarding unity on Earth? Let me ask you a personal unity question: How are you with your family? We have asked this before and we'll ask it again: Whom won't you speak to? What energy do you carry around that is inappropriate? You know what I speak of, don't you? What won't you release that separates you from love? What energy will you hang on to and hang on to and hang on to? You will not have unity in your own heart or your own biology until that old energy contract is dismissed. It takes two to write a contract, you know. Sometimes it's you and you!

Are you still abusing your body? Why? You might feel that this is a small issue, but it might also shorten your life on Earth . . . making you a far less effective healer or Lightworker. Did you consider this? What about the family at work? What's going on there? Are you joyful when you go to that vocation of yours, surrounded by those whom you would never have personally picked to be with? You think what's happening there is an accident?

What about the one at home? What about your partnering? Now we're starting to get to the hard parts, aren't we? *"Kryon, why do you ask this? What does it have to do with peace on Earth or the rebuilding of the third temple?"* What can you do for Earth? It sounds too simple: What about unity between you and you? We have broached this interdimensional issue in past Kryon channellings. We told you that part of you is on the other side of the veil. All of you is not here! I would like to tell you who came in a little while ago and sat next to you. Were you aware of a feeling of home flooding into your space, perhaps? Was there something very special? Who was it? You came to sit with you! The entity that has taken its place before you is the one on the other side of the veil who also has your face. Here is what that entity wants to ask you, dear Human Being: How much do you smile when no one is around? Do you really know who's inside? Are you letting the duality work overtime?

How would you like to peel that onion of duality around you and expose your spiritual core? Do you laugh when you're alone? Is there joy when you're alone? If the answer is no, then you haven't discovered who is there! For if you truly knew about the core, the unity, the angel inside, you might be astonished to realize it is a child! Angels never grow up, you know. They're always one age—youthful, joyful, playful, laughing, and smiling. That's who's in there. That's the one who can create unity on the planet. How about you with you? Will you let yourself go there and let yourself do that? Blessed is the Human Being who understands where the angel is—the consciousness of joy and celebration.

This is the Human Being who will create unity on the planet. This is the Human Being cooperating with the new grid system, with the tools that can create the third temple of consciousness, that can create The New Jerusalem on the planet. With this understanding, all of the other things will fall into place. When *you* unite with *you*, it is the beginning of laying the cornerstone for the last temple. It will also gird you against anything that may oppose you . . . fear, sorrow, or the last gasp of old energy. This is the Kryon message and always has been.

As we close, let the healing begin!

And so it is.

Kryon

Can you find peace within your heart now, even for those who perpetrated the events?

Can you think inter-dimensionally? These are the spiritual questions that will separate those who talk about spiritual growth, from those who actually understand and practice it.

Taken from the messsage of Kryon, channelled on September 11 and transcibed via the Internet to thousands all over the earth.

Shown on page 188

9-11

The Tragedy of
September 11, 2001

From Lee Carroll . . .

On September 11 we were on the fourth day of a "Kryon Cruise" around the Hawaiian islands. This was the second annual Kryon cruise event and included Jan Tober, myself, facilitators Barbra Dillenger, Michael Makay, and Canadian musical recording artist Robert Coxon. Our cruise hosts, Mary Ellen and Len Delekta, were on their honeymoon. The day was planned as a "play day," without any scheduled Kryon events.

Due to the time difference, those who awakened very early saw the Manhattan and Washington, D.C., events in real time. The rest of us were actually watching history after the fact . . . videotapes playing over and over. I remember Jan calling my cabin and saying, "Turn on the TV!" I did. The impact on all of us was profound, just like it was for most Americans that morning.

The ship was named *Ms Patriot.* Each morning at breakfast we had started the day by standing and honoring the playing of our U.S. national anthem. This day was different. The theme was more meaningful to most of us, and we knew the world had changed . . . we had changed.

The captain graciously allowed a shipwide announcement for the Kryon group, inviting any who wished, to attend a meditation in the "Eagle's Nest" lounge where we had been holding our Kryon events. The meeting began. As leaders of the group we spoke briefly, then all of us just meditated and comforted each other. We sang some songs. We prayed and some wept. It was good to be with family.

Sadly, this was the last voyage of the *Ms Patriot*. The 9-11 event, and all the economic fallout that went with it for Hawaii, bankrupted the cruise line. We didn't find that out until we docked in Honolulu a few days later.

The ship had e-mail capability, so after the meditation Kryon channelled a response at the computer. I sent it to Gary Liljegren, our Website manager; Barb and Rob Harris, our Emagazine editors; and also to *The Sedona Journal of Emergence* (the magazine where the Kryon channellings are presented each month). The message immediately was sent to thousands of people through our e-mail "marshmallow messages" and was placed on the font page of our Website. Later it was also published in *The Sedona Journal.* We know that many saw it and were comforted by Kryon's words.

It touches everyone, you know . . . every Human on the planet. But within our group we had one mother whose daughter worked at the twin towers, and who was supposed to be at work by 6:30 a.m. Eastern time. This placed her at her desk in the high-rise when the plane struck. The mother had been trying to call the daughter for some hours. The lines were busy (as you can imagine).

She called and called. Adding to the frustration was that the ship was not equipped with cellular technology, and the phone system was a ship-to-shore hookup . . . a very old and limited way to communicate. She continued . . . hoping to hear something from someone about her dear one. She finally connected. Can you imagine her joy of finally hearing on the phone that her daughter had "accidentally" missed the event? She had overslept! She had rushed to work and gotten to the base of the building just in time to see the first plane hit. Her reaction? She wanted to rush inside. Instead, her boyfriend, who was with her, literally carried her away from the scene. We all celebrated this miracle at a time when there was so much sadness. It helped us all.

I had been in New Jersey two weeks earlier giving two meetings. It was just on the border of New York . . . just across the bridge, and many who attended were from New York, some of whom worked in Manhattan. I am gripped with the thought that all of them might not be here now. I will never know that. I took a United flight home to Los Angeles, and it's still in my mind what those on a similar flight experienced. We circled the city as I left, and I saw the twin towers—the last time I will ever see those American icons of strength and commerce.

A heartfelt channelling was given on our ship on September 13. Kryon asked us to visualize all those who had died. He wanted us to see them returning home, with joy and purpose. Right before they make their final transition, they turn around and face us. Collectively they say, "We loved you enough to give you this push . . . this gift of action. What are you going to do with it? Make it count for us! Make love count for us!" Then they turn and disappear into the divine forms of God that they are—forms that we are in when we are not here. With their disappearance, however, is also the assurance that we will eventually join them. We always do.

My heart still cries with concern and empathy for those we lost . . . six months later. At the same time I hope that this will make a huge difference on our planet for a future generation of children who just may not ever have to go through anything like this again. What will we do with this?

In this new "war," those who gave their lives this week may very well be seen someday as veterans and unwilling combatants, but ones who helped preserve the world's freedom. Yes, there will be a memorial, and I hope to someday attend it and tell them I love them. In the "now," they are all still here.

I would also like to present the thoughts of Jan Tober that day (my presenting partner and cofounder of the Kryon work). She sums up the feelings for both of us. After that, the actual message from Kryon on September 11, 2001.

From Jan Tober . . .

Through the grace of Spirit, the crisis of September 11, 2001, found 70 people on the *Ms Patriot*, an American flagship, sailing the waters around what were pieces of the continent of Lemuria, now called the Hawaiian islands. Lee and I, along with our dear friends and teachers of many years, Barbra Dillenger and Michael Makay, were hosting the second annual Kryon cruise. It was intended to be a "Back to Lemuria" experience.

We started the cruise on Saturday afternoon and by Tuesday, September 11, had already been given two powerful channellings by Kryon, and explored the island of Kauai. On the morning of Tuesday the 11th, I switched on the television in my cabin to find out the activities of the day. In total shock and disbelief, with millions of others, I watched the surreal tragedy as it was being rerun again and again, digging a deep groove of pain into our consciousness.

Lee and I quickly gathered our Lemurian family in the room at the very top of the ship's forward section, above the bridge. As we joined together, someone in our group reflected that September 11 was "911," the call for help. We also realized as we were sailing out of the waters of Kauai, that somehow we were placed at the westernmost part of the United States, about as far away as you could be from the tragedy and still be in the States. This was also an area where we had been able to rekindle the love we felt as we had in Lemuria, as integrated Human Beings.

All of us in the group that day felt the shock and sadness, not only for America but for the world. We had a difficult challenge before us. As I moved into a channelled, guided meditation, we were told that it was appropriate and important to move out of our heads and into our hearts. We were reminded by Spirit of the instructions on how to return to the heart space so we could hold only the intent of Love and Light . . . only the feeling of Love and Light. It was a challenge under the circumstances, but we began.

We started by moving into our heart space in a conscious, deliberate manner. We then envisioned New York City and the WTC towers intact, as before the incident, and filled with gold, shimmering light. We asked Spirit, our teachers, guides, and angels, to support us in amplifying the golden, loving energy. We then moved this Love to Washington, D.C., the Pentagon, the crash site in Pennsylvania, and to all the people who had lost their lives.

If we found ourselves moving into fear, tears, or sorrow, we gently but firmly replaced our intent to Spirit, the one power which is Love. It was difficult at first since we were so emotional, but as the Grace of Love filled us, it became easier. We felt those who had passed on joining us in the room. It was extremely emotional. We then saw angels in the streets of New York helping people who were making their transitions, and also helping the loved ones and families who were remaining. With the support of the angels, we then placed our intent on all the leaders of the world to join together from a level of unity, with their Higher-Selves being in charge of all their decisions.

As our group disbanded so that everyone could also do their private prayers, we were then asked by Spirit to consciously make the effort to return our intentions to the feeling of the Love we had created while together.

On Saturday morning, we docked back in Honolulu. As I looked around, I realized that I was in the waters of Pearl Harbor . . . the event, up until now, of the worst American national attack. How ironic this felt to me. On Sunday, September 16, 2001, we were able to catch a flight home to San Diego. I was reminded by Spirit of the astrological configuration that many of us knew about . . . that in the skies above the Middle East (above Giza), a Star of David would be formed, astrologically. The intuitive information that many of us had been given was that after this portal had been opened, nothing would be the same. Humanity was done being complacent with the old ways. How right that was!

Those of us on this Kryon cruise thought that much of our sojourn would be pleasure as well as processing. We didn't expect to be put together at such a momentous time on the planet, but it was so perfect. The magic of Lemuria was present. I, for one, was so thankful I had been part of this beautiful group of Human Lemurian angels as we all did the work of Spirit in those peaceful islands we called home.

May peace prevail.

Namaste, Aloha, and Om Shanti

Jan Tober

Kryon's 9-11 Message

Dear ones, today you mourn for the family members who have made their transitions and who are still in the process. For many of you, the question is this: "Why didn't we know?" or "Shouldn't Spirit have told us of these things?"

We want you all to know that the words we gave you sometime ago are now here: "There is no Human or Spirit who can tell you what's going to happen tomorrow," we said. This is part of the new dimensionality . . . that all things happen outside a linear time frame, and that humanity is totally in charge.

What you saw today is the result of what we saw and reported to you as the potential for 2000 and beyond. We told you that you would see spiritual rage, and that there would be forces who would not let go of the old paradigm —the way the world "used to work." Now, you, in your country of America, are also involved in actually feeling what this means. The battle begins in earnest, and now you know why you're called "warriors" of the light.

With the millennium change came a new responsibility. Part of that revolves around this question: *What will you do now?* Can you lift yourselves above the anger? Can you see anything more in this than rage? Are you going to join or separate? The chasm opens, and the choices become harder . . . such is the beginning of new wisdom for the planet.

The family who transited in this event, on this "11" day, agreed to be part of this Human horror potential—something that could have changed yesterday if humanity had so decided. You agreed to go forward, however, and the result will make you part of the world family more than ever before. Perhaps this will bring you all closer to agreement? Perhaps this will eventually make you decide on world events differently? Perhaps more will go to your knees? Perhaps more will understand the "world family"?

Kryon's 9-11 Message

If so, then the Humans who came home today will have a grander party than they expected, for it will have advanced planetary healing. All is in divine order, and all is appropriate, even though such statements are not understandable while you're in sorrow. Can you find peace within your heart now, even for those who perpetrated the events? Can you think interdimensionally? These are the spiritual questions that will separate those who talk about spiritual growth, from those who actually understand and practice it.

Blessed are those family members who remain, for they're feeling the pain and suffering of incredible loss. For now, send your energy and your love to them. Remember: The thoughts of the few can change the reality of the many. Hug them from afar. Bring them into your rooms and weep for them, for they need your help.

Then, when enough time has passed, bring about wise decisions from a new resource of Humans who can now tap in to the masters, the ones who are bringing their energy potential to the planet.

A call to action has been sounded in a land that was happy to just exist and watch the others work it out. Now you're all involved in the same challenges. The result? Human free choice will decide all, just as it always has. Only now, there is a profound urgency that wasn't there before.

You're not alone in this, and legions stand with you to bring about solutions to what you all know is now very real—the old vs. the new.

Love is infinitely more powerful, dear ones. Use it today! We are with you in your sorrow, and the potential profound wisdom that can arise from it.

You are dearly loved!   *Kryon*

Birth of a New World Consciousness?

From Kryon: December 2000

Listen: This baby whom we invite you to celebrate is the returning consciousness of the ascended masters all coming together into the energy of one child—a child being born and celebrated in the hearts of many Humans right now. "Which master?" you might ask. "After all, they all represent different belief systems." Really? Take a look at the core information of each one. Take a look at the source of the information they gave you. Take a look at one divinity and one message!

Kryon — Kryon Book 9 — The New Beginning, page 140

From Princeton University: September 2001

After "The Global Consciousness Project" had *measured* the 9-11 event on their equipment . . .

Groups of people, including the group that is the whole world, have a place in consciousness space. Under special circumstances they—or we—become a new presence. Evidence [from the 9-11 response of the 39 sensors around the world] shows that both individuals and groups manifest something we can tentatively call a "consciousness field." Pursuing the speculation, it would seem that the new, integrated mind is just beginning to be active . . . Perhaps the best image is an infant slowly developing awareness.

Source: Princeton University, The Global Consciousness Project, Roger Nelson, director

[http://noosphere.princeton.edu/terror.html]

Live Channelling

"The Circle of Energy from the 'Ordinary' Human"

Channelled in
San Francisco, California/
Denver, Colorado
October 2002

Chapter Eight

"The Circle of Energy from the 'Ordinary' Human"

Live Channelling
San Francisco, California/ Denver, Colorado

The live channelling that follows was transcribed as a combination of two events with the same message . . . given live. It has been edited with additional words and thoughts to allow clarification and better understanding of the written word.

Greetings, dear ones, I am Kryon of Magnetic Service. There will be those in this room who do not understand the preciousness of this time. There will be those who will say that the energies here are of the Human, not Spirit. Let us say to you, as we have said so many times previously, that the energy that flows into this place and that presses upon you from the front, the back and the sides, are from those who have come to wash your feet. Let that be the proof that this is not *ordinary*.

It is a precious time that allows Spirit, and the family of Spirit, to flow into this place. There are those who might come into this place this evening whom some of you didn't expect. Some of you have said that the entourage of Kryon is always the same—these who come and wash your feet in honor. For those of you who do not know, we tell you that this entourage is *never* the same! This group has *your* name upon it. We knew you were coming, for you had given intent. Even those who just decided this very day to come into this room had an energy potential of being here days ago. Let me tell you this, and it may give you pause, dear Human Being, *ordinary* piece of God—perhaps now you might understand exactly who came to see whom!

There is an entourage here that has been waiting for three days. Preparation of this room for the visitors and the readers began three days ago. The posturing for the names who would come in and for the "angels" who would walk through the door [Humans] started three days ago. Some of you have realized that we have created a very peaceful sanctuary, like a bubble isolated from the rest of Earth temporarily, letting you slowly remember who you really are. Feel the love of Spirit and family slowly break down the barriers of the intellect and biased reasoning of all those things that you call the veil. Perhaps it can crack open that shell, the shell of duality—the one that keeps you from truly feeling the love of God.

And so it is that you sit here in an energy that is new for the planet, an energy that lets these messages flow out even better than they even have before—an energy of love that is finally able to reach out and grasp you and say, "Now, family, do you remember what the potentials were?" Some of you have had your hearts opened in these last few weeks [following September 11]. We will talk of such things in a moment, for the energy of this time is different from the last time we were in this place, dear Human Being. There is potential like there never was before. An opening has occurred, one that was not predestined, but a powerful potential—one that we had hinted about to you over and over throughout the last decade. We gave you information about the chasm opening, and now you stare into it. We gave you information about the decisions for humanity "getting off the fence," and now you're looking at the fence. What none of you expected would touch you is now something you must live with for the rest of your lives. The decision is yours; the action is within you. That is what we wish to talk about this night.

You might say, *"Dear Kryon, we feel so ordinary in this world. We watch the unfolding scenario, and it is abominable to our spirit. Some of it we understand the necessity for, but we feel helpless because we cannot change anything. We're so ordinary! We have leaders of the earth and watch their progress through our various systems through which news is given. We wring our hands and weep. We visualize and pray, but we feel so ordinary."*

It is this evening that we're going to title this particular message to you: "The Circle of Energy from an Ordinary Angel." There is nothing *ordinary* about who sits in the chairs before us or who finds themselves casually reading these words, dear ones. It does not matter your age, what you feel are your talents, or where you are in some spiritual path that you seem to have as your own priority. It has nothing to do with any of those things.

How many of you understand the "now"? How many of you understand that this time in history in absolutely unique? Perhaps this time will be the only one that will allow you to open to Spirit in ways you never would have before? Perhaps this is the moment that you might give permission to do something that you never would have before?

Let me tell you about a profound spiritual process. It is called "The Cycle of Energy." I am here to tell you about something that has been known—something we've talked about and targeted over and over in our communications, but which may have not been clear. Dear *ordinary* Humans, you are the ones who are going to determine the outcome of what is before you in the news. When we say *you*, we mean the family of humanity—those listening right now in your *now*, and also the readers.

Dear reader, we speak to you now, for we see the eyes on the page and we see the mind we are connecting with. We ask the family who is in the room listening to reach up and take the hand of the reader. The ones listening, although they are not in your time frame, understand fully that there will be many more who will read this message than those who are listening. We are "here" with you, reader, as you pretend to visit the past through this transcription. The family who is here listening now reaches out in time to those through the years who will read this message over and over. For this is the circle of energy created by the *ordinary* Human Being.

The Circle of Energy

There is a circle of energy that operates and affects the planet. It is created almost solely by what the Human Beings do on the planet, as pieces of God, walking this Earth in duality. It is not about judgment, for there is none. We have given you this message over and over. It is not about works—who did well and who did not. It is not about social status—who became a leader and who did not. It is instead about *solutions*. What have you solved lately? What have you discovered lately? What are the spiritual and interdimensional things that we have told you about that you've grasped onto and begun to make a part of your life? How many of you are more peaceful today than you were a year ago or the year before that? How many of you are more joyful? How many of you can elicit those feelings at will, even in the face of pain, sorrow, suffering, or profound empathy?

I would like to tell you about the circle of energy. When you solve the problems, when you do certain kinds of spiritual things, when you become interdimensional and begin to connect with Spirit and peel that onion of duality to discover your divinity inside, energy is released. We have labeled this energy many things in the past, but it's an energy of the divine Human

Being who does the work of solution on Earth. This may sound odd and strange, but in a day when the actual energy field of consciousness is being examined by your scientists, it may start to make sense.

When this energy of solution is released, it goes to two places . . . if you really need to identify a location. This is when this explanation becomes difficult in your four-dimensional lives. For the energy goes to a location that is not in your experiential spectrum, and I cannot explain it well. I can tell you where the energy goes, but you may not fully understand it, for it's a circle.

The energy goes two places and then returns. It goes into the magnetic grid system of the earth, and also into the dirt of the earth—two directions, above and below. What it does there, dear *ordinary* Human divine being, is to change the actual measured energy of the earth! For those of you familiar with the messages of Kryon and with how these things work, you know that the *earth* is measured, *not* the Human Being—the physical living earth is measured every 25 years. These measurements are why you're here: Can pieces of God—angels disguised as Humans—come to planet Earth on an even-consciousness playing field, not recognizing who they are while they're here, yet discover love or spiritual awareness? What will they endure and go through to change the planet? What reality will they choose? What solutions will they discover within? When the test is over and the energy of the earth is measured, the result of all of the eons of preparation—the tens of thousands of cycles of past lives and lives ongoing—will be taken and applied to another place in the Universe that you have no concept of.

While you are in this Earthly body, you will not know any of this. I am going to tell you that the energy that you provide for what you do now and how you solve things now is going to affect millions in places you cannot even fathom. This is the truth. It is the test of the "only planet of free choice." The circle? We will get to that in a moment.

Let us speak about some of these things, especially the new things. Let us speak about what creates reality, changing energy from *ordinary* Human Beings. The first item seems to be a review, but we must tell you again, for this first one is critical. There is the Human and there is challenge. When these come together and create spiritual solution, energy is released and is the "third energy" in what we have called "The Third Language." We have told you about The Third Language repeatedly. The information is old enough now that it has been published and read by many.

We are telling you that there is a language that is interdimensional—a language of the avatar. It's a language that can be yours with a 100 percent walking connection with Spirit. It's a language that transforms physics, and goes beyond the laws of your 4D. Here is what may be new to you: When we say Spirit, we mean *you* with *you*. Some of you will understand what we mean this time.

The piece of God that you are—which is on the other side of the veil—reaches through and wishes to touch you. It is not unusual, and it is not frightening. It is a reunion of the highest order. Some have made this look frightening in the past, since the veil firmly hides this. Do you know what *you* with *you* can do with this revelation? It creates a partner! This Third Language is a connection energy. *"Kryon, are you saying we should do this instead of meditating?"* Absolutely not. Spirit loves ceremony and loves to be loved. The family loves to talk to you and have you speak to them, but this is beyond that.

When you stand up and walk from this place, or the place where you're reading, we're saying that there's a language or energy that can be with you that's a constant connection to God. As you remove your body from this area and get into your vehicle and go about doing seemingly mundane tasks in your ordinary day, dear Human, it's still there. When you reach up and take the hand of the Higher-Self, you actually create energy! When you say to Spirit, *"I would like to know more about this. I wish to be connected as the grid finishes its scheduled move and the bow is tied on a new earth-energy gift at the end of 2002. I want to cross this bridge of swords and be counted!"* This creates energy! It's profound, spiritual, and affects the earth itself.

The real Kryon work begins in 2003. The grid will be settled, and the solutions of unsolvable items on your planet will have begun to move off their peg of impossibility. The Third Language is here and is an interdimensional energy that says, "Connect with me, and when you connect, you'll know it." That's just one way that the *ordinary* Human creates energy that changes everything.

Oh, there's so very much more. Some have said, *"I'm so ordinary that I'm never going to meet these leaders of Earth. I can't affect anything. Nobody is going to listen to any wisdom I might feel I have. Not only that, but in my life, I feel stuck, going places I don't want to go, having to do things I really don't want to do. Dear Spirit, I can't have that 'Third Language.' You don't know where I work!"* [Laughter] Oh, yes, we do!

Ordinary, you're not. Some of you go to very dark places every day. We have said this before. Some of you say to Spirit, *"Oh, please remove me from this place. It's not commensurate with the magnificence of God, and I'm not accomplishing anything here. People don't understand me here. It's not for me. Get me out!"* Do you want to know how light-energy is created? Do you want to know how energy goes into the grid and into the earth? It happens when you go to those places you don't want to go to and spread your light! You may be the only one there who knows about the light!

Let me remind you how you change lives, for you do not impose your energy upon the other person. You never have to communicate it verbally. You can just go and "be the light," and in the process of going to a place where you think you don't belong, you're right where you asked to be when you gave permission for God to place you in your sweet spot! You're right there helping other Humans. Oh, you may say you're not and they don't even really know you at all, but we must remind you that in those dark places, you may be the *only* light!

We must remind you again of this phenomenon that we've talked about over and over, but maybe you didn't understand. It's about the energy created when you fill a room with light. It lets the others around you see their choices more clearly. You never have to verbally communicate with them. They may never know your name, and you may come and go many, many times. Your presence actually might enhance their paths—not in an evangelistic way, but in a way that allows them to see things they may not have seen before in the dark. They may make better choices for themselves due to what you brought. And while you're creating that solution, you're praying to be released from that place. [Laughter] Do you really mean it? That's what a Lightworker does. And so we say to you, if this is your plight, we've heard your prayer. We ask you to celebrate where you're going every day. There will come a time when you're finished spreading light there, and you'll move on to a more appropriate place, but while you're there, do the work and enjoy the journey.

There may be darkness, negativity, confrontation, and sadness. But you might be the only one there with a bubble of energy where these things can bounce off of you, and instead, you'll place light in that dark place. How many people around you are afraid wherever they walk? There is much fear right now—everywhere! It's a great time to show them your joy. It's a great time to walk with confidence. Oh, you're sensitive, compassionate, loving, and you mourn with them also about the events of the recent past, but there's something different about you: You've got the light of Spirit within you that shines light in dark places. When you do that, energy goes to the grid—to the earth—and creates the cycle of energy. That's all done by angels, calling themselves *ordinary* Human Beings—the ones who have been here over and over and over. There has never been a more profound setup to help change the planet than right now!

Let us speak about being afraid. *"Kryon, what are we going to do about fear? There's fear everywhere we go right now."* Perhaps you're noticing that you can't remember a time when you saw more people afraid on a collective basis? We say something to you that we've given you over and over. Perhaps now you can put it into a context that fits into life's puzzle. Blessed is that Human Being who understands what fear is. It's an appropriate energy. It's a balance. It's a shade of love that presents itself to the Human Being in all correctness and challenge, and it's powerful. For those of you who have analyzed it, you know where fear starts. Listen: Fear does not start at the crown chakra! That's where it's headed, however. If you let it, it will go there, and it will control how you think and will paralyze your mind and take over.

You have time from the place where it starts, to where it's going. You have time to recognize it, identify it, and say to it: "Not this time. Get behind me, for I'm driving today!" And the vehicle you're driving is your life! It's how you choose to feel about the things around you and the spiritual connection that gives you peace. It's not about what the emotions will do "to you," which can overcome and control you. Those days are gone.

When an *ordinary* Human identifies and cancels fear as it creeps up, interdimensional energy is created . . . lots of it! It is absolute energy that flows to the grid and the earth. Now you may say that one person's energy is minuscule and very small and that it cannot play an important part. This is where you're wrong! This is far more potent than you realize. How many times can you put fear away? Every time you do it, you create energy. Energy is solution. The one who is holding the hand of the

Higher-Self via The Third Language is able to help the planet, themselves, and everyone around them. There will come a time when as you wake up in the morning, all you do is send energy to the grid and to the dirt of the earth, dear *ordinary* angel! Then . . . you may begin to understand what ascension truly means.

"Kryon, we've heard you talk about co-creation. How does that fit into this?" It fits very well! How would you like to co-create a meld that you didn't think possible? We keep talking about the Higher-Self. It is a misnomer. It truly is not the Higher-Self at all, but rather, it is your "other self." It is equal to yours and is on the other side of the veil. It's *you* with *you*, a phenomenon that you still do not fully understand or recognize.

All of you is not here, as we've said before. Sometime ago, we gave you a picture in history that we'd like to revisit. It is of the Prophet Elijah, walking into a field with his assistant, Elisha, looking on. For Elijah told Elisha that is was time to go and he was going to ascend. And in 4D, Elisha witnessed this ascension. In the reality of his Humanism, Elisha reported the ascension of the master, Elijah. You can read it in your scripture history.

There were bright lights, seeming vaporization, energy everywhere! Elisha said that Elijah ceased to exist as he witnessed it. In that energy from those days, I would like to tell you what took place: Elijah was not taken by God. What Elijah did was to claim the spectacular energy of The Third Language— to touch the hands of the Higher (other) Self. The two parts of Elijah joined and became the piece of God that we talk about. Therefore, what Elisha reported was a meld of a total spiritual being, not an ascension or a departure. The Human Elijah, plus the connection energy, plus the Higher-Self of Elijah—three energies—combined to give Elijah his whole divinity . . . an energy that could not stay on Earth at that time.

When the meld took place in those days—in that older energy—the interdimensionality of it seemingly vaporized Elijah. Now we're saying that the earth has changed—the grid has changed—the consciousness of humanity has changed—even the weather has changed! All has created a new reality so that you can hold more energy and stay here—and even do almost what Elijah did: create tremendous energy by a melding of the selves. In your case, the energy that Elisha saw is still real, but you do not vaporize. You stay and walk the earth as a potential to shine light into dark places, and help this planet move into its next phase. We would not tell you these things if they were not so, and we say, co-create the meld!

Here's a big one. How would you like to create amazing energy? It's time to straighten out some of the relationships in your life, family to family. We say it again: Who is it that you won't talk to? Dead or alive, who is it that you won't talk to? Now we bring you the news of who is in the room, or by your chair. The pieces and the parts of those people whom you have issues with, stand around you. It would be the right time, would it not, to solve this? Then watch! Sparks will fly and the energy you create through solution will go to the grid and to the living earth.

Dear *ordinary* Human Being, this energy vibrates so high that it will continue to move the consciousness of the earth. Some of you continue to say, *"That's all very well for me, but it doesn't change the decisions that our leaders are going to make or help the wisdom factor."* Oh, yes, it does! Perhaps you have not yet understood clearly what we're saying. The more of you who hold this vision, the more energy is created. It shines light into dark places, on paths that have yet to be trod, on decisions yet to be made. It goes into those inner offices where those leaders are, famous ones who you may never meet, dear Human Being. It places light in a place where they would not have had light. In the process, it does not push upon them in any way. Instead, it enhances things for them. It's placed on the ground where they walk, metaphorically—the light of Spirit, helping them to see more choices in their path. All because you solved a problem in your life—because you had The Third Language—because you created a meld. And that's the way it works.

Some have said, *"What can we really do to enhance our understanding about God?"* I will give you an answer that perhaps you didn't expect: A beautiful energy has arrived on the grid *this year*. Things happen in balance, even though it may not always appear so. When there is tragedy, there is also miracle. We would not give you problems without solutions. There would never be challenges without answers. We have said this before. There is always a balance.

With the event that you all know as September 11, 2001, before it ever happened, there was another event. On the grid arrived all of the masters that have ever walked this Earth who said they would come back, and all the ones who were expected for the first time as well. Not in the flesh—better than that—unified together and posturing a potential that will respond to your action. It's part of the grid change that is the sole reason the Kryon grid entourage came in 1989. It's part of why the grid is important, and is being shaped and coming to completion in 2002. This completes it.

Almost every religion on your planet was expecting a master to return or come for the first time, and they have arrived. Part of reaching up and touching the Higher (other) Self is also reaching into the grid and understanding what God really is. The returning avatars—the returning masters—the prophets—are all here as a direct result of the 11:11, that time after the Harmonic Convergence where you gave permission to move beyond the track of an Armageddon and instead changed your Earth paradigm of spiritual reality. Your tragedy of September 11 was not the beginning of anything you ever were given in your old prophecy. Instead, it was a beginning of what you gave permission for within your new one.

These masters and avatars, almost too numerous to count, all together holding hands, are looking upon this planet and communicating with you together as one energy. There has never been a resource—a well of wisdom—like this on the planet... never. It is the interdimensional Human who starts to search, who gives pure intent for divine communication, who will reach up to touch that energy. And the wisdom will flow into that Human, and then the energy of this profound decision will go to the grid, to the dirt of the earth, and it will shine light in dark places ... all created from the *ordinary* Human angel.

The circle? Some have figured it out by now. As this energy is sent into the grid and the living earth called Gaia, it changes the fabric of what is possible, of what a Human can call "reality" and can collectively accomplish. It circles back to the earth through the connection called The Third Language—a perfect circle of divinity for the *ordinary* Human! Your solutions cause energy, and the energy enhances your connection. Notice that it has involved the earth and the sky, and the life force that is in between. Can you change the reality of your planet? You just did.

I'm going to explain something that has happened to some of you that perhaps you haven't understood. There is a dichotomy in the emotions of some of you regarding September 11, 2001. You and many others felt incredible grief, horror, and shock. An outpouring of love took place—yes, even a rearrangement of your priorities, perhaps. A fuller understanding of what is taking place on the earth, perhaps. But there is one seemingly dichotomous emotion that so many of you are having that you cannot explain. It doesn't seem to align with the other emotions and might be confusing.

Some of you have not even breathed a word of it because you could not "go there" in your minds yet. In your own psyche, you can't understand what's taking place, and it doesn't seem to be commensurate with the grief of the tragedy. We will tell you what the word is, and some of you will honestly know when I tell you that the word is: RELEASE.

The world has been stuck in old challenges, and we told you that there would come a time when things would unstick themselves and involve the entire planet [*Kryon Book Eight*]. This has been the Kryon information since 1989, and was even enhanced in the year 2000. This was *your* plan in your new reality, and in this process, there has been tremendous release! An anchor has been broken—an anchor connected to the past paradigm that you have been in for ages. Your event of September 11, although horrible beyond Human comprehension, released an energy that now has allowed things to move forward at an accelerated pace. Was it foreseen? Yes. Go back and find the Kryon energy around 9 and 11, given even in 1989. Our message in 1989? That you had changed the paradigm of the planet, and were moving into a new reality. We began moving the grid, and now you're beginning to understand how, as the grid begins to settle, this puzzle is coming together. See the synchronicity of the 11's everywhere, but know that nothing is predestined. Instead, you manifested the potentials that we saw and reported to you over a decade ago. When this planet starts to move forward with an increasing pace within this new decade, there's nothing ordinary about what you can now do with it.

Let me close with this. On the morning of September 11, 2001, *ordinary* Human Beings reporting to work in several buildings around your country. At some level, there was cellular information that they would be in the right place at the right time, and they all had free choice to be where they chose. Naturally, none of them, with information from their four-dimensional reality, would have knowingly gone. But in a spiritual way, they made an appointment and were there, as planned.

All of them were *ordinary* Human angels. Now, what you see on the earth as a result is what *ordinary* people chose to do on that day for the planet. Right "now," they file one at a time into the "Hall of Honor," and we sing their spiritual name in light and take our time recounting the lives they have been, where they have been, and where they're going . . . and the beautiful children they will be as they return again. I don't know if you've thought of this as being beautiful, but let me tell you . . . it is. *They* are okay. *They* are joyful! Do not mourn for them. Pour your prayer on those who are left.

I don't know if you can conceive of this in the context in which Spirit sees it, but the September 11 event was a "marker." In Tel-Aviv, Israel, in 2000, my partner [Lee] told you that before the earth could move forward and before there could be solutions in the Middle East, there would have to be a "draw to zero." This was channelled information. Almost all of those who sat in that assemblage [Israel] felt deep grief. It reflected their own challenge, and they wondered what "draw to zero" meant. All of them felt it might be some prophecy as to what they were going to experience in Israel. None of them saw the "draw to zero" occurring in lower Manhattan. None of them realized that "ground zero" is what was meant. How does an event in America start a solution in Israel? It's the circle of energy, and you will soon see.

Here you sit, a family member with the earth—with the challenge of the old and the new before you. How *ordinary* are you? You are spectacular! When we "see" you at the various times that you come into the "Hall of Honor," and when we sing your spiritual name in light, there is nothing *ordinary* about the angel who receives the colors. The interdimensional being that you are is veiled completely from you while you're here!

And that is the message of Kryon—there has never been a time in Earth history with more potential than right now. There has never been a grander time for solution than right now, and all of it will happen with *ordinary* Human Beings within the circle of energy—sending it to the grid, to the Earth-spreading light, walking through challenges, connecting withThe Third Language, shining light into places where kings make decisions, shaping nations, and bringing peace and promise to lands that thought they would never see it.

Ordinary? Hardly. That is why we love you the way we do. That is why we say that "you are dearly loved."

And so it is.

Kryon

Basic Kryon Message since 1989 . . .

The tilt [of the magnetic grid] that has been foreseen is my job. It is a magnetic tilt, and will be the realignment of the grid system of the Earth to provide for your final time . . . Your magnetic north will no longer line up with polar north. It really never has that you know of, but its tilt will now become significant.

My process will take ten to twelve Earth years to accomplish. From now through the year 2002 will be the gradual change. Around the year 1999 you should know exactly of what I am speaking. Governments are run by men of power . . . not all of them are enlightened. Their inability to deal with the consciousness alteration could imbalance them, and the result could be chaos.

Kryon Book One - The End Times - Lee Carroll
   Page 22 and 23 - 1989

North Magnetic Pole
Could Be Leaving Canada
by Richard Stenger
CNN - March 20, 2002

(CNN) --The North Magnetic Pole could soon abandon Canada, migrate north of Alaska and eventually wind up in Russia, according to a Canadian scientist.

The magnetic pole, which has steadily drifted for decades, has picked up its pace in recent years and could exit Canadian territory as soon as 2004, said Larry Newitt of the Geological Survey of Canada.

If the pole follows its present course, it will pass north of Alaska and arrive in Siberia in a half century, but Newitt cautioned that such predictions could prove wrong.

"Although it has been moving north or northwest for a hundred years, it is not going to continue in that direction forever. Its speed has increased considerably during the past 25 years, and it could just as easily decrease a few years from now," the geophysicist said.

Richard Stenger for CNN Website: "North Magnetic Pole Could Be Leaving Canada" Entire article not shown

[http://www.cnn.com/2002/TECH/space/03/20/north.pole/index.html]

Kryon's message was the beacon lighting our way through darkest night, slowly guiding our footsteps to the new harbor where we dropped anchor. Since then, an eternal feeling of gratitude and indescribable joy has taken up permanent residence: the serene joy of knowing for sure that things are well founded and fair, and the joy that resembles an outburst of laughter when you discover at last the extraordinary beauty that lives behind the dramatic comedy that is life. That joy is nothing other than Love of Life . . .

. . . and a feeling of total confidence and abandonment in the arms of Spirit who, in the new era, takes command in our cockpit.

Fété & Clément

From *The African Experience*
page 345

"The Evolution of Earth and Humanity"

Channelled in
New Hampshire
November 2001

Chapter Nine

"The Evolution of Earth and Humanity"

Live Channelling
New Hampshire

This live channelling has been edited with additional words and thoughts to allow clarification and better understanding of the written word.

Greetings, dear ones, I am Kryon of Magnetic Service. We greet the family, whom we have seen previously—those who have been to this room before, and those who have sat in front of Spirit before.

Let me tell you something that we have not told many up till now—something that you may not even recognize or realize is so: Three days ago, when this room was dark, it was humming. It was singing. There was preparation, and some may even call it rehearsal. In some ways, some of the entourage was poured into this place, and it never left. Some of you felt this energy when you walked in. Perhaps you felt the hug of God, or the *family*, take your hand as you sat down? Perhaps you heard that still, small voice that said, "This day is special"?

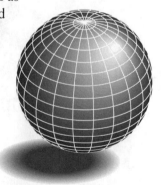

Today, angels disguised as Human Beings will walk into this place and sit down [the audience]. Some of them will leave later, but you won't recognize the ones you actually "saw," even though you spent lifetimes together in the past. Such is the energy of the veil! Why would we come three days early? Why would we fill this place in this fashion? Let me tell you something that is happening right now: There is an entourage pouring into this place, and some of them have rehearsed in order to be here!

There has never been a time in Human history like this. The veil has lifted even more profoundly than it did a year ago at this time when we were together in this room. Awareness is starting to come from so many places. Awakening and remembrance is the "order of the day," and there are so many Human Beings who are awakening to the core issue of their divinity. They are beginning to look back upon their lives and say, *"Now I understand why I went through this—why I went through that."* They're rising above the victimization, above the blame, above the hate. They are starting to have revelations. *"Oh, now I understand,"* they are saying. They are starting to see purpose in their lives.

Twelve years will have gone by since the first words were uttered: "Greetings, I am Kryon of Magnetic Service." This is part of what we want to talk about tonight. How did the energy get to this stage? What has the evolvement been of humanity? Why would Spirit show up three days ago and rehearse? Here is what most of you don't even realize: We are here to see *you*. You think you have come to hear wise words? You think perhaps there will be a message for you tonight? Oh, there might be . . . both for the listener and the reader, but energy is pouring into this place for other reasons, too.

The Third Language will be present. There will even be healing tonight. You know who you are and why you came here, or why you might be reading these words. And you also think you know what you need. I'm saying to you that this energy has come forth to start processes in your body that some will call miracles! It's because you gave intent to come and *be*, and to sit and have a family reunion with those who came to see *you*. It's about energy, but it's really about family! It's about holding hands between my side of the veil and yours. So, who came to see whom? That is the question. The answer? A reunion has both sides arriving to see each other. That's why we came early. That should give you some idea of the energy here between us, hearer and listener.

Dear Human Being, this is real. You are eternal, you know. As you look at yourself in the mirror in the morning, how many of you remind yourselves that you are eternal? How many of you look into your own eyes and say *"I am that I am"?* How many of you remember the *family?* How many of you think of us? The duality keeps this from happening on a regular basis, and instead, you walk about your Human existence and your Human lives as you always do, day by day—consumed with detail about living your everyday lives.

It's different now, however, isn't it? [speaking to American citizens after the September 11 event]. How could we have ever given you the knowledge in the past that today you would be in an energy that would be so profound with the potential for solutions? And yet here it is. How could we have told you that the entire earth would participate together and have you believe it? Actually, we did, you know. But it did not mean the same to you as it does now. Now, perhaps, you might understand what the *gift of the few* has meant to the many.

There has never been a time like this time . . . ever. Some of you can see colors. You can see colors of energy. We tell you that during this time this evening, you're invited to actually see the colors coming from this place [the stage]. They're different from the last time we were together.

The entourage has taken its place. It's next to all of you. For some of you, there will be physical evidence of tonight's energy, and for some of you, there will not. It has to do with how much of the veil you wish to "peel away" as you listen and read . . . and what you allow yourself to believe. Could it really be that Spirit wanted to come today and speak to you? The answer is yes, yes, and yes!

Beyond the ones who are listening at this moment, there is a vast number who are reading—two eyes on the pages—joining you right now. Two ears hearing this, and two eyes on the page. This is whom we speak to, and this is whom we talk to—all of you. We tell you this: There is energy created now that will go beyond the words on the page— that will go beyond the hearing. You can capture it and call it your own within your own body. There is an emotion of love from this side of the veil, pouring itself to you like never before.

Humanity has willingly walked through a challenge that is tremendous. Some of you have indeed felt the *release* that it has given, and now, here you sit. It is no accident that the grid finishes at a time when it is most needed to finish. Let us tell you about that. Let us tell you about the earth. Let us go places regarding instruction that we've never gone before. Let us give you a chronology of humanity. Let me give you the whole picture. I'm going to talk about the chronology of the earth. I'm going to talk about the evolution of Human Beings and the geology of the planet. I'm going to speak about the evolution of the *consciousness* and the *biology* of humanity, for they are very separate. I wish to give you the whole story.

The Evolution of Earth

How can I tell you what was present more than 12 billion years ago right where you sit? I actually don't have to tell you, since you were all here! But even though I can give you information, some of you won't believe it. You don't remember, and due to the duality of humanism, it won't make any sense. In addition, your linear setup will tell you that what I say is impossible. Even so, I will say that all of you watched, anticipating the setup for the test to come. I was with you. This meta-phoric neutral playing field called Earth is where *angels pretend-ing to be Humans* arrived and performed a test of energy. We have given you this scenario before.

The Bang That Wasn't

Although it may seem unfathomable to you, more than 12 billion years ago the universe was born. If I take you back there, you will see something quite different from what your science says took place. We have spoken of this before [1995], and again we are going to reiterate what took place. We told you that there was no such thing as "one event" that came out of nowhere, which started everything. There is a bias in your scientific method. Even those who would pretend to be the least biased—who honor the scientific method to the fullest—are biased. Your scientists are constantly looking for the beginning, and there was none. The entire thought of linear time is a 4D Human construct for you, and it sets up a premise that everything has a beginning and an end. It doesn't.

You are eternal in both directions, and Lightworkers know that. At the cellular level, you know that there is no end to your life—there is only energy transformation. Hard to prove? Very few ever come back and tell you what it was like, do they? And yet it is so . . . that you are eternal. You always were, and you always will be.

Scientists will tell you that there was a beginning to all that you see, and that out of nothing whatsoever, everything was created. Not only that, they tell you that it happened all at once—in an instant—from nothing to everything. Not only that, they will tell you that in the process of nothing becoming everything, it violated all of the physics rules known to man! And that was the beginning. Quite a story, don't you think? In all fairness to them, they didn't make it up. They are trying their best to reconstruct what happened by looking at the 4D evidence, but it simply doesn't make sense. That's because the real evidence is outside of 4D.

Again we'll say this to you: There was no such thing as *The Big Bang*. Oh, there was motion and there was speed, and you will see even in the relativity of motion to speed, it will appear as though there was an explosion . . . a beginning. There was not.

The Universe always was. The best way for us to speak of this for your understanding is to say that it, like you, changed energy! And whereas the Universe *always was* and perhaps *is*, invisible in 4D, it became 4D out of something else—and although it seems to have taken place all at once, this process actually started a multicreative event—something that is impossible to describe to you. Let's simply say that it's still happening.

We invite the scientists to go and look again. They will have to support a premise they are not ready to accept, however, to find the truth . . . that maybe the Universe *always was*. So whereas the scientists would call it The Big Bang, this event was actually a change of energy, a shift of dimensions, and a cyclical event. Everything showed up at the same time, seemingly. Not a big bang, but a revelation. In that 4D revelation was the material that Earth would become. That was the *beginning*, and you were there.

If there is darkness for a very long time, and then suddenly someone turns on the light, does that mean that what is revealed in the light was created when the light went on? Do you assume that when there is nothing but darkness, there is nothing to be seen? Or does it perhaps imply that what was revealed might have always been there, and that the creation event was really about the light—not what was seen after it went on? In other words, it was about energy changing dimension, revealing what was always there—your Universe.

Family has always been *family*, you know. How does it make you feel to know that someday, when the earth is simply a burnt cinder, a distance of time beyond your reasoning, you and I and the others will still be playing together in the Universe? Can you fathom such a thing? How does it make you feel to know that the core of the reality of God and of the Uiverse is a simple thing you've called *love?* Do you think there's a measurable consciousness field around you? Do you think there's a consciousness field around humanity? There is. It's what you call the emotion of love and the essence of God. It comes to you through the veil, unaltered, and you feel it at the heart level.

We told you 12 years ago that at the heart of every atom you would find love. We told you that the secret of the Universe was love. It seems oversimplified, but it's not. Now your scientists tell you that at the heart of every atom they have recently found interdimensional energy. Your *meta*physics is becoming physics, simply through wisdom and discovery. Someday, who knows, they may even find interdimensional life there? That's another channelling!

The Arrival of Water

Let me tell you what happened regarding water. Earth is a water planet. It had to be a water planet in order for the biology to develop in the way you scheduled it to. Yet in the beginning, there wasn't enough water here. Similar to the other planets you see in your solar system, you didn't have much. The water planet had a delivery, however, and this is not a metaphor. Again, we speak to the geologists—go find it—the evidence is there. The water did not originate here. It was delivered. In those early days when things were whizzing around and colliding, you had a delivery to Earth of most of the water that is now on your planet, almost all at once. It was cataclysmic—and needed. These things sound odd and unusual, and you're not going to read it in your history or science books. Perhaps someday that will change?

The Arrival of Biology

Now we talk to the biologists. You want to see a big bang? Explain this one: Five hundred and thirty-eight million years ago, life began all at once on your planet. Five hundred and thirty-eight million years ago—that was yesterday! All over the planet, seemingly at the same time—not through millions of years of evolution—not even through tens of thousands of years—but only a handful of years, life populated the entire earth, all at once. Unbelievable? Go find the 4D evidence. It's there.

You might ask, "How did such a thing happen? Is there proof?" Oh, yes. Ask your biologists. They will find that this is so. Everywhere they look, at one point there was no life. The rocks reveal this. Suddenly, seemingly out of nowhere, there *was!* And that's because it was *delivered* here! In those early days, the essence of life (which permeates the Universe) was delivered on schedule. How else would you explain such a biological explosion? It was by design, and you, dear ones, were here and watched it happen.

This is a finely cooked meal, this earth, which took billions of years to prepare so that you could sit in the throne of its completion. Seemingly, within the last few seconds of Earth's history, humanity came to bring about a profound test of energy—one that might make the Universe change energy once more. This is why we love you so much.

The Big Asteroid Hit

Yes, indeed, there was an astronomical event 60 million years ago. This was discovered and is now accepted. It was designed to move around the crust of the earth, and it did. In the process, it took some life away, appropriately. In the process, even much of the polar ice melted and shifted the weight of the planet, allowing the crust of the planet to rearrange itself—and even to cause a slight wobble to begin.

The Arrival of Humans

And now we're getting closer to what we call the present. One hundred thousand years ago, we had Adam and Eve. *"Kryon, you're going to talk about Adam and Eve?"* Yes, I am. There is an argument between the evolutionists and the creationists. The argument goes like this: Evolutionists say that Human Beings evolved over a very long period of time in the life cycle, which was normal and natural on the planet. It brought about the modern Human, and it also evolved consciousness. It was called evolution. The creationists say that the word of Spirit proclaims that the breath of life and consciousness was given to Human Beings all at once. Who is right? The answer: Both of them!

The biology of humanity was developed over the same duration as all of the other life on Earth. However, something unusual happened. Take a look at something odd: We have told you this before. Counterintuitive to the evolutionary process,100,000 years ago, Humans changed. Within the normal evolutionary process, there had been more than 17 kinds of Human Beings, all going their own separate ways. In the evolution scheme, all the primates under you have many kinds of categories and types. Whether they're gorillas or monkeys or apes, there are many, many kinds and variations of these primates. One hundred thousand years ago, there were also branches of the way Human Beings would develop, much like all the other primates had. Instead of Humans developing the way all the others did, all the variations were stopped but one

. . . and you're looking at it in the chair next to you! [for those in the audience] How is that for a counterintuitive evolution? It does not make sense to the scientific biological process on Earth. Only one type of Human was allowed to develop.

The Arrival of Divine Consciousness

After this occurred, and when the one kind of biological Human evolved to a place that some call Adam and Eve, there was a specific kind of DNA alteration that took place—a consciousness was delivered to the planet. In this, the creationists were right! There was something that happened all at once. Yet, the evolutionists were right, also, for the biology was prepared over a very long period of time. So, you did indeed have an almost instantaneous delivery of consciousness, a beginning DNA posturing, and it came to you from the stars. This flies in the face, does it not, of natural selection? There is evolution, and yet there's also appropriate spiritual cosmic delivery. It even continues to this day, although you do not see it in the same light as you saw original creation.

Another Asteroid Hit?

Ten thousand years ago, an event took place that scientists do not agree with yet. There was another asteroid hit. It is not nearly as large as the one 60 million years ago, but indeed, it still made a big difference in the planet. One of the things that it did was to partially melt the ice caps again. It also moved portions and pieces of the land around, and it flooded most of Earth for a little while. Some of the Human Beings survived, but they had societies and civilizations that were completely terminated. Most of them had to begin again, and this new beginning, dear ones, is where your modern history starts. Your anthropologists haven't yet discovered the great civilization that existed more than 10,000 years ago. They don't believe it—yet.

Many of you who sit in the chair listening and reading were here on Earth as Humans at that time. Sometimes you equate your spirituality with pain and death, since you felt that God had destroyed the planet just at a time when you were finding so much science! You were here! I'm going to give you some information that you may find laughable until it is proven. There were civilizations that were grand more than 10,000 years ago. These were civilizations that most of those on Earth are completely unaware of, and are not part of your history. Some do search for this, but the evidence is buried so deep that you will never find the main artifacts. But there *are* some artifacts to find, and we're going to tell you where they are closest to the top of the earth, where you can find them. It's in your own country, too [speaking of the U.S.].

The artifacts to find that will give hints to the science of the civilizations more than 10,000 years ago will be found in Arkansas. And when this takes place, remember where you heard it! [Laughter] And when it takes place, perhaps you will think of these other things we just told you—unbelievable things—and perhaps you will realize that they are true, too.

The Grid

Now here you are. The meal of Earth had been cooked for ages, ready to eat. The earth was prepared. The angels that would inhabit it stood by and watched, and prepared to become Human. When the earth was cooling, we laid the grid lines. The magnetic grid was begun. The core of the earth was involved—the sun was involved, and all the pieces and the parts that went into it, I oversaw. That is why they call me "The Magnetic Master." I want to tell you who helped me. They're sitting here in this room, listening and reading! It is why some of you awaken—some of you experience synchronicity. It's why there is so much remembrance. There will come a day on the other side of the veil when you remember all of it fully. Together we will commiserate about what it looked like, and remember the grandness of it all. I promise.

The Evolution of Human Consciousness

Now it gets good! We would like to tell you about the evolvement of Human consciousness, the overview. Perhaps we have not discussed it in this fashion before. For some of you it's a review, but not for all. For a hundred thousand years, humanity evolved and developed. You know much of the history, and if you look at it, you'll see that the consciousness of humanity remained pretty much the same. Prophets for thousands of years were able to "look out" and predict what might happen due to the static nature of the energy that was carrying humanity down a reality track that had predictable consequences. Like a Tarot reading for an individual, the energy-stamp of the planet was tied to the reality track that humanity was on, and it was unchanging. That made it easy to read.

Right up until certain ones of you arrived here in your own lifetimes, the consciousness of humanity remained on the same track. This planet has only come off this track of consciousness recently—very recently. Almost all of you were here as the Humans you are now. How does it make you feel to know that the biggest shift on the planet—the one no one could have foretold of—took place while you were here?

The Harmonic Convergence

There was a measurement of this planet in 1987, which you have called the Harmonic Convergence. It was a regular scheduled measurement, taken every 25 years, the last of which will be 2012. We've told you this. This convergence, however, showed that the earth had changed its vibration, and not marginally.

Like the Universe itself, created by moving from one dimension to another, your Earth was about ready to shift in an interdimensional fashion—a reality paradigm of life itself was about to change. That's what was revealed in 1987.

Now you're starting to understand the grand plan of why the grid entourage took its place when it did. *The Kryon* has always been here, and always will be! The grid *entourage* that arrived in 1989 to work with the grid will leave at the end of 2002. It is this entourage that took its place in 1989. Within our messages, we told you who they were, where they were, and what they were doing. In all of this, we spoke metaphorically. For those of you who have not heard this, we say that all of the metaphors should now make total sense.

First of all, why the grid? What does it have to do with reality shifting? Because in this new reality, this interdimensional communication device called the magnetic grid of Earth needed to be shifted and changed. The grid postures the veil! As goes the magnetic grid, so goes that thing you have called duality— the veil that separates *you* from *you*—the higher *you* from the lower *you*—the Human from the angel.

The grid had to be adjusted in order to create the potential reality of what you had given permission for, which we called "The New Jerusalem." All things would change, and we began to tell you that all was different. We began to tell you that the prophecies of old would not take place . . . and they didn't. We told you 12 years ago that the earth itself—the geology—would shift in reality, and that the weather patterns would be different . . . and they are. All of these things started to manifest themselves in 1989.

Where would you go? What would you do? How long will it take? What's the grid all about, anyway? I'll tell you that in the metaphors we gave you, we said that there was an entourage contained in a ship called *Excalibur,* and we told you that it was in the orbit of Jupiter. These were metaphors, of course. It is not in the orbit of Jupiter at all. We referred to the orbit that Jupiter takes around the sun, and that's a metaphor, too. What is the energy of that? Go to the astrologers and ask them about the role of Jupiter in the new millennium. When you know that, you know the purpose of the entourage of Kryon! That is what the entourage's energy is about, and why the ship is called Excalibur. It's because this is the sword in the myth called Camelot. It is the sword of love. It is the sword of alchemy. It is the sword that was pulled out of the rock by the boy who would be king. Do you remember? Excalibur.

It is what happened to the Human Beings these last few years when they reached out and did the impossible—when alchemy took place. Each one of you is the boy who would be king. He did the impossible; he reached down and pulled the sword of truth from the stone. That is why we named it Excalibur. The sword became wisdom, and a kingdom was developed that created unity, tolerance, and peace for its inhabitants. Remember?

The 11:11

Then came the 11:11. This very day it has been explained [in the seminar before the channelling]. But how many of you really understand the 11:11? Even before the 11:11, I explained the meaning of the "9." It means completion. We told you that the "11" was a master number. I told you that it was the number of the grid entourage. And now it plays a bigger part in your lives, does it not? How many of you find it synchronistic that 12 years ago, Kryon would speak to you of only two numbers, the 9 and 11? What does that tell you about your current events? The 11:11 was the permission window of interdimensional change . . . a new Universe of potential was born, and humanity gave permission to walk through it.

The 12:12

The grid was in progress, and then came the expected 12:12. On the 11:11, humanity gave permission to move forward into a new reality—a new plan—that would awaken all to the point where everyone had to pay attention. We told you of this potential in 1999 and 2000. More Human Beings live on your planet than ever before. They have a potential of more peace than ever before—is that counterintuitive? Yes, for the old paradigm. The 12:12 was when the torch was passed to the mass of humanity on the planet, allowing you to actually steward the earth. This is difficult to explain. The grid began to move in 1989, and the 12:12 was the opportunity for humanity to take the full essence of Gaia. Some of the guardians of the canyons left, even some of the devas of the gardens. Some of the most sacred places on the planet, which had always held certain kinds of energies, became different as the placeholders—those who always held the sacred energy—departed. In their departure, they handed the torch of their energy to the Human Being who was starting to feel the shift of the grid and take the full mantle of the earth's life force.

The energy was passed one to another—the Human Being was taking a part of the divinity of their own angels, and that was what was going on. In this consciousness process of the last decade, tens of thousands began to question: *"Is there more? Is there more? Tell me more about God,"* they said. *"I feel things stirring inside I've never felt before. What is happening?"* There's been tremendous acknowledgment of remembrance, and for those of you who have been around for a while, you know what I'm talking about. For today is not anything like ten years ago.

The Time Line—a Review

Let me review something with you that I have given one other time—a time line that is the "energy reading" of what is happening at the moment. This can change tomorrow, but at this moment, the energy of what you have planned goes like this: The year 2000 was a year of celebration and rest. In general, 2000 was not truly "the marker." The year 2001 was the marker. Indeed, there was no year-zero, so 2001 became that place where the millennium began.

In an energetic way, you sit in 2001 right now. It is the year of the three, and those of you who know about numbers know what *three* is. It's creativity. Time to create. *"Oh, Kryon,"* some may say, *"it doesn't look like we've created much here. It looks like we've created death and destruction and sorrow."* Lift yourselves above this! See the bigger picture of what is being created in the release energy of the events in this, your new millennium. The learning starts now.

Lightworkers everywhere are going to be the frosting on this cake of creativity. They know where the light is; they know how to direct it. They know how to visualize; they know how to go to dark places and know how to go to work in places they would not necessarily want to go to—perhaps creating the only light there. They know how to heal their bodies—and know how to rise from the chairs of a place like this and feel joyful even when others are feeling sorrow. They have an overview of wisdom. They have a head start, because they were there when the earth was created.

When you were on the other side, did you know about this— the potential to change reality? Yes, you did. You lined up waiting to come in to this lifetime, and you didn't line up to die in Armageddon! Think about it. You lined up so that you could help with this process, the promise of peace on the planet. That's why you're here.

At the end of 2002, the grid is completed. Much will be pasted into place. The grid "talks" to your DNA. It enables things that were not enabled before. The grid allows for knowledge; it allows for healing; it allows for life extension. The grid allows for Human Beings to cut through the veil in a way that they never have before. When it is set and is in place, there will be a celebration. The grid actually allows for another dimension to be actively pursued by regular 4D Humans!

Most of the earth will have no idea what is taking place; like so many other things, we say, "God is slow." But in retrospect (after the fact), you will see it. Lightworkers will know it. Many of the things that you have seen for yourself (visualized as your potential) may be manifest in the year 2003. The year 2002 is about grounding. The grid has moved, so it would be a good time to connect with the planet. Some of you know what I mean. It would be a good time for you to discover the energy of Gaia. It would be a good time for you to reconnect with a living partner. You don't think about it much, but your indigenous ones did. They never lost this connection, and they still know about how it works. Seek out their advice. Understand what the energy of the land is. Understand how it wants to contact you in certain ways. Feel it! Some of you already know what I mean, for you're in love with the earth.

The year 2003 is a five [in numerology]. Changes begin. More changes. Doesn't it make sense that there would be changes after the grid had arrived at its final completion of energy? The year 2003 is one of change. Don't read anything negative into this change. It can be manifestation! Change can be co-creation; change can be healing. Change can be facilitating the love of your life.

Some have asked, *"Kryon, when are we going to have a solution in the Middle East?"* Your leaders are right. It will take a long time. You cannot undo history overnight. Attitudes change slowly. Sometimes proof is necessary, and long durations are needed to allow a generation to trust another one. Just ask the Asians. The year of the potential of solution in the Middle East remains 2008.

The year 2012 is the final measurement of the planet. Your indigenous ones told you that time would cease to exist in that year. Depending upon what you do, I'll tell you what that means. It is not going to be the end of Earth. What if, instead, it was the end of the *old* time? It's another marker, one that historians might go back to and report about, saying: *"By the time 2012 hit, civilization had determined what they wanted . . . how to define themselves. They moved forward as a group of very diverse people with different cultures and different beliefs, but ones that had solved the unsolvable—ones that had thrown history's puzzles away. It became a new kind of planet, with new adventures."* Wouldn't that be something? Well, that's what the energy spread of Earth says right now. That's what the potentials are.

Lightworker, what are you going to do with it? In all of these years and all of this creation, you've done the unexpected. The culmination of everything Kryon has ever talked about through all of these years sits in front of you right now. Some of you have clarity now. Kryon does not leave in the end of 2002—only the grid-change Kryon entourage. My real work begins at the beginning of 2003! All of this has simply been a warm-up. Hand in hand, partnering with God, you have been taught how to claim the divinity inside and move forward—to shine your light. Now the work begins.

Visualize this planet as being free from hunger. See those in Africa having conquered disease, smiling at one another—at their families. See them in the country that you call Afghanistan with solutions, with smiles. See the children playing; see them all together in joy, with food. It is not a fantasy that is unattainable. Do not pay any attention to what they tell you about what the past gave them or what the past must dictate is their plight. Pay no attention to someone's ideas of what *should* be. Go beyond it. But in your visualizations, do not tell Spirit how it's to be done—just see it as finished. That is the visualization.

Take yourself into the Middle East and see thousands of years of misunderstanding, hatred, and mistrust start to evaporate. It will be because solution has been reached.

Regarding the planet's tribal wars: Instead of teaching hate, see generations beginning to have understanding and tolerance until there comes a time when enemies are no longer enemies. It has happened before on the planet. You've seen it even in your own past wars. Former enemies don't have to stay enemies. It may take a generation—it make take a lot of children to change the planet, and that's the truth.

That's the message today, all encapsulated into a short amount of time—the evolvement of the planet and its consciousness. Now, here we are at the end.

Thousands of people have passed in these last months. They're being greeted in the Hall of Honor. I want you to see them right now, and for one moment, they're all going to stop. They're going to stop their process and turn around and look at you in this room, all in real time. Reader, are you with us? They're looking at you as well, as your eyes are on this page.

All of those who have participated in this gift to Earth— they're looking into your eyes at the moment, just for a moment, all of them. Collectively, here's their message to you. They say: "Make our gift worth it!"

As you rise from this place, take the energy of their gift and go to the next level. Don't miss a day without the visualizations for planetary healing, unity, and tolerance. Your energy field is awesome, and your power is absolute. You can change reality and physics. You can heal yourself, and you can heal the planet. That's the legacy of the evolved Human Being.

And so it is,

Kryon

Live Channelling

"Explaining the Unexplainable"

Channelled in
Newport Beach, California
December 2001

Chapter Ten

"Explaining the Unexplainable"
Live Channelling
Newport Beach, California

This live channelling has been edited with additional words and thoughts to allow clarification and better understanding of the written word.

Greetings, dear ones. I am Kryon of Magnetic Service. Some of you are aware of the flutter of energy here. We say this metaphorically, because many of you are very aware of the angels in the room. There will be those of you whose energy will be shifted and changed in a peaceful way this day, since you gave permission for it. Let the peace of Spirit and the love of God enter you in a way that is pristine and pure. May it bring you to a point of understanding in this message. All is well.

(Pause)

Dear ones, right now this room is being prepared for a sweet message—one that has not been given before—one whose subject has not even been broached before. It is a message in its sweetness and also in its profundity, and one that may be very difficult to understand. The message of today is difficult to give you because it is out of your dimensional understanding.

Before we teach, we ask that the room be prepared—that the angels who are here take their places next to you and give you peace. We ask that what you feel here be that of a family reunion, nothing odd or unusual—and that you will understand that those who are standing next to you are family. That's where we begin this teaching. Oh, perhaps you were not aware that we knew who would come to this place? Even before we start this teaching, we say that perhaps some of you are not aware of how personal this is.

We speak to two ears in the "now" of this room. We speak to two eyes on the page. It has always been this way. Although you assemble in a group and you feel the energy as a group, instead this is a one-with-one-consciousness communication that we offer. This energy comes to you because you've asked it to be this way. It always takes a little bit of time to "press upon" a group such as this—the two ears such as this—the two eyes such as this. It's needed for you to feel the energy and to understand that you're in a safe spot. Nevertheless, all of this does not help explain interdimensionality to a four-dimensional Human Being—our task today, and also one in future communications.

From the moment the first word from Kryon [as channelled by Lee] was put on a page almost 12 years ago, we knew of the energy that was potentially going to be here at this moment—in this country—on this planet—in this city and in this room. The *now* is not explainable to you. We were here, potentially, even back then. We "saw" you here. You might say, *"Well, how could that be, Kryon? I did not understand any of this back then. I was a different person back then. I've only just discovered this spiritual energy recently and have come to this meeting."* We will tell you that the potentials of the path of every single Human Being is understood and known. You can also change it tomorrow, you know. Without predestination, we will tell you that there are predispositions in the room—that is, potentials that you are likely to fulfill due to your current intent. We knew of your awakening—what would drive you to be here. We knew what some of you would go through in order to come to the place where you sit or read . . . and you wonder why we love you? Where do we begin?

Review

We've spoken of The Third Language for more than a year. Almost every time we've come before you recently, we've spoken of the "language of the three." We've told you that this language is like a walking channel—a continuous connection to the other side of the veil. It's something you participate with in an interdimensional way, a way we cannot explain to you but one we can invite you to feel. But you really don't understand.

So we call upon the veil to be lifted to some degree for your divine understanding on this day, during this time. The Third Language features a four-dimensional Human Being with one foot in another dimension. You can call it the fifth dimension if you wish, but that's not accurate. We told you long ago that when you get past the four dimensions you're in, you cannot number them beyond that. They're a different "flavor." You don't number flavors or smells. You experience them. Indeed!

The metaphor of having one foot on the other side of the veil is not only a potential, but also a reality. There are those in this room and who are reading this page who have this! They've learned what this is like, and it has taken them some time. Some of them have learned by experience, some of them by teaching, and some by intuition.

Here is what they may tell you: They've moved from the "two to the three." We're going to give you an example in a moment of what that means, but their experience is this: To become what you've called a fifth-dimensional Human Being (which we will call a multidimensional Human Being), is to become one who exists in both places, not just a new place. Also, interdimensionality doesn't mean that you throw away what you have in order to gain what you choose. In other words, you can have added dimensions given to you while you remain in the four.

How many of you are aware of those who have crossed that interdimensional barrier, only to also throw away the four they were in? They felt that they were so spiritual that they must be finished with the old Human 4D. In the process, they threw away the core of their reality and became no Earthly good at all. Did you notice? They can no longer think or operate well within your culture. They can't go to work, can't take care of their children. Many of them actually have to be looked after. Yet when you look at them, they're blissful and happy. They've entered into another dimensionality and left the one they came from behind.

This isn't what we're discussing. We're talking about The Third Language. We're discussing an ability that is profound at this moment, more than any moment in the history of humanity. It's a potential of walking a path that's dimensionally different from anything previously—keeping what you have and creating another reality from the one you're most familiar with.

Some of you have taken a look at the *veil*—that odd separator that keeps humanity at an arm's length from core spiritual truth. It's interdimensional, you know, since it's a piece of the fabric of God. Yet some of you have decided that the veil is either black or white. You're either on my side or your side. That's not the way it is at all. The veil is miles thick [metaphor]. Part of what the grid system is doing as it moves is to recalibrate the veil—to lift it—to make it thinner. This is so humanity in general may awaken to new prospects, especially the one that we're trying to give you this very day—an interdimensional message that says you can claim a reality that you don't have now—one that's divine—one that will give you an overview that's far different in energy from what you've ever experienced before.

The veil is thick and without an actual barrier. It's not a wall. It's a cocoon—a surrounding of every molecule in 4D. It isn't a place, either. There are some of you who swim in it during your meditations. You often come back to your four-dimensional ways not remembering anything. There are pieces and parts of entities in this very thick veil that you completely and totally misunderstand. There are those who are interdimensional who visit—who come and go—just part of this *magic* veil that you cannot understand.

There are those who anchor the earth, whom you've called "the entities in the earth," who are part of this veil. The fabric of time is part of the veil. It stretches as you enter, and structures as you return. As you broach this interdimensional energy you've discussed between spirit and humanity, you move aside the reality that you're used to, adding a brand-new flavor to it, changing it to something else.

What Is "Normal"?

All this is difficult to explain, and one of the things we have to discuss before we even get into the start of this message is the following: Dear Human Being, I want you to think right now to yourself as we sit in front of you, and answer the question, *"What is normal?"* What is *normal* for you? When you think of your life and you think of what you've given yourself as the master of yourselves, what have you told your cellular structure, as you walk around this planet, is normal?

How many of you have actually spoken out loud that your normalcy is to be depressed? *"I don't feel good today,"* you might say, and *"That's typical."* Well, that's your *normal*, and you just defined it. How many of you have told your countenance that it's less than joyful, and that being less then joyful is the Human condition? I'd like to tell you about *normal*. There is a life force that the cells in your body *listen* to. You're the master of each one of them—the "boss upstairs," the one that is the controlling force in the head of the Human Being—the one that informs the body of what *normal* is. The cellular force within your body will do its best to comply with "the boss." Therefore, what you've decided to tell your structure is *normal* will become the goal of your cells, and your reality. Count on it!

Calibrating

I've just given you a shade of reality. This is difficult, very difficult to explain, for the *normal* that you give your body is a *reality set* that it will then strive for. It's so difficult to tell you what is afoot! It's more than The Third Language. This interdimensional potential that visits you in this moment, as the grid is being finished, as the world reacts to a release, is new. In order to go to where it is and add to the existing dimensionality that you're in, you're going to have to *tune in* to that new invisible broadcasting station, and that station is not the one you're listening to now.

We use the metaphor of tuning to a broadcast because that's exactly what we're asking you to do. You're moving from the two to the three. It is the Human Being who recognizes the reality therein and is wishing to find it, who represents a Human that did not exist 12 years ago. We're telling you that you're broaching the same abilities and asking the same questions of the past avatars!

The last time we were together, we gave you a review of the consciousness evolution of the planet. We spoke about 1987, and we talked about the window of opportunity called 11:11. This was the description of permission you gave to move to another reality—to another level—and you said yes to that permission question. The ball started rolling, as you say metaphorically, and the grid started moving. Almost in its final year of adjustment, the grid represents magnetics of the planet that are posturing this interdimensional veil, allowing you to have answers to more profound questions. Things are beginning to move on Earth that may seem similar to much of the information we gave you over two years ago. We told you that this battle between the old and the new would affect everyone—that no one would escape having to make choices. We told you that men would use God as a shield for their spiritual rage. Now here you are with exactly that situation.

With all of the items on Earth that seem negative right now, we're giving you the most powerful, inspirational, hopeful news that has even been given—that the veil is being postured to be slightly lifted—reduced to a place where you can move into another dimension, keeping the one you're in. In the process, wisdom will replace chaos, and answers to eons of strife may be revealed.

But in order to move forward with this, you're going to have to tune to that new station—the one that you can't see or hear— the one that's beyond your senses. Let's call it what it is: You're going to have to *calibrate* to the new Universal energy. This is not a new attribute of Earth. This dimensionality has always existed on the planet, but it has been out of reach to everyone but the avatar or shaman. Until now.

This is the message of Kryon in 1989, and it still is. Except now, you sit on the edge of the ability to fulfill much of what seemed odd and strange when we began to speak of it back then. There are now those who have been given the methods, the phases of understanding—those who have stewarded this information well, and we celebrate them. There are also those who sit here and read this who, even without the teaching, will be able to feel it and intuitively perform the correct steps to find and calibrate to the new energy. This is the way Spirit has always worked. There's an entire spectrum of different kinds of teachings, some intuitive, some not, to match the various paths of those who seek the truth of spiritual enlightenment. There are many ways to achieve the same goal, and yet so many of you wish to say there is only one. Celebrate the differences, and celebrate the Human who seeks through his intellect, as well as the one who seeks through his heart. Both may find the same exact solution, and it will be the love of God.

An Example

We'll give you another example of moving from the two to the three. If we continue to put this explanation in your dimensional experience, you won't understand it. Therefore, let's go down a dimension or two. Pretend you're a cartoon on a piece of paper. You're now in two dimensions. You can move left and right and forward and back, and that's it—two dimensions. You cannot move up or down, and you exist on paper, outside of time. Pretend you're on a piece of paper that extends thousands of miles in all directions and you *walk* anywhere you wish.

One day you hear a voice from above you that says, "There's more! There's more than your reality of two dimensions—there's more." The two-dimensional being on the piece of paper doesn't know where to look. Where is that voice coming from? It's not coming from the left, and it's not coming from the right. You see, the two-dimensional creature on the piece of paper can't look up! There is no "up"! Three-dimensional action is seemingly beyond the two-dimensional cartoon on the paper, so it sits there listening to the voice in total confusion. It travels to the edge of the paper. It goes through procedures; it goes through lessons. Finally, it cries out to God, "I know there's more, but I can't do anything with what I have. I've looked everywhere. I've done everything. God, tell me what it is I should do!" And the voice from God says, "Look up!" And then the question from the cartoon is, *"What's up?"*

Slowly, however, that two-dimensional creature figures out how to look up. Intuition, training, and gut feelings all come into play. The cartoon creature scans the unknown and the realm of the unexplainable, and finally calibrates himself to "up." When that two-dimensional being on the paper finally is able to grasp what *up* is, he becomes three-dimensional. He looks up and he sees that the voice was coming from another dimensional energy in "the three." Due to the cartoon character's investigation and wisdom, he's no longer a cartoon. He has instead entered an entirely new dimensional reality, and he can fly! Indeed, there's more. Now there's a voice talking to you, but it doesn't say, "Look up." Instead it says, "Look within. There's *magic* inside!" It's an interdimensional voice, or whatever you wish to call it. It's divine.

Return of the Masters—Revisited

Now let me explain a little more about what we've told you in the past that may interface with this in a way you didn't expect. Over a year ago, we sat in front of those in Tel Aviv. At that time, we told them that every master, every avatar, every prophet or shaman that had ever lived and was expected to return, had indeed returned. We told you at that time, dear Human Being, that the avatars were encircling the globe and that they were within an energy that we called "the grid." We told you that you could pull upon that energy anytime you wanted to. We told you that their arrival was part of the final completing energy grid adjustment [due to be finished 12/02].

I will tell you this, and it may seem like a dichotomous statement—one that's filled with opposites: The event on September 11 could never have happened without the masters of love and unity being on the grid! You may say to yourself, "How can this be?" What you asked for within the past 15 years—a change of reality—an awakening to the love of Spirit—could never have taken place without *all* of you being involved. Do you understand now that everyone on the planet had a place in this event?

Let me talk about energy. Do you understand why the masters are here? Do you understand why the grid has the masters within it? We've talked about new information pouring into your cellular structure. We've talked about your "looking within" for interdimensionality. Do you want to know what you're calibrating to? It should be obvious! You're calibrating your own reality to the masters who have walked on this earth— that have your energy and theirs ready to be intermingled. This is so you can look within and find the divinity to do things you had no idea you could do regarding energy within this lifetime.

We could write books on energy, but let me tell you about just a few of them in your life. Perhaps these are energies you may have never thought of within your day-to-day existence.

Energy of Conversation

What about your conversations? Are you aware that one person with another is sharing energy when they speak? There is all manner of conversation possibilities. There's idle conversation, polite conversation, and there's also confrontational and abusive conversation. What is the energy that you feel when somebody says something to you that you don't like, or who doesn't agree with you? What is the energy of those who are put above you in a place of importance as they *talk down* to you? What is that energy to you? What do you do with it?

In four dimensions, I'll tell you what often happens—it often goes right into your heart. Then that's where you have to deal with it. In your four dimensions, when someone asks you a question, there's a strange thing that takes place. There's an energy that says you have to answer it! Did you ever think about that? Almost like a tennis ball coming across the net, it carries an energy of demand. Have any of you ever realized that you didn't have to answer? You don't have to return the tennis ball or even play the game, so we have to ask you this: What is your *normal* when it comes to conversation?

"When that person says something, it always wounds me," you might say, or *"It makes me feel bad to hear this or hear that."* Oh, how can I tell you this, dear one? As "chief of your cells," you've just informed your body of what your normal is! If your *normal* was calibrated to what you're calling the fifth dimension—the next phase—no matter what is said to you would go into a place where it would not hurt—where it would register only the things that make sense to you, where you will rise seemingly above all conversation. You will be in charge of it, for it is your truth to answer, or not to answer—to be affected or not be affected. I bring this up because some of you in four dimensions are a slave to conversation! You've never known that you could rise to a place that is within—to claim the power to control that tennis ball. Instead, you often use the energy you have to tell your whole structure that you're always wounded! When you move past this, it feels so comfortable no matter what you say and no matter what is said to you. That's energy!

Energy of Choice

You know what another energy is within your life? It's choice. *I choose to do this; I choose to do that.* How many of you have decided that your *normal* is, *"I always choose the wrong thing"?* What did I tell you about your cells? They will listen to the "boss," and every cell of your body will strive to give you what you've stated is your *normal.* Think about it. Your body has heard you tell it that you expect to choose incorrectly! Therefore, any intuition regarding selecting and discerning the energy of choice has an anchor around it! The ability to tune in to that new station is what we were discussing. Another dimensionality is available that creates a Human Being that can begin to relax about discernment opportunities. When the Human Being begins to relax, something else starts to take place—a dimensional shift, a *normalcy* of joy. Fear of making the wrong decision will be a thing of the past. You won't even remember it, since you're tuned in to a new station that features answers and stability.

Energy of Creation

What about creation? Not co-creation, but creation? This very day, the presentation that you heard was not accidental [the scientific validations of the power of Human consciousness, given in the seminar]. This information was provided so that you would fully understand what is now being said. What did you learn about water? Perhaps, just perhaps, water is reactive to a force field of an individual Human Being? Perhaps it's even sensitive to more than that? Now I want to ask you this: What are you made of? Your cells bathe themselves in water. The essence of your biology is water. You are a water being. Within the water in your body there's an interdimensional life force—one that you will never see, but one that will react to the Human who *creates*.

When that Human creates out of the restrictions of four dimensions, and calibrates what they consider to be *normal*, the cells listen to the "boss." Years ago we gave you something that sounded unusual. To this day, perhaps some of you haven't fully understood what we presented back then. Now, with your new wisdom, you may begin to understand when we say that all things ingested into your body may be changed molecularly before they get into your system! If you can change the essence of water with a word [information shown in the seminar], think of what you can do with intent! Almost all of the food ingested in your body has interdimensional life essence within it. It's your medicine of growth and your sustenance. It's also responsive to Human life force! So again we're telling you, Human

Being, that you have the ability to create a molecular change in everything you ingest—making it safe [not necessarily nutritious, but safe].

For your sustenance, we're saying this: It's time to understand The Third Language—moving from the *two* to the *three*. You worry where food was prepared, about the preservatives or about what scientist are doing to it genetically? Let me tell you, that's a political subject, not a personal one. It won't matter for you, since you can calibrate it to your body. All you have to do is send your interdimensional divine energy into that food or drink matter before it's ingested. Speak to the life force within the matter, and greet it. Bring it to your vibration.

We must speak more about your cells. The cells of Humans are beginning to recognize the new energy. Some of the cellular structures of your own bodies are yelling at the boss! They're saying, *"There's something more here! You should look at it!"* How many of you sit there in pain? How many of you have unsolvable things going on in your cellular structure? I wish to tell you something: What you're experiencing is only within 4D. It's just like the speed of light. You think that's absolute? No. That's only the speed limit in 4D! Once you step out of the 4D reality that you've lived with all your lives—the one you were born into, things that you felt could never happen, can happen! Your cellular structure is almost all water. By the way, so is the potential disease in there! Did you think of that? Did you know it's listening, too? We would not give you this information if it were not so.

However, these actions we suggest aren't like turning a switch. It's not going to be all that easy to grasp the unexplainable. You're going to have to strive for new methods to implement this new paradigm, but it's there waiting. Calibrating to a new energy for the planet—one that is before you in a profound way, is the goal.

Healers, listen. I'm certain you're aware that you heal nobody, aren't you? All you do is set a balance of energy. You balance, and the individuals before you then have the ability to take this balance and heal themselves. You've spent your lives facilitating this balance. It explains why you can go through the same process of energy work on many Humans, yet some are healed and some are not. Even among those who are healed, some are marginally helped and some profoundly. All you can do is lead them to the balancing table. Then it's up to the Human Being to heal or not. It will always be this way. It gives complete free choice to each Human. But I tell you this for a reason. It's the healer who knows how to move energy around profoundly. It's the healer who will show you how bodies can accept an interdimensional force field of balance.

Look at the history of the avatars—they changed matter! Some of the avatars even had situations where, after their deaths, their cellular structures didn't even know they were dead! The cells continued to live and rejuvenate for weeks after the "boss" left. What does that tell you about cellular structure? In the case of the avatars, the cells really "knew" what *normal* was, and they strived to keep it *normal* long after the body "died." What does that tell you about a potential Human consciousness field? What does it tell you about intent? Some of those avatars are the ones who are on the grid right now, wanting to take your hand, wanting to be the ones to show you where that new calibration is.

Money

So, healer, if you're used to moving energy, why can't you move money? What is normal to you? Where have you told your body is *normal* is, regarding money? Let me give you an example: You cannot pay the obligation that's coming up, and so what do you do with the energy of that? Do you prepare to be destitute?

Do you somehow posture your countenance *not* to have the money the next time either? Do you tell your cellular structure, *"This is the way it is"?* Or do you drop those vows of poverty you took in the past and try to grasp on to the new energy?

I'll tell you the dichotomy in the room: The ones most used to moving energy are the ones who don't understand the energy of money! Money energy is far more simple than balancing a Human Being! How many of you have the freedom, when you cannot pay an obligation, to celebrate the fact that you can't pay it? You say almost none of you would do such a silly thing? Well, perhaps it's going to take some silly things to make you understand where the new energy calibration is.

When you *tune* to that new station, your consciousness will understand that obligations and money are only energy—and like those who are healed and not healed, it will come in its appropriate form and in its appropriate way. When you no longer draw in drama around having it, it will be there! Now, isn't that a lot like the ones who don't get healed? Even with balance, many fear the healing, or wish to keep the drama of the discomfort.

It's the one who's understanding this new dimensionality—who's starting to be calibrated, who looks at conversation and choice and creation, who speaks to the cellular structure of his own body, who's the one totally in control of his reality. Not one who's just in control of reality, but one who's filled with joy. You can't have the love of God in your life—the love of Spirit in your life—without laughing out loud! Did you ever think of that? Doesn't this make sense?

Parable: Wo and The New City

We have a parable as we close. It's different from any parable we've ever given, and we've given many. Wo, our main character, is living a life in 4D. Now Wo is not a man or a woman. Wo is a *wo-man*, representing both genders. It's you! For the purpose of the parable, we will call Wo, *he*. As all our parables are, this one is also totally metaphoric.

Wo was living in the old energy and truly felt that there was something more to life. One night in a deep meditation, Wo was given some profound information. Whoever it was that he felt he was talking to, Wo didn't know. However, the truth was that Wo was talking to Wo! It was Wo's Higher-Self, the part of him that he longed to be married to, and the part that Wo missed the most.

Did you know, dear, lonely Human Being, that when you develop The Third Language, you're beginning a hand-hold— a marriage ceremony to the missing part of you? That's where the joy comes from!

Wo received information: *"Wo, it's time to board the train to the new city. The old city is gone, Wo. It no longer represents who you are. It's time for the new city. Get on the train called the "intent express." In the new city, you'll find golden streets paved with your intent. Miracles are possible there. Your life will be extended; you'll be filled with joy; you can help many people there. You'll find passion there. You'll do things that you never thought you could do. There are things waiting for you in the new city, Wo. It's time to get on the train."*

So Wo purchased a ticket and got on the train, and indeed the tracks of intent led him to the new city. It was a one-way ticket, and he knew he could never look back; he could never go back to the old. He knew that, and he thought about it very carefully before he ever made the decision to go.

Wo was on the train thinking about it all. He knew he would take his place in the new city exactly where he lived in the old, but that everything would be different. He could hardly wait to see it! Finally, Wo arrived in the new city. He got off the train and was astonished by what he saw. It was almost identical to the city he had just left. Wo began to look for the changes. He wished to see what differences there would be from the old to the new—and to find those streets of gold.

But everywhere Wo looked, he saw . . . old energy!

"What's going on?" Wo asked. "This city looks and feels just like the one I came from. Where is all the new stuff?"

There he stood, confused. And right there, dear ones, is where the parable suspends itself. This parable is different from all the others we've given. We're going to freeze Wo right there, and we're going to give you this information: *You are Wo!* The parable is in the *now*, and its ending is your ending. Or is it your beginning?

The *new city* is hiding in the old one! Many of you have purchased the ticket. You have taken the train, and for some, it's been a difficult journey. Now you're sitting in an energy, that's confusing. Part of you are saying, "It's the same as it always was!" Then along comes information from your Higher-Self, the other part of you that is divine, which says, *"The golden streets are paved with your intent. Your intent to calibrate is what will reveal the new."*

Wo is still here, so we will ask him this question: "Wo, what is your normal?" Wo thinks a moment. Here is his answer: *"My normal is in a dimensionality I have yet to discover. However, as I gradually calibrate to this new energy, I will see the golden streets; I will see peace on earth. I will see changes in those around me."*

Wo knows there's work to do, for it will not happen overnight. Wo knows that he's going to need *second sight*, that there's another kind of a feeling and energy that's afoot—one that humans want to call "number five," but it isn't. It's simply the next dimension, which also contains the ones you're in.

"Kryon," some are saying, *"you've told us a lot about this new dimensionality, but you're not giving us much information about how to access it."* This is so, and it's why I'm trying to place a higher

dimensional instruction set into the limitations of 4D. The metaphor remains: Can you see the broadcast you tune in to on your radio? No. Do you know the frequency? No. So what do you do? You begin to calibrate the receiver and look for it. You scan until you lock on to the signal. This is the way of it, that the new dimensionality we're trying to explain to you is one that you must search for and calibrate to. Also, like the broadcast, it is invisible, but all around you, filled with a new program—one that has your name on it.

As you sit in these chairs, dear Human Being [speaking specifically to those in attendance], you're closing the "year of the three." This is the year we told you would be so profound when we brought you the message back in your month of August, and it has been. We've given many statements over the years, but one that we will revisit right now is right in your face: "As go the Jews, so goes Earth." Perhaps some of you are beginning to realize what that meant. The entire earth will be involved in solving the unsolvable. The entire earth will be involved in straightening out the place where the old reality was going to create Armageddon. But today that place is different. Oh, it may look the same, and it may have sorrow and death and unspeakable hatred still hovering there, but there's something different now. There's a broadcast coming from the grid—from the masters. There's a "hidden city" with golden streets paved with intent. Underneath is "The New Jerusalem."

All that has happened to you in these last months has been in preparation for you to be involved in creating peace in the center of the Universe called the Middle East. And now you know that you're part of it [speaking specifically to those in America]. Watch for something profound in 2002 in that place. The leaders who are there cannot make peace, and those leaders won't be there for long. A new energy is afoot—one that so many of you are aware of and feel deeply.

And so it is, dear ones, that we pick up the bowls of our tears and we leave this place. The tears are our tears of joy that would allow such a thing to take place—washing the feet of a Human Being—a Human Being who exists in an energy that has never been on this planet before. The ones listening and reading are the ones who are ready to recalibrate to a new reality. How many of you wish to leave different from how you came in? How many wish to walk the old streets, but live in joy on the new ones? I think the answer is obvious.

And that is why we love you so.

And so it is!

Kryon

Live Channelling

"Time and Reality"
Part III

Channelled in
Orlando, Florida
January 2002

Chapter Eleven

"Time and Reality"
Part III
Live Channelling
Orlando, Florida

*This live channelling has been edited with additional
words and thoughts to allow clarification and better
understanding of the written word.*

From the writer . . .

Where are parts I and II? The live channelling of "Time
and Reality" Parts I and II are the first two channellings in
Kryon Book Eight, Passing the Marker.

Greetings, dear ones, I am Kryon of Magnetic Serßvice.
This is a special time for us. It is a sweet spot, we might
say, in this moment of your linear time. A *moment* to us
is *now* and always will be, and since the now is always there, this
moment can last forever! Since it is
forever, this *moment* also exists as a
storehouse so that you can call
upon its energy anytime you
wish. Perhaps this is difficult to
understand? Just wait until we
continue this explanation!

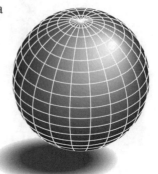

For these next moments, we
wish to pass the sweetness of
Spirit to this room, and to
the room of the many readers. Indeed, this is a sweet, sweet
place.

I am Kryon. I speak to the family member before me. I will call you "Two-ears." For those who are reading before me now, I will call you "Two-eyes." We do not speak to groups; this is family, and the communication is one-on-one. Although you pretend to meet as part of a group in the physical four dimensions, indeed there is one consciousness here—one pair of ears and one pair of eyes. And that is whom we wish to address... you!

We'll say something we have said many times before: You have no idea of the preparation of this room [this time speaking of the live seminar]! Long before you arrived, we were here, and although this appears to be in your linear time, we present it in this fashion so you will understand the importance and the profundity of it. You think you came to hear this? You think you came to feel this? I will tell you something: You are confused about who came to see whom! For there are far more of *us* than of you here.

This family that surrounds you is not a group to be frightened of. It's not anything too ethereal or beyond the grasp of your Human understanding. If fact, some of us are touching you even now. You might experience some of us at the heart level, and some of you will feel us at the intellectual level, for these are the places where we appeal to both, combined to create emotion within the Human Being, and to validate the presence of God through the compassion that follows the emotion.

We define God as "the angels in this room pretending to be Human Beings." And so in these opening moments, even before the teachings begin, we say to you again that there's more here than meets the eye or ear. This is a gathering that's a reunion, a unique group that will never be here again in this exact way. Like one of your snowflakes, it's unique in its design and spectacular in its beauty. Although the meetings are common, the energy is unique. It is for you to see this, or not, as is your power of discernment.

Join the family even within the messages and the teachings of this day, for the teachings are about a subject we have been speaking of for months! But now we open new vistas of understanding with the metaphors we bring.

About the Teachings in This Channelling

The teaching remains this: To try to broach to you, dear Human Being, what we need to tell you about interdimensional things. Again we say, how can we present the unpresentable? How can we teach the unteachable? How can we explain the unexplainable? The answer is that it must be absorbed using what we have called "The Third Language." Breathe! Ask for understanding at a level you do not possess in four dimensions. Then smile as you receive it! This message is about your actual reality.

Time—a Variable?

In this particular teaching, we're going to explain the best we can about *time and reality*—some of the most misunderstood concepts you have. To you, your time and reality are absolute. Everything seems to be time-stamped these days by your technology. You have photos in books to time-stamp your memories along a time line that you see as stretching from horizon to horizon—a straight, linear track that you're always on, always in motion. That's your *time*, and within it you live in a reality that seems unchanging.

We've told you that time is variable. Even your scientists have brought you this concept, yet to you, who must live within it, it doesn't appear that way, does it? Long before, we gave you the "relativity metaphor" where you're on a train holding a watch. Over time, the train speeds up and some of you begin feeling the rocking side-to-side movement of the train car you're in on this "time-track." The engine is pulling you faster, yet when you look at your watch, its motion remains constant. So the absoluteness of time seems to be relative to the car that you ride in, but outside of that car you're unaware of the things that have changed around you. You feel it, however, don't you? How many can say to themselves that their train of time has sped up in the last few years? The answer is that it has! Yet the clocks you carry in your train car remain the same.

Outside your train-car, things are going by faster than before. You can see it out the window. The earth is changing faster than ever, and the solar system is reacting, too. Your reality is changing, and you're beginning to have new awareness as well. Yet your clocks remain the same.

Even before we can begin to talk to you about time and reality, we must broach an issue never before mentioned. Perhaps you might look around. We've told you of the new energy of Earth. We've told you about an advancement—a speed-up of time within your solar system and in your part of the Universe. It was brought about by the consciousness of those who live on Planet Earth. We told you that you had elected to change reality, to change dimensionality. Now let me ask you for a moment: Do you think that when you gave permission to change the earth, it would be isolated and alone in a vacuum by itself? Did you think somehow that this reality and time would only change on Earth? The answer, of course, is no.

Now we invite you to see these things within your solar system as well. It has been reported that there's a change happening to the other planets within your system. All of them are reacting to what you've done here. There are magnetic shifts, thickening of atmospheres, and other clear signs that this solar system of yours is different than it was a decade ago. You now have the tools to look into this, to find it, and to expose it; and the astronomers will shake their heads and ask, "Why are these things happening now? Why not before?" Odd as it may seem, the answer has to do with your consciousness! You've never been closer to discovering the "big secret" than you are now . . . that Human consciousness can change reality, time, and yes . . . even the solar system around you. If this were not the case, we wouldn't have told you this more than 12 years ago. Now you may look around and see it manifested.

The Treadmill Metaphor

We're going to give you three separate kinds of metaphors to explain time and your reality. Each is very different from the one before, so you can't use one by itself. We give you this, however, as steps of understanding, so that you might put them together later for full disclosure of the concepts we're speaking about.

The first metaphor is going to be about the *now*. For this exercise, throw away the metaphor of the train . . . but keep it close, for we'll return to it. This new metaphor is different.

Pretend you're on a treadmill, similar to the automated exercise machines that some of you have but seldom use [laughter]. In this metaphor, you're walking and walking and walking. Now, in this visualization, you're staying in one spot, are you not? But you're walking and you're walking. If you had a device that measured your steps, it would tell you that you had perhaps walked a mile, maybe even more in the time of this message. But you're in one place, aren't you? Even perhaps in the same room?

This is a metaphor about the *now* portion of time. Let's extend this visualization for a moment, and instead of a moving belt beneath your feet, consider this—you have the entire earth beneath your feet as the exercise belt. As you take your steps, it's the terrain of the planet that moves under you in a continuous belt, and you're always in one place! No matter what the measurement of your clocks or what the instruments tell you about how far you've walked, you're still in one place . . . in one room. Not only that, now consider those exercise controls in front of you. You control the exercise plan, don't you? You can make the earth go beneath your feet as fast or as slow as you wish. You can even "dial up" the difficulty—elevating the track and creating challenge . . . all of this, staying in one place, and in one time.

Make this even more profound. This huge belt goes in any direction you face! Go left, and the belt moves to accommodate your direction. Go right, and it does the same thing. The only thing it *seems* you can't do is to stop the belt or make it move backwards. This, of course, is a false premise. But go with it for now, for it suits your 4D linear mind and is the way you see yourselves in life.

For the purpose of the lesson today, I want you to extend this metaphor into two complete and totally different frameworks of mind. One is you, walking the earth in your reality. The other is the Human race, walking in its reality. They're very different. Your reality is what you create day-by-day—how you feel about things—what things come to you on the treadmill depending on which direction you wish to walk—what things are conquered and what things you wish to keep as challenges. You dial these in very clearly in that place where you're seemingly alone, where you've chosen to walk the treadmill.

Here's the confusing part: The earth also has a treadmill of its own. It represents the consciousness of the entire planet—where it's headed within the fabric of time—what's going to happen from year-to-year based on the choices it makes, and the potentials for additional challenge or celebration. And when you put these two concepts together, there's magic! For the thing that the individual Human Being does with his or her life is a piece and a part of the entire consciousness of the whole. Therefore, what you choose to have pass under your feet as you walk in that one spot, in the *now*, has a profound influence on the whole earth's treadmill. Not only that, but your influence of the whole is not linear. That is to say that the ones who more fully understand the *now* have a grander influence on the whole of the *now*. Did I tell you this would be easy to understand? No.

What I'm telling you is that what you're hearing and reading from Kryon today is also what the physicists have said about your reality and your ability to change it [information given within Lee's AV presentation in the seminar regarding the "Global Consciousness Project" at Princeton University]. Your reality is a comfortable one if you choose it to be. The temperature in the room where you walk never changes if you choose it that way. You can be as joyful as you wish or as angry as you wish. You can also select to be bored, where nothing happens at all! You can *dial up* the hardest incline or not. You can go as fast or as slow as you wish. This is the metaphor of your ability to stay in one place, yet proceed in what appears to be a linear path of time.

One of the hardest things for any Human to understand is that no matter what the controls were set at when you arrived, you can find them and reset them! No entity, guide, helper, friend, healer, guru, or angel can reach out and dial in a better control setting. That's reserved for you . . . in the now . . . right where you sit. It's *Two-ears* and *Two-eyes* who do the work. It's the individual Human who makes the changes that then result in the way the entire world walks its own treadmill. Yet there are so many of you who simply accept the settings and continue to think that somehow God has placed a burden on you. Somehow you feel that God has asked you to *endure* it! Did you ever think that, instead, it was a test to find and *change* it?

Multiple Realities—Do They Exist?

Let's add to this puzzle. Now we are going to change that metaphor completely and take it back to your concept of linearity. You're on a train again. Ahh, isn't it nice to be back to linear time? [Kryon laughter] The train track goes forever and you're moving along at a nice clip. We're going to tell you about *multiple realities*, the way it works. We're going to tell you about reality potentials.

There is a train called humanity. In the late '60s in your linear time line, this train slowed down. For whatever reason, the Human consciousness that had been established and known, one that was predisposed to fulfill its own planned destiny—one you called Armageddon—started to slow itself down. And those on it looked around and did not like what they saw. Although this is a metaphor, I can tell you that this is the reality of your earth—that in the late 1960s, this train almost stopped! What happened is very much like the creation of the 4D Universe you see around you. It's that profound! Although it wasn't something that you were aware of, you changed tracks! When you did so, you changed to another reality level, and the reality that was the track you were on, lies there unfulfilled and unmanifested.

The track of Armageddon—the track of old prophecy—the track that you had been on for a very, very long time, was left behind, or perhaps continues beside you? When you changed tracks, you manifested an entire new plan for yourselves. You established a consciousness shift that was so profound that it wouldn't just affect humanity, but the weather, planetary alignments, magnetic grids, the solar system planets, and even the sun! The joke, of course, is that you look out into the cosmos and you believe it's controlling you. You have it backwards, you know. All of it is a reaction to the controls on the treadmill that you've chosen.

This train of humanity started to speed up again, and you're now on that track called "Reality number two." Now, I wish to explain something very clearly. There are those who would say, *"Well, that means that there are multiple realities—that somewhere in all this there is 'me' in another dimension fulfilling another reality.*

Therefore, there are many tracks and many of me." This is not so. Indeed, there are many tracks, but there's only one train. When you move off of one reality, all of the potentials that existed on that old track, stop. They lie on the ground, dead . . . never fulfilled. Think of it this way: You are the power for *all* reality. Without you on the track, there's nothing. You supply the power for the train, and also for the reality of the track you're on. Think of yourselves as "The Third Rail . . . the one that powers the train." Therefore, when you ask the questions, "What if this" or "What if that," there's no answer. It is unknown of God. There's only one reality, and that's the one that you choose *now*.

There are those who would say that "if only I had done this or that, things would have been different." Not so! I will tell you this: There is no manifested reality that sits next to you that's different because you missed an opportunity, or because you didn't do *this* or didn't do *that*. What you have *now* is the only reality in the Universe for your entity. It's the *one*, the track that you're on.

Bush and Gore—the Florida Legacy

There are many of you who have asked about synchronistic things—the "what-if" scenarios that have occurred recently. The most profound one is that which rests right here in this area [in Florida, where the seminar is being held]. It's an energy that's very strong here. Do you think that it's an accident that you have the leader that you now have? Look at what happened. Look at it carefully. You have brought to the helm of your country, seemingly almost by accident, one who may not have been elected by the popular vote! Do you really think that's an accident or a "near miss"? Do you think it's an accident that it was decided here? Let me give you some metaphysical truth. The whole potential of this election was manifested in the late '60s on the track that you chose as your new reality as the train started to speed up. Although metaphoric, listen: There will be much of this kind of thing where the normal becomes abnormal—where the things that have worked a certain way forever seem to jump away from you. Some will look at it and say it was a "close call." It's not a close call at all! Others will understand and see it for what it is . . . the manifestation of something new. In that uncomfortable process, sometimes your new reality will seem "forced."

I bring you this information for many reasons, for there are those who would say, *"What if the other candidate had won? Where would we be now? How would he have handled the situation in front of us now?"* The answer is this: It's not even known by God! For that reality never manifested itself, and therefore it's all conjecture. There's no parallel reality next to you that you can look at or tap into, interdimensionally. There's only one reality, and that's the track you chose to be on. So the leader that had the potential to lead you during your challenging times *is* indeed the one you have. All of you agreed, even though it might not seem like it.

There's no such thing as predestination. We will speak of this in a moment. You've set yourself a course that you're predisposed to follow as if you were in a comfortable groove, until you wish to change it again through active intent.

The Twisted Ribbon Metaphor

Now we're going to get complicated. A third metaphor is presented to you, one that's going to start explaining more and more about the true energy of the *now*. Return to the treadmill idea, but instead, think of it as ribbon—a wide ribbon in a loop—shaped much like that of the treadmill you were walking on. The ribbon is in a loop, a circle, and is seamless. We're going to combine the first two metaphors. You're not walking this ribbon, but instead, your linear train is on the outside of that ribbon, moving along on a track. The inside of the ribbon is bare.

Now in this visualization, I want you to take scissors and cut the ribbon. Put a one-half twist in the ribbon and put it back together so it's again seamless. Now I want you to try and visualize where the linear train and track will go with this new configuration. You may find it oddly amusing that although the train seems to remain on one side (the one you're on), its movement will eventually trace a path on both sides of the ribbon! This is complicated to visualize unless you've seen it. To add a further almost impossible visualization, the treadmill ribbon is still moving, and the linear train is now the thing that seems to stay in one place!

In mathematics, this particular ribbon model is a categorized shape. In your language [English], it is known as The Mobius Strip. This particular metaphoric model creates a situation where there's always one track, but the startling part of it is that beneath your track is another track on the other side of the ribbon! It's actually the same track you're on, but one that you've traveled recently. It also represents where you're going! So you have the odd circumstance of one track that goes in a pattern that isn't a circle, but is still closed on itself. A real circle will not have you always next to where you just were, or where you're going. But this Mobius ribbon let's you actually see or "feel" the existence of your singular reality in duplicate, since it's also on the other side of the ribbon. This odd circumstance lets you closely examine the energy of where you just were and where you're going. I told you that this might be difficult, but if you're able to grasp this, then you'll begin to see how the true *now* reality works.

Why do we bring this up? Some of you are aware of what "past and present" means to your life. You know that if there's only one track, then you keep running over the same energies. It becomes more complex if you think of the *one track* also on the other side of the ribbon very close to you. It represents the singularity of the *only* track. Not only do you keep running over the old energies that you manifested long ago, but that "other" track that's right below you adds another dimension to this experience. It's *you* with *you*. Now you're starting to be taught the concept of "layered time."

No Such Thing As a Past Life?

Now, go back to the treadmill where you're standing in one spot. The reason we bring this forward is this: There's no such thing as a *past* life! If you're always in the now, do you understand that everything you think of as "past" is actually *now?* And here's what it means to you. Every life you've ever lived on that track is being lived now! Next to you, on that treadmill, are all of the other "you's" that you've ever been! The only one you actually "see" is the current one, but they're all there. They have to be. Physics demands it. The treadmill just got wider! It has to now accommodate all of the "you's" that ever were (in your mind), and you're walking side-by-side with them, creating your own reality.

Now it gets complicated (as if it weren't already). How can all of these lives together, walking in synchronization on the treadmill, be right? Who's in charge? Who's going to set the treadmill speed or the difficulty level? The answer? All of you will, but the one in the singular reality will actually do the work. What that means, dear Human Being, is that surging through your DNA, through the 12 layers, are all of the other lives that you're currently living! They have permission to affect you—your decisions—and the remembrance of the vows you took. Each of these who walk the treadmill with you help to "dial up" the difficulty and the speed of your current treadmill.

Ghosts and Hauntings

Oh, it gets better: We'll explain now what you often call "weirdness." I'm going to talk to you about ghosts! There's a big difference between what I'm going to speak of, compared with what some of you see as "communications with the other side." We're not speaking of that. Instead, we're speaking of ghosts and hauntings—those places on the planet where scientists gather to measure the "weirdness."

There are places that are "haunted" where you seem to "see" the same apparition day after day, or year after year. Some are seen often, and some less. Sometimes they may be coming down the stairs, dressed the same way, going somewhere . . . over and over. Some just walk from here to there constantly. Some of these areas are so potent that energies are manifested that actually interact with your 4D world. Things move, temperatures change, and magnetics are atypical. These are the things that stir fear in the souls and the hearts of men and women.

What are they? I'm describing simple energetic soul passings that are happening all the time, because they're always in the *now*. They're on a treadmill, just like you! And when you intersect that *past* energy, you often see or feel it clearly! Here are some validations that this is true: First, notice that this particular repeating scenario plays the same way every time, just like a loop of tape or a film spliced to itself. Ghosts are not changing their clothes over time or having children [laughter]! In other words, you're seeing the same event every time. This ought to hint at what's really happening.

Instead of a ghost visiting you, you're visiting or intersecting an energy on the track where something happened. Perhaps it was so profound that it seems to be held there physically, or at least to a point where it somehow intersects your reality. Who are they? They are family who are in a 100 percent state of "always leaving," except that the actual entities that represented the energy have long gone. Only the imprint they made is still there. The reason we brought in the confusing Mobius strip is to tell you that it's the interaction of "layered" time that creates this interchange. More than just running over the same track again and again, it's complicated by the singular reality that is also on the "other side" of the one you're traveling.

You might say, *"Well, what are we supposed to do about that?"* The answer is: You don't have to do anything about it if you don't wish to. For they're gone . . . long gone. Yet you could say, *"Well, if everything is in the now, they never left, did they?"* This is what makes the intersection of linear and nonlinear time so difficult for a Human Being to comprehend. It features seeming dichotomies of logic where things may leave before they arrive, or exist and not exist in the same "space." It also raises the logic question of who came first. The answer is that existence is absolute and singular. You're simply seeing the edges of it at different "times."

For those of you who wish to know what you might do about this repeating energy, we say, "Clean the track." Then the Human asks, *"How?"* Claim the teaching that we've given you again and again: Human pure intent carries an awesome energy of action. It creates compassion, and compassion is the catalyst to almost every action item on your spiritual list! But you knew that, didn't you?

Affecting and Changing Your Reality Track

When you start cleaning your track, no matter what you think happened in your *past*, eventually, as you imbue your energy into that track on this Mobius strip, there will come a time when *all* of it has your new energy. The energy of your intent and compassion as the Human Being you are *now*, supersedes the energy of those on the treadmill with you.

We're going to tell you something else in a moment that may surprise you about what you consider to be unchangeable. But for now, let us speak about your current life in the *now* on that treadmill or on that train.

Your life right *now* has to do with the energy that you put into that track. What if, on those dials in front of you, instead of an "inclination of difficulty and speed," the dial read, "Peace, joy, abundance, sustenance, and love of life?" What if you had a dial that you could turn for that? I'm here to tell you that there is! But that dial hides until you completely visit the dimension it's in. And when you're there, you must "own it."

When you speak about *joy*, do you say to another person, *"I try to be joyful. That is my countenance. I want to live my life in joy, and I try my best. I'm always thinking about it"?* Let me ask you this: When the angel from the other side spoke so clearly to the prophet, did the angel, as a piece of God, say those profound words: "I AM, THAT I TRY?" [Laughter] No. The phrase was, "I AM THAT I AM." Do you know what that confusing phrase means? Do you know why it's confusing? It's because it's on a Mobius strip! "I am, that I am, that I am, that I am, that I am, that I am, that I am." It's a circle, isn't it? In fact, it's a statement that actually has no beginning or end.

Try this: I *am* joy. Joy *is* the energy of the track. Don't *try* to be joy, Instead, own the idea that you *are* joy. Then you might say, *"Well, then, if I am joy, why are there difficulties at all?"* Those difficulties, dear ones, are due to that fact that you walk on an earth with other Human Beings around you. So the challenge is not just with you, rather it's you with *them*. Isn't that always the puzzle? In addition, we've just told you that it's also with you and the other yous! Take care of yourself first, and all these things will be added to you. Make your track joyful. Say, "I *am* joy."

You've heard us speak about abundance. Let us define it, since there's often misunderstanding. Some have asked, *"Kryon, when you said we could have abundance, does that mean a storehouse of money someplace? Perhaps it's something to help break a financial fall, you know, if there are problems?"* No, it isn't.

I just told you that *you* are in the now. If you're in the now, where there's no past and no future, how can you have a storehouse for the future? So what is abundance? I will tell you: It's "immediate sustenance." It means that the *now* may always be taken care of. It means that on that treadmill, you never have to worry about, or think about, anything but *now*. I'm not speaking about your ability to pay the rent in a week. I'm talking about *now*. Are you feeling loved right *now?* Do you understand what's taking place *now?* Speaking of the rent, can you disengage from the worry about what will be the *now* in a week? The better you grasp the actual interdimensional energy of this concept, the more abundance will flow.

Do you know of the spiritual seeds that are being planted here? That's abundant! Do you have any concept of what's going on in the room where you sit? There's an abundant love! Some of you understand, and that's the abundance that we speak of.

It's sustenance—emotional, financial, environmental. It's what we showed to the tribes in the desert each day. They got used to it every day for years! They would have been shocked if the food had not arrived each day in this miraculous way.

Every day they were fed in the wilderness, And I'm telling you that no matter what you think about your wilderness, you can be fed in the same way. The family feeds the family. That's what sustenance is.

What about your health? So many of you are asking for healing, and you repeat, "I am that I try." How about, "I *am* healed"? This is the visualization. This is what we tell you to do in your meditations—to project this energy on your track. "I *am* healed." We're not telling you to go out and do foolish things, for you must return to your 4D. What we're telling you is that you can change the 4D eventually, but just like any protocol in any learning—in any schooling—it's going to take time to learn. Slowly, this affirmation creates an energy of change in your cellular structure. It creates pure intent and compassion. Understand and realize that you *can* change your cellular structure! But I will tell you that there's no quicker fast-track to do that than, "I *am* healed." Own it. Imbue yourselves with that consciousness, and your cells, which are also enlightened, will follow your lead.

Let me give you a hint of something you may not have realized in today's teaching. Cellular structure is made of water. Today you saw the scientist's examples of how water is sensitive to a Human's consciousness field. Was that profound for you? It's what we've been teaching for over a decade! Do you understand that all disease is also made of water? What does that tell you? It should remind you that *all* biology is ready to respond to you. All of it is waiting to change! There's nothing too hard for the angels calling themselves Humans in the room—walking on the treadmill—dialing up their own difficulty.

Changing the Past?

Here is the final metaphor—the last teaching for this session. It's the information that we told you might startle you.

Again, visualize that you're on the treadmill. You're walking in place—in the *now*. Your reality slips beneath your feet as the tread you're walking moves and moves. Think of this: You're holding a jar of liquid. You can name this liquid whatever you want—solution, peace, abundance, health, love of life—anything that you need. Then you slowly pour that sacred liquid of intent and compassion onto the track right beneath your feet as you walk.

Now ... take a look. Which direction does the liquid on the tread go? Look: It goes behind you! The fluid spills on the track and disappears behind you into whatever mechanism is responsible for the engine of the treadmill. But it doesn't take long, does it, before it appears in front of you, since the belt is endless and is in a loop. And this happens no matter how long the track is. Eventually, as you pour the fluid of intent, the entire track will change ... the whole thing!

What we want to show you is this: The first thing that had to happen on that metaphoric treadmill was that the fluid you poured cleared what was *behind you* before it ever got to what was in front of you. Become interdimensional with me just for a moment. Understand that all of those whom you walk with, affect your DNA. I'm again speaking of those past-life *you's* who are walking with you, who are really *present-life* energies. They're walking on this treadmill with you, and they affect your DNA ... the parts of DNA that are spiritual and carry lessons and setups and emotional baggage.

When you slowly dedicate energy to clearing your *now*, your past changes first! It's hard for you to grasp this, since you're so 100 percent linear! But the truth is that you are in the *now*. Everything is happening at the same time, so there are pieces and parts of you who will be manifested in the future that are also there as potentials in your predisposed form. But by giving divine purpose where you walk now, you purify all of it to the degree that you become *one* consciousness. Therefore, what you do now changes the past and the present of *you*.

If you can grasp this concept, dear ones, you'll understand that there's nothing you cannot change on Earth. Perhaps you thought that "the past is the past"? No. Thousands of years of strife can be solved on that treadmill if you wish. But instead of pouring hate and rage on the track, over and over, someone's going to come up with the idea to change *the fluid in the jar*. If you change it to the energy of compassion, and pour it on the track of Earth, you change the past and the future. And that, dear Human Being, is the beginning of the creation of the metaphor called "The New Jerusalem." It solves the unsolvable. It changes *all*.

The Future?

In light of what you've been through, many have asked: *"Kryon, from what you know about our track—this train that slowed down in the '60s and changed tracks—can you tell us what is in front of our train? You said that we knew, and had the potential of September 11 on our track all along. Is there another one coming? Is there something like that?"*

Here's what we say: If it's what you need to create—what you've decided to manifest—then the answer is yes. Do you need this right now? No. I will tell you this: Like a parent—a Higher-Self—you'll do what you must to manifest the track of intent that you've put in front of you. But there's something odd happening right now, and I say odd because even a year ago we would have said this wasn't happening: The train is beginning to slow down again! We don't know what this means. It may just be a "look around" to say, "How are we doing?" It may be that the train must slow down to imbue the track with a greater energy, or it could mean that the train wants to change yet to another reality—something even beyond what we can know and what is here at the present. There's no entity in the Universe that can tell what the "only planet of free choice" is going to do next. And that's the truth, angels. The only predictions that can be made are ones that validate what the energy is right *now* . . . and even that's changing as we speak.

What is it in your life that you believe is uncontrollable—that is always one color and always will be? What is it that bothers you the most where you have given verbal credibility to the fact that it can never change? Do you have something like that? I want you to remember the words: "I *am* that I try." Then perhaps you'll remind yourselves that the track is really quite, quite short. What you do with it *now* will change the *past*. Then that energy will come around to change the future—all of it taking place in the now as you walk in one place.

"They're only metaphors, Kryon!" Yes, I know. But they're metaphors that tell about a powerful Human Being—one who has a masterful potential. The avatars of the earth have *all* told you this. This is not new information. What *is* new is the positioning, the energy, the magnetics, even the solar system that you live in—now all changing because the Human Being moved reality.

Then, perhaps this year you may understand for the first time in all of our teachings some of the weirdest, strangest parts of the Kryon message—who are you, really? Could it be that you truly are a family member of the collective you call God? Could it be that you're eternal? Could it be that this Earth experience is like a play? Oh, powerful one, I will see you someday back where you're complete. Listen to this, Two-ears, Two-eyes, I know your name! I *am* in love with the Human Being before me, for I love the family. Call it what you wish—the love of God—the love of an angel, but this is the part of the message that reminds solid: that you're never alone!

God is not in a vacuum. We know who you are and why you're here. We know the parts of you who are on the other side of the veil. We know the challenges you've selected and the potentials in your life. It's why we came to see you. It's why our love goes deep into you as you read the words on this page.

And so it is that we give you this loving message: Reality is what you dial in, dear Human. Take your cue from the masters who walked the earth before you, for this Human power is yours, also.

And so it is that we take up the bowls of our tears of joy— the ones we have from washing your feet . . . and we walk away through the same veil that we came through . . . and this is our difficulty, since we love you dearly.

And so it is.

Kryon

Live Channelling

"*The Nine Fears*"

Channelled in
New Orleans, Louisiana/
Lyon, France
March & April 2002

Chapter Twelve

"The Nine Fears"
Live Channelling
New Orleans, Louisiana/
Lyon, France

These two live channellings were edited and combined with additional words and thoughts to allow clarification and better understanding of the written word.

Greetings, dear ones, I am Kryon of Magnetic Service. There's a sweet energy that is pouring into this place, an energy of those in an entourage of love. They are brothers and sisters who have no beginning or ending, just like you. As they pour into this place, we will again reflect: Could it be that something like this is real? Is it possible within the Human experience that God could talk to humanity so directly, with so much compassion, with succinct messages of love and hope? Could it be that the voice that's being heard at this moment—the one that's been heard all day long and now has another energy combined with it . . . could speak for Spirit? Could it be?

We give you this reminder: Everywhere on Earth, scripture was given to you in this manner. The most profound information and prophecies that have ever been given to you have been passed from Human Being to Human Being. Think back. None of the angels who have come forward in the history of Earth actually *wrote* the scriptures! No. Instead they gave messages to the Humans, who wrote down the words that later became recognized as divine.

All of the love, all of the counsel, and all of the wisdom has been given Human to Human. That's the way it was, and it remains this way today. You gather here at this time, perhaps to hear teachings, or words of wisdom. You come to participate in the energy within this room. Yet you know, don't you, that the core of who *you* are is as divine as anything that you can imagine?

Some of you might say, *"Well, I would like to come back and experience this again. A profound energy develops in a place like this."* Again, we say this: It's never necessary to come back to a meeting like this to gain spiritual energy! For you have this same energy when you're alone. We've spoken about this before, and we will speak of it again, even this evening. But before we start the teachings, we wish to remind you who's here. It's no accident that finds you sitting in the chair, dear one, listening or reading. Regardless of what you think about all of the messages of this day, or the personalities [speaking of the Kryon conference and the lectures of the day], we now invite you to feel the energy of a very loving family. Spirit pours into this place and covers you with love.

There's a sweetness here that's so sweet that it's thick! Some of you here will feel "pressed upon." Some of you will feel your hands being held, and some of you will feel your feet being washed. Although we often speak in metaphors, we say that this is real. It's real for us, and it's real for you. It's where the multidimensional meets your reality, the 4D. That's what makes it so special.

The duality of humanism is where the challenge is. You see, we have no duality at all. We come into a place of this kind, with your permission, touching each one of you, knowing you by name. We remember the last time we saw you. There's no duality strong enough to keep us apart. That's why we flow in so freely and so easily, and that's why we can "touch" you. That's why we invite you to feel the touch of Spirit. The Human Being has free choice, you know. You have the choice to sit here and say, "This can't be real," or you can also say to yourself, perhaps, just perhaps, "It is."

For the last 11 years, while the grids have been shifting, we've been giving you information, filling places just like this over and over with love. We've broached information that has now become commonplace. We've given you information on the way things work; we've talked of your physics; we've talked of the energy lattice that hides; we've spoken of calibration to another dimension; and we gave you information about the world and how things might happen. We told you how you had changed your reality—just in time for the physicists to tell you that all matter has a choice to change reality! Some of the things that we discussed early on with you sounded so odd and so strange and so unbelievable . . . yet now many of these same concepts are being brought to you from your own scientists! They've told you that time doesn't exist, and that there are many dimensions within your own body material. They've discovered faster-than-light attributes and reverse-time anomalies. Now, here you sit with the unbelievable being common . . . with spiritual concepts being accepted as science. Here you sit in a *new world!*

Tonight we wish to give you teachings about a subject that you need to hear. It's one we seldom speak of . . . but now we can. The energy is different now. There's an understanding and a wisdom that hasn't been here before. It's a wisdom that's becoming interdimensional, allowing humanity to start thinking out of that "box" where it's been for so long. Humans are starting to see things in a more tolerant light, in a different light.

It's a new reality track, and within this new track, free choice is still the operative system and always will be. We've discussed *ascension* with you. We've discussed becoming a *lighthouse* with you. We've discussed *work* with you. Now, we're going to give you a concept that perhaps in the past would not have been understandable. For suddenly, even within your science and what was given to you today in lecture, we're broaching the subject of Human power. You call it consciousness. We've always called it power. We're going to speak of *dark and light* again.

We've given similar kinds of messages before, even one called, "Dark and Light." So this one will be about "Shades of Light." To further qualify it, we should say that we're going to speak about the shades of *fear*—that is, an explanation of nine elements that make up common Human fear.

Now, this isn't a message that will depress anyone. This is an uplifting teaching, but we *will* talk about fear. For, dear Human Being, now you're beginning to understand what fear is and also what causes it. In order for you to understand fear, we must first speak of light. I'm going to give you some information that may seem unbelievable at this moment: If you go to the darkest places on this planet, places you would never, ever want to visit, to the lowest consciousness possible, the unbalanced of the unbalanced, you're going to find Human Beings exercising free choice. The energy that these Humans have chosen is simply a shade of light being produced . . . a shade of balance.

Dark is the absence of a brighter light. There are many shades of light, but from the brightest to the darkest, we're here to tell you that all of the Human experience—*all* of it—is created by Humans in a free-choice atmosphere. Therefore, as we've said before, it's a choice of the Human experience to bring the planet to a sense of balance. What is the mid-shade of light, you might ask? Of the whole spectrum of light, where is "normal" supposed to be for Planet Earth? It is this shift in the "normal" that has brought you out of the Armageddon and into the energy where you sit at this very moment. Therefore, the answer is that this mid-shade, or average middle point, has shifted to a higher shade.

You are *family*, and you are eternal. You've come here by free choice, and all of you can develop whatever energy you please. This, after all, is the test, isn't it? And here is the message tonight ... nine attributes of fear that you should see. It's an exposition, a revelation that the Human Being can create any shade of light or dark it wishes. Some of the things that you're most afraid of ... you will find that you're responsible for! You, and no one else. This is information that perhaps will fly in the face of the doctrine that you've studied, or of some of the "boxes of thought" that you have come out of, which are profoundly spiritual.

So, please listen. We'd like to tell you about nine attributes of fear. As we go through each one, we're going to show you where they come from, and how they can be transmuted into light.

Seed Fear: A Review

The first is a review. We gave you this information 12 years ago, and it's still here. It's an energy that surges in the very veins of your being—the interdimensional layers of DNA of your body. The layers of the DNA carry this, and it's prevalent in this room and in those reading this! It's called the *seed fear*.

So many of you came into this particular lifetime with feelings and attributes of a "searcher." And here you sit in a place that reflects your choice. Some of you found very early on that you weren't comfortable with the explanations of spirituality. You weren't a joiner. You didn't do things the way you were "supposed" to. So you developed your own spiritual philosophy, and many of you sit here because you've claimed the power of a Human to find his or her own divinity. You know where your core is; you know where *the prophet* is; you know where *the book* is. These spiritual elements that every religion on Earth has are all inside you. You're exercising the integrity of "peeling the onion" of duality until you find your own spiritual core and use it. You know that inside, there's honesty, appropriateness, integrity, manifestation, and joy. You're a Lightworker.

Perhaps that's you? If so, we can tell you that you've gone through this awakening before, but not all of you realize it. Some of you are awakening only now to these philosophies and have walked into this room perhaps not even knowing that there would be a channelling! Yet something brought you here, didn't it? An accident, perhaps? Let me tell you about *you*: You've been through this before! This isn't the first time you've awakened. Does it feel familiar? Does it ring true? I'm talking to the monks and the nuns and the shamans and the medicine men and women. I'm talking about those who died at the stake for it! I'm talking about those who spent their lives doing practically nothing but spiritual work. I'm talking of those who sacrificed everything for it . . . and here you are again.

The feelings of this planet are now moving into an energy that you only personally experienced before—one that was sacred and wise—an energy that is worshipful, whose truth belongs to the shamans. Yet here it is for the masses! You're hearing the very "secrets of the mystery schools" revealed on your everyday bookshelves—and many of you are afraid!

It's the seed fear. Some of you want to put this knowledge on the shelf and forget it. Even now, some of you in this group before me are wondering, *"How long is this channelling going to last? I'm not going to listen to this. I don't want this information."* I'll tell you why, because you've been there and you've done it, and when you did, you suffered for it. Some of you lost your lives for it. It wasn't pleasant—not at all. And here it is again, and you feel it at the cellular level. Many of you silently decided years ago not to "pick up the mantle." You decided that it wasn't necessary this time to follow a spiritual path. Well, I have news . . . that fence you sit on, where you "know" the truth but don't wish to speak about it . . . is being torn down. You'll have to face it eventually.

The seed fear is the fear of enlightenment, the fear of peeling that onion of duality. It's the fear of "finding the prophet inside." And that's the truth. What we say to you about this fear is that it's a false one. It's given to you to keep you constantly wondering what's real and what's not. It's often responsible for the very fence you're on. The joke is that you're an actual angel of God! Yet there you sit wondering if any of this is true. We know your names, you know. I'm not talking about the names that you came in with. I'm talking about your eternal name. I'm talking about the ones we sing in light when we see you each time you return. We know what you've been through, and who you really are. All this is hidden from you while you sit there on that fence.

Some of you carry within you the DNA layers of your own body, memories of becoming enlightened, which then generate the four-dimensional fear that you're "doing it again." It's different this time, dear one; it's different. This time will not bring calamity, or a personal catastrophe. This time will not bring needless death. This time around is the reason you came! All the lives you led up to this point helped create this new energy. Let me ask you this, dear Human Being: Does it make sense to you that you would elect to be born on this planet with the potential of Armageddon that looms so large? What's wrong with you that you would be here at this dangerous time? Can you see yourself standing in line on the other side of the veil, waiting to return? Perhaps you said to the angel next to you: *"I can hardly wait to get back to Earth. I'm going to live through hell, be squashed like a bug, be burned alive, with all my children with me. Let's go!"* Does this make any sense to you? Yet here you are.

It's for this very reason that some who don't understand the love of God feel that being a Human must be some sort of punishment! You have to ask yourself at some point: *"Why did I come back, knowing that this was the time when all the prophecies would converge to create Armageddon?"* We say it's because there was part of you that knew that in reality, change could happen. Because at the cellular level, you knew how things work! You knew that you had the power to change it, and you did. Now you sit in the new Earth with a promise of new energy, one that is seemingly tearing itself apart with change at the moment, bringing down the old foundation so that it can rebuild on level ground.

If this is you, then be aware . . . you trained for this. This energy has your name on it, and it's finally time that you claimed it.

For Women

There are other fears that are common to humanity, and two of them are mentioned next. We bring them here to this enlightened group because we know they exist with you, too. They come in with the duality, and they surge through the veins of all Human Beings. They're present in the DNA, within the interdimensional layers, and they're part of the humanism that's given to you.

Women, you have a fear. Well, let sister Kryon talk to you! So many women are afraid of being abandoned. This fear is present all the time. Oh, not for all of you, but for so many of you that it should be mentioned. You have to look at what that fear is about. Abandonment by whom? "Other Humans," you might say. Really? Well, I have some information for you. Do you know what the *soulmate* is? Do you know what the *twin flame* is? You live all your lives for that one person who will satisfy you, who will always be there, who will never abandon you. You want to fall in love with this energy. Does it exist? Could it exist? You may be happy in a relationship, but deep down you wonder whether you missed it. Did you miss finding the "real" one?

Now I will tell you something that we've revealed before: You're not *all here*. You knew that, didn't you? I mean by this that what you think is you as you look in the mirror . . . is not. It's a piece and a part—the four-dimensional part of you—the part that walks in duality. There's another part of you that's apart from you—around you all the time. You call it the *Higher-Self*. There are pieces and parts of you that are even within your own energy! You're not all here. There are pieces and parts of *you* on the other side of the veil—parts beyond what you can see, doing things that you can't even imagine. This is all part of the plan of support for your free will and your free choice. Now, let me tell you this: The energy of the twin flame, the soulmate, is the profound desire of every single Human Being to fall in love with the other pieces of *you* and join together. It is a spiritual quest, you know, and it always has spiritual overtones when you think of it, does it not?

When that marriage is complete at an interdimensional level, you have calibrated yourself. It's a meld through the energy of what we've called the universal cosmic lattice that reaches through the veil and touches the hand of *you*, a piece of God. Once you do that, dear Human Being, in this new energy, that handshake remains solid. You have just met another piece of *you*, a piece that will never go away, a piece that you can be in love with, a piece that will never abandon you ever! You will never be alone—never.

You can walk this planet and never have another thought about abandonment, for it's impossible! The energies that really matter are holding your hand, and they always will. That creates a balanced Human Being, without fear. So you realize that this fear is not of missing some hidden opportunity with another Human, but something that's always available through you. And that's the truth. That was the second fear.

For Men

For the men in the room, brother Kryon wishes to speak to you. Number three is the fear of failure. In this particular culture, it's paramount. You have your own expectations, your culture's expectations, your family's expectations—they all expect you to succeed. That's presented in a linear fashion, by the way.

How do you know what failure is? You're too goal oriented! Men, listen: There are many careers to be had. There are many success stories, and they all lie on top of each other in a *now* time frame. Yet you can't see that. What you consider to be failure oftentimes will bring you to your knees . . . so you can get on with the work you came here for!

When you walk around thinking that perhaps you failed, or you're afraid of something that may be happening in your life that may cause you to fail, we're telling you that perhaps, just perhaps, it's leading you to a place that you actually asked to be in! Perhaps it's leading to a crossroad where you can finally take something inappropriate and move past it—moving to something else—which is why you really came. All the time your heart is being churned up, saying, "I'm failing, I'm failing," But it's not the case. There are so many of you men in this room who have given intent to follow a path, but you consider it progressive—leading and graduating to something of your own linear design. You don't see the beauty of the timing of it all, and you don't understand that in an interdimensional way, you don't need to learn one thing before another. Sometimes what you think is stupid now will later become the core! Don't judge yourself or mark a scorecard. Instead, celebrate the exact place you're in now.

You know what? This is also related to fear number seven [in a moment]! To me, all nine attributes are happening simultaneously. Now, when we get to number seven, you're going to see how this relates. Oddly enough, when you add them together

[3 + 7] you get a "one," which stands for the *energy of beginning*. It's all interrelated, you know. All nine of these fears are presented to you in a circle. Go ahead . . . add 1+2+3+4+5+6+7+8+9. The answer, when reduced, will show you the "circle of the nines."

Men, are you listening? Not all things are as they seem. What you consider in your four-dimensionality as a path, as a goal, or as success, may only be the start of something else. There are things you don't know. There are things that are going to be revealed to you as you walk the path in your linear way. So, don't judge yourself. Stand before Spirit and say, "Tell me what it is I need to know." Can you celebrate where you are in your life no matter what's happening? Can you reach your hand up and claim that all is appropriate? Can you say, "I am divine"? Blessed is the Human Being who understands this, for this is the one who also understands that the calibration to the lattice brings success and manifestation in the eyes of God. Then who is it you think you've failed? This fear is a Human setup, and is voided with spiritual understanding.

Another point: Did you try things along the way and discard them when they didn't work? Did you throw them away, thinking that the energy back then didn't produce anything from your efforts? Do you remember the "clock of Spirit"? It's timeless. Never tell yourself that what you did or tried in your past won't work now or in your future. Think of all the time you spent! Perhaps it's time to revisit some of those things. Perhaps they didn't work then, but might now. Get out of the linear time frame!

Numbers four, five, and six all have a common theme; they're related, believe it or not. We're starting to get into the *shades of light*. We're starting to expose some of the things that you normally don't talk about.

First, be clear on what we're telling you. Humanity creates whatever shade of light it wishes. Human Beings create the energy they wish with the co-creative power that's theirs. All Human Beings can go to the darkest or lightest places imaginable and start creating with whatever shades they wish. And they *will* be able to manifest dark power if desired. Yes, it's true. Did you think for a moment that the power of Human consciousness would only be restricted to those things that are light? The answer is no, not in free choice. It can be any shade. It might take more of them to create darkness, but indeed, it's done all the time, and has been the way much of your planet has been shaped. The old paradigm has mass consciousness enslaved in fear—enhancing the power of the dark.

The choice of humanity to begin with was to decide what "normal" would be—what energy would be on the planet— what vibratory rate the planet would settle into through history . . . culminating with your present millennium. That's why you sit in this place in history, which no one could imagine. So number four is *fear of self.*

Fear of Self

Now, fear of self is not a seed fear at all. This is very four-dimensional. There is a part and a piece of you that knows ever so well that you could create darkness if you chose to. You're afraid to go there because you think perhaps you'll do it!

There are some of you here in this room who have had a situation where you've gone into a place of depression. You've seen it up close. You know what the countenance is and the horror of what it does to the rest of the brain. You know what the thinking and the thoughts are in that place, and you know what it feels like. Having been there, you're afraid to go there again. This is fear of self. This is not for all of you, but there are certainly enough of you, including some who are reading this right now. The realization that the Human is powerful in all the shades of light and dark often creates a fear that you might go into the darkness and stay there . . . fear of self.

Some of you may say, *"Well, that's not me."* Perhaps, but again, surging through your DNA there's the option to choose any part of a light scenario you wish . . . darkest to lightest. Some of you who have come from places that are dark know what that is like. You never want to visit those places again. And that's what I'm talking about.

Here is your hope: The Human spirit will not stay stuck in any place where there's intent to change it. There's no force working against you . . . but you. You may be sick or depressed for a time, but never will your consciousness remain in a state that isn't the one you wish it to be. Even in the darkest depression, there's a part of you that's yelling, "This is *not* me." This thought alone will slowly bring you back. Sometimes lighthouses shut down for repair. Sometimes they need a rest. But they're always lighthouses, placed in areas to help others find their paths. Even when the lighthouse is dark, it knows what its purpose is.

Fear of the Dark Side

Now we get to the area called "fear of the dark side." We're going to give you information right now . . . something that you've always known intuitively: There's no such thing as the dark side.

All through your Human history, in all of your cultures, Humans have assigned darkness and its energy to another entity or another power. The teaching goes that this other power is one that wants to come up and grab you and pull you down! All through your childhood, you feared the monsters and other entities that were "out to get you." Some wish you to think that a soul that's not believing a specific way is going to be captured by dark entities, or that you're always in danger of being possessed. That's not the way of it, and it never was.

Humans create their own dark side. Humans have power in the light, and they also have power in the dark. Let me be specific. Some have asked, *"Kryon, is it possible for Human Beings to take a shade that's so dark that they could create darkness around someone else?"* The answer is yes! Let me give you an example: What happens when you're trying to find your way through a dimly lit room? Suddenly even the smallest amount of light that's been helping you vanishes. You freeze. What if this path you're searching for is your lifeline? You become afraid. You can't move. Without any light, suddenly you wonder what else might be in there with you! You start hearing things. Fear begins to possess you. Look at what has happened. They simply turned off the light. But *you* created the fear that enables fear to flourish.

Is there a group of Humans from another place that has sent darkness into your area? Yes. They have always been able to do that. Doesn't that make sense, dear Human Being, that you would have free choice to choose dark or light? Doesn't it make sense that Human consciousness would not be limited to simply sending light? But here's what we also have to remind you—it's a review of sorts.

The story we just told you may seem to be frightening, unless of course the person in the dark place had an extra light. You see, there's no equality within the shades of light. Each one of them has an energy of its own. You can manifest any shade you wish, but the shade you manifest has an energy specific to itself. Long ago we gave you the information that light is active and dark is passive. The shades have vastly different energy! When you're in a dark room and you open the door, dark does not leak out! Instead, light flows in. What does that tell you about the power of light? A higher vibrational shade is more active and more powerful. It takes less of it to generate a specific energy. It takes more Humans to create a lower shade than a higher one.

If you take a totally dark room filled with people and you have *one* Lightworker who enters it, the whole room illuminates! For those of you who are afraid of the dark side, I will say this: The only reason you're afraid is because you've never understood the power of the energy you carry to build a lighthouse. You can stand in the middle of the darkest scenario anywhere. You can have those around you—dozens and dozens of them— trying to create dark around you, yet one enlightened Human Being will void all the darkness!

And you wonder why we're excited? Because that shade of "normal" for the planet these last two years has just ratcheted up an entire notch! You love to create plateaus in your three-dimensional linear thinking, so we'll just help you with it and say this: Collectively, this planet has decided to lift up what it thinks is normal to another shade of light. That's why we're here today, and that's why the grid is being adjusted.

The difference between dark and light and the average thereof, has become higher than it's ever been. The ones who continue to try and create darkness are having a harder and harder time finding places where there's no light. Do you understand? Every single entity that has ever come to you from across the veil has given you this information! You're enabled, dear ones, to create whatever shade you wish. There used to be a time when almost everything had a dark side . . . so dark that secrets would hide for centuries. Noticed anything different lately about secrets and conspiracies? They don't remain for long in this energy! You think all the revelations you're seeing are just a coincidence? The highest levels are being examined, and the secrets aren't sticking to any dark area. They can't, since you're shining the light there! It's happening in politics, business . . . even at the level of leaders of countries. Responsibility is now the issue. There's no hiding anymore. What does that tell you about light and dark—and balance on your planet?

Fear of Other Entities

Number six is related, isn't it? Fear of actual entities. Many wish to assign darkness to an entity. Many are afraid of anything that's outside of 4D. No matter what it is, if it walks through a wall, it must be evil. Don't you understand that this is the core of who *you* are? You are interdimensional! Do you know the reason that you're not all in a body? If you were, the laws of four-dimensional physics wouldn't work for you. Multidimensionality is your natural state, as you might recall. It's only because you volunteered to have it reduced and hidden from you by your duality that you think you're only 4D. Remember, every divine angel who has ever appeared before you has said the words "Fear not." For the divine entities on the planet are well aware that Human Beings tend to fear what they don't understand.

There are some of you who fear dark-side entities. The truth is that there's no such thing! Oh, there would be those here who would argue. They would say, "I've seen this or that." I will tell you that this is a projection that a Human Being has put upon you—or perhaps a Human with the help of others standing silently behind. It's fear enhanced by your own fear, in cooperation with them. Can fear manifest magic? Yes, if you cooperate with it. It can show you anything it wants to, since there's no light for you to see the truth. What does this mean? It means that you can actually help those who wish to send you darkness if you will "buy into" the fact that they can do it. If you turn off the lights willingly, they'll all be there, and any show you want can project on that dark screen. The dance that you'll perform in the dark has many faces, and they're all very frightening. That's your choice. But this is what you should know: It's all Human, all the time, no matter what face you think it has. And that's the truth.

There are many who fear what's going on today—right now. They would say, *"There's an entity named Kryon, one who has possessed a person, and he's speaking through that person at this meeting."* Let me tell you, that's not what's taking place today. What are you feeling now? Is it fear or safety? Can an entity that is family fool your heart continually year after year? Are you that weak? No. Instead, there's a meld going on—one of love—a Higher-Self and a brother, a sister, giving you messages of love from the other side of the veil. And what do we say to do with it? We ask you to discern for yourself. We always hand the decision to you. Does that sound like a trick? Does it sound like we have an agenda? Our only agenda is to increase your awareness and love, then we retreat and let the Human do the rest—some trick.

It's time to remember the light that you hold and what has happened on this planet. You move from place to place—you vibrate higher, yet you don't even know it. The issue was broached today that some of you walk in dark places and you don't like it. You have difficulty with it, and you pray for it to be removed. You think of it as inappropriate, and you think you're just "marking time" until God answers your prayer. Again, we tell you that maybe the places you go to work, or even the places you go home to, need that light you carry. Are you listening? What if *you* are the only light there?

That is the *work*, Lightworker! And you'll never know how you might have touched a person when you were standing next to them. You'll never know how those around you benefited by being next to the lighthouse that has your face. The lighthouse sits there all night long in the dark, rotating and rotating and rotating so that the skipper of the ship can steer into a safe harbor. The skipper never meets the lighthouse keepers—never knows their names or who they are. Yet you want to fear the energy of the entity that is you. You fear the entity that is Kryon. There's a big dichotomy here. We're celebrating your light at the same time you're fearing the dark. How 4D of you! And that was number six.

Fear of Not Finding Your Path

Number seven relates to number three, as I indicated earlier. It's the fear of not finding your path. Oh, listen to me! You walk inside a sphere. You think you're on a straight line, but you're not. This path of yours is *not* straight. You think that you do one thing after another, and you place them in a two-dimensional row. You wonder about the future, and you consider the past, but you never see them together. Some have asked, *"Kryon, when am I going to find my path?"* Some of you are sitting in it!

It's exactly why you came, yet you constantly look to the future and say, *"Well, maybe later, maybe in the future I'll find it."* You walk on the inside of a sphere—that means that at an interdimensional level, you can see all the paths you ever walked and ever will walk just by looking around. They're all together! It's just like your idea of success and failure. It's the wise Human Being that understands that not all is as it seems—that there's more.

When are you going to find your path, you ask? What if the lighthouse thought this way? *"Well, nobody has called me lately to thank me for shining my light. I haven't had any skippers of any ships tell me they were thankful I was here, too. I think I'll turn off my light and leave. Time to move on. I'll keep searching for what I'm supposed to do."*

Is that what you really want? The fear of not finding your path is related to the seed fear, too. It's also related to number three, the fear of failure. It's very linear, so we give you this information again: Celebrate where you are, every minute of every day! Piled on top of what you consider a linear time are all the "nows." It's difficult to explain interdimensionality to a single-digit dimensional Human Being. But we see you differently than you do. If we could only give you that brilliance and show you what you've done . . . and what you're going to do!

It's not what you see in the mirror, dear Human Being. It goes way beyond that. That's why we love you the way we do. You literally walk around without being able to see what's around you. And this takes courage. That was number seven.

Fear of Disease

There are still those among you who are enlightened, yet who say, *"You know, it's out there, don't you? And it's going to get me! I've got a friend. It got him. It's going to get me! The disease is out there!"*

This is not so. Listen to this: It doesn't matter how predisposed you are genetically to get a disease. No matter what you were told in an old energy about the way things work, the bigger picture was not seen. Throw away all of the old biological explanations and accept the new way that things work!

Through Human consciousness, you can talk to cellular structure; you can renew it; you can enhance it; you can awaken it, you can heal it; you can clean it. You can even talk to the disease. Earlier this day, the question was put: "Biologically, what are you made of?" And the answer was *water*. What is disease made of? The answer is *water*. Then it was shown to you that Human consciousness can profoundly change water! Did you draw the logic from this? The same consciousness that can change crystal patterns in a jar of water that sits in front of you is the same consciousness that can greatly change water in a Human Being—your cellular structure. No matter what you've been told. And that's the truth.

If you wish to sit in fear, you may do so, and that's free choice. If you wish to do the opposite and celebrate where you are and where you're going and what might happen, that creates light. Then you start to laugh at the fear and realize what a joke it is. Blessed is the Human who understands that there's no limit to the influence you have over your own cellular structure! It's the new way of things, and the yogis and shamans of old showed it to you. Now it's your turn! And that was number eight.

Fear of the Future

Here is the final one—we've saved it till last—number nine. The energy of the *nine* is well known. Nine is *completion.* The energy of eleven and nine? The energy of the *eleven* is the energy you sit within. It is a master number that represents a new Earth. The energy of the *nine* is all around you. It is the jar that *eleven* sits in. It's completion of the old—completion of an old paradigm, an old energy. And yet as you sit here with all this before you, which is so grand in its scope and its potential, you fear the future.

"Kryon," you ask, *"what will happen? That last event took us by surprise! Is there another one like that one on the horizon? What are we to do?"* Let me point out something that perhaps some of you have not really seen fully: Have you noticed the soothsayers coming out of the woodwork lately? They do that, you know. They follow fear. Did you notice that there weren't very many of them before the eleven-nine event? But after that, even six months later, they're all around you! They feed on your fear, you know. They're here willing to enhance it if you let them, with scenarios that will create even more fear. These are the ones who want to drag that "above-normal" energy you worked on so hard, back to the way it was. They want that shade of light and dark to become what it used to be. That's the difference between the old and the new, dear ones. Those are the ones who will be left behind.

Remember our teachings so long ago? You can't take energy to a less-aware state. You can't willingly "unknown" anything. The earth cannot "unknown" its enlightened state. The earth cannot "un-invent" what has taken place in the last few months. Yet the fearmongers will try, and they will tell you all manner of things to watch out for: "Be fearful!" they will say. Then they'll give you dates and times in advance of your doom. Planets are coming to smash into you . . . asteroids will get you . . . alignments of astronomical influences will destroy Earth. Of course, nothing will happen, but many won't realize it, and they'll ask for new dates of doom and gloom—being addicted to the energy of fear. Look back. Their messages never changed from the ones 1,000 years ago. Isn't it time to move on?

If you go along with it, however, your light is diminished. Do I have proof of such a thing—that there are more of them today than yesterday? No, I do not. But let me give you something to ponder: Where were they on September 10? The answer? Still lurking under their fear rocks . . . inventing false things to fear—and they missed the big one. What I'm telling you is this, that it was the manifestation of something frightening to you that allowed them to do what they're doing now—being listened to. Some are very well aware of this. What does it mean to you? It means that nothing has changed regarding your power and the battle before you. It's just that everyone may now see it. The battle really has begun.

Earth is now going through something we told you it might: awareness. A battle between the old and the new is now part of your current events! Decisions about getting off the fence are before you. Where do *you* stand? There's an issue that no one even talked about a little while ago: What do you consider to be "normal" in civilization? We brought you these exact questions in 1999, and to many of you back then, it was just "interesting." Perhaps now it might be worth another look?

You sit in the energy of a new reality track without any prophecy. It's wide open. Along come the soothsayers to create a fear scenario for you. They're here, just as they should be, to present you the choice between dark and light. But you know something they don't—the grand potential! Oh, how many years have we said to you that the potential is "The New Jerusalem"? And you thought that was some kind of mysterious or historic phrase? Look at your news! What do you think that it means now?

You've heard it over and over from Kryon and those before Kryon: Jerusalem is not just a city in Israel. It's also the metaphor for an Earth solving the unsolvable, and moving to a level that was unexpected. It's the rebuilding, for the third time, of a temple of consciousness. It is a new planet—a new Earth.

There are many metaphors in this, and we say to you: Don't be afraid of a future that *you*, Lightworker, are controlling and manifesting. You're the ones who aborted the Armageddon; you're the ones who are seeing the 11-11 on the clocks; you're the ones who are hugging Spirit right now—creating the light of the world.

The nine are complete. The entourage realizes that it will not be long before it's going to go back through the crack in the veil, which a moment ago they came through. The invitation has been open for you to feel them next to you, around you, moving through you, pressing upon you in various areas and ways. In this message of the nine fears has been the invitation to marry the Higher-Self, to fall in love with that part of you that is divine, to calibrate, and to celebrate the future.

The message of Kryon is one of hope, isn't it? Yes. The message of Kryon is one of enhancement, isn't it? Yes, it is. But it's not actually a "Kryon" message! Instead, it's a Human message, giving four-dimensional Human Beings their own message of an interdimensional Human future. It's *your* message! It hides so convincingly. That's why we're here.

No matter what you're facing in life, when you stand up in a moment and exit this place, the invitation is to leave this place differently from how you came in, with a new awareness of how things work . . . the potentials of how things might be working. Even if you believed nothing of what you heard, perhaps you're now at least ready to ask questions on your own. Investigate the truth of what's been said. Try out the energy—even pray and meditate. When you do that, you create compassion, and that creates an "energy handshake," the beginning of the process of calibration.

And so it is that in these few minutes, we've visited family, and we've had a reunion. We've enhanced what you already know. Many are "peeling the onion of duality." Oh, there are other words for it, too. One is "remembering." So you might say that for these moments, we've been here to enhance your own memory of who you really are. And that's the way it is. Did you notice which fear was *not* in the nine? It was "fear of death." Why? Because intuitively, Humans do not fear going home.

So the entourage picks up its bowls of tears—tears of joy it used to wash your feet, and it's exiting back to the crack in the veil where it came from—to that place you call home. In the process, we celebrate you; we celebrate the event; we celebrate the energy of this place, and we celebrate the family. We know you all very well—all of you.

Just before we leave, again we would like to remind all the Humans in the room, the family members, the angels . . . you are never alone—never. And so it is.

Live Channelling

"The Fourteen Questions"

Channelled in
Reno, Nevada
February 2002

Chapter Thirteen

"The Fourteen Questions"
Live Channelling
Reno, Nevada

This live channelling has been edited with additional words and thoughts to allow for clarification and better understanding of the written word. It represented the energy of the crowd that was in front of Kryon at that moment . . . and the questions they collectively carried with them.

Greetings, dear ones, I am Kryon of Magnetic Service. This is a greeting that I've given you for almost 12 years. It's a greeting that's filled with more than the energy of just a greeting. Rather, it's an energy transfer. For even though the veil is thick, there are those of you who will understand this greeting and say, "I am sister, I am brother, I am family."

I will say again that this moment is precious—a precious moment due to the fact that you've chosen to invite this entourage into your energy. Some of you felt, when you walked into this area, that this was a safe place. Some of you felt it when you sat down to read this. Some of you walked into this physical place and remarked, "This is what I expected. I don't know what's going to happen today, but I wish to sit here in a safe harbor within this energy." A safe harbor? Yes. There is safety here, spiritual and emotional. There's a welcoming here; there's love here.

And so it is that we take our place within you and prepare to give the lessons for today. If you only knew what's taking place at the moment! There's a thickness of energy on this planet, which has never been here before. There are changes taking place that we've never described, and it's here because of you. If you're one of those who "signed up" through intent to be what we call a Lightworker, then you're feeling it. That's what we wish to talk about.

Here is a departure from the channellings and messages of the last months. We've talked about interdimensionality; we've talked about physics and science and calibration; we've spoken of the enexplainable; we've talked about things that we couldn't talk about because they weren't understandable—yet we did it anyway. We spoke of circles within the circles—and now we're going to rest that subject as much as we can.

Today we speak of personal things. We're going to answer some questions—14 of them. These are questions being asked specifically in this room and also from some other groups at the same time, right now. We'll do our best in this dimension to answer interdimensional questions. Every single one of these items may seem to be in your reality, but the answers are not. Get used to this. That's the way it's going to be from now on, for you've given permission to move beyond what you're used to . . . beyond the old reality . . . beyond 4D.

Many of you ask Spirit: "What about this? What about that? What am I supposed to do here? What about how I'm feeling?" The answers you expect to come to your ears are in a reality that is yours. What if the answers were slightly out of your reality? Would you hear them? Are you one of those who has waited and waited for answers, but only get silence? Answer this: If a sightless Human asked for light, and it was created all around him, would he know it, or would he continue to sit in his own personal darkness? We will try to give you answers that make sense, but they're often above the reality that you're used to. These answers aren't always easy to comprehend or understand, but that's the way of the new energy.

Blessed is the Human Being who understands that they do not see all that there is. We have said it before—that things are not always as they seem! Now, on this planet, this is a profound statement. You sit in the thickness of potential for huge change. Fourteen questions . . . and here is number one:

Question 1 – Why I am so tired?

"Dear Kryon, I'm tired. I'm more tired than I've ever been. I'm a Lightworker, and. I've done everything that I think I should do. I anchor the spots I'm supposed to anchor. I go to places I'm supposed to go that I'm aware of—I try my best. I meditate. I walk through life with integrity, but I'm tired. Is it supposed to be this way? Will it change? What's next? What can I do? Is this normal?"

Dear Human Being, let me tell you this: On the 11th of September, you manifested a leap for this planet—an "exposure" of what it can be. Think of it as being an opening—the beginning of some profound solutions. You may look around the earth and say, "This doesn't look very promising right now!" We say this to you: You don't know everything! You don't see everything! Patience! It's because you gave permission for it on the 11:11, Lightworker, that the weight of what you've just accepted has doubled. You knew that, didn't you? What happens when you take physical weights and clip them onto you and march around day to day? You become tired. The weights that you've taken are the new weights of the potential paradigms of interdimensionality that you gave permission for—the very ones we told you about almost 12 years ago! It won't always be this way. This year [2002] will mark the completion of the grid shift. It will be the beginning of a pattern that stays and remains . . . a pattern that will no longer shift and move as it does now.

Do you know what is so difficult for a Lightworker? It's the fact that just when they start to get used to one energy, another is presented! This fact is going to come to an end soon. Some of you may say to yourselves, "Glory be! It has been a long 12 years." Blessed is the Human who understands that what they're feeling now is not forever. What they're feeling now is not the new paradigm. It's transition. You bear a heavy load—heavier than ever. Your anchor is heavier than ever. Your concern for the planet has deepened and intensified every morning and every night. The angels that surround you have matured; the guides are no longer guides . . . but a different kind of enabler.

All of these things speak of another kind of planetary potential. Here you sit as a lighthouse, as the new planet steers itself among the rocks. Is it any wonder you're tired? Here's our advice: Endure until the end of this year. We're telling you that at the beginning of the year of change, much will be settled. The end of the grid shift is this year—the year of grounding [2002]. The year of change [2003] is the year of the stabilization. That sounds contradictory, but it is so. Spiritually, things will become more stable, but physically in 4D, your planet will begin to change. Think of it like this: The new textbook is finalized so that the teachers may have a syllabus to begin the changing of the energy of the planet. Much will begin to clear for the Lightworker. It's different for each, but that's the truth. Endure. There is hope; there is a new paradigm to follow.

Question #2 – How can I communicate better with Spirit?

"Dear Kryon: What am I going to do about communication with Spirit? You see, it hasn't gotten any better. I try so hard to recapture the

feelings that I used to have. That was my measure of connection. That's what I considered to be "normal." I know when I'm speaking to Spirit because I can feel it in my heart—my cells. I tingle a certain way, and I know it's happening. When is that going to come back?"

Lightworkers, say "good-bye" to that! You're going to have to look for new signs in a new energy in a new Earth. We told you about this early on. The energy being developed is the beginning of something you could never have imagined. It didn't start out the way you imagined either, but here you are in a position you've never been in before—a communicating position. Our advice? Disengage, relax, and love Spirit! Sit on the floor, if you choose, and have a "meditation moment" where you say, "Dear Spirit, tell me what it is you want me to hear—what it is you want me to know." Then I'll just be quiet. Disengage and love the family. You're learning "The Third Language," which we have spoken of many times . . . a continual marriage to a piece of you that enables a communication that is 100 percent of the time . . . not confined only to specific "meditation moments."

Something happens when you develop compassion. That energy marries the intellect and creates a window of opportunity. It's a time-space where there's a tremendous amount of information given. It's going to take compassion to create action. Feel free to weep if you wish, because you're dearly loved— because the earth is changing—because you asked for it— because you've eliminated the energy of "the Armageddon," and because you've changed tracks of reality. Weep with joy because you're in love with the earth! Weep with joy because the earth can talk to you through your feet. Did you know that? You're so stuck in that odd paradigm that everything comes from above! It must be shocking to know that so much comes from below! [Laughter] It comes from your partner, Planet Earth.

Question #3 – What am I supposed to do here? I'm tired of waiting!

"Dear Spirit, dear Kryon: When am I going to find out what I'm supposed to do here? I've been looking a long time, and of course I'm making an assumption that what I'm doing now sure isn't it!"

Really? Oh, dear Human, let me tell you something that maybe you never considered. You're too goal oriented! You want a time line for everything. You think you're climbing some ladder, and when you get to the top, you're going to breathe a sigh of relief. You think you'll reach a summit or plateau. Perhaps there will be some kind of a cot there for you to rest? Then you will announce to Spirit, "Oh, thank you, I'm here. I know what I'm doing now!" [Laughter]

That's not the way it is. Every moment of your life is what you're doing for the planet. Oh, yes, some of you are working toward something specific, but remember the axiom: As you work, as you vibrate higher, as you walk on this planet and change the vibration where you move from place to place, you're working it. Perhaps that's why you're surprised that you're tired?

Many ask, "When am I going to find out what I'm here for?" Here is the answer: You're here for now . . . not something coming up. What have you got going on in your life that you don't like? What's happening right now that you wish would move out of your life? What is it that you don't understand? Perhaps you ask yourself each day, "Will it be better tomorrow?" Dear ones, make *this* the day that's the summit. Take the situation of today and mold it into something that's beautiful for you now. In dire, difficult circumstances, anchor and celebrate all that's around you. Claim the love of God, and let the compassion of Spirit fill you. Then keep on going . . . even in doubt. Instead of striving for something at the top of the ladder, strive for understanding the circle of energy that makes up your new "now" reality. When you see the circle *"I am that I am,"* do you understand that it's a statement of nonlinearity? Do you understand that it's a statement of you and the family? Be the angel, the lighthouse, each moment of your life.

Question #4 – When am I going to get a break from the people around me?

"Spirit, Kryon, family: When are these people around me going to change? I'm really tired of tolerating them. How long do I have to go through this?"

You think we don't know? You think that somehow Spirit is in a vacuum? So, you think that when you have challenges, somebody has turned off the "God spigot," and when you feel real good, it's on again? No. We sit with you and hold your hand through all of it, even the intolerable.

Let me give you the answer to this question, very clearly: Dear Human Being, dear lighthouse, you give intent and take on the anchor energy, the lighthouse energy, and here's what happens. The emotional "buttons" that you've allowed to be pushed, that make you intolerant and angry (and tired), slowly dissolve. Those people who, you wish would change . . . may never change! It is *you* who will change.

There may come a day, in all naiveté, when you'll announce to Spirit, "Thank you for changing those people!" The humor in this is that all along, what happened, dear Human Being, is that you changed to such a degree that they no longer bother you anymore! What they do no longer pushes your buttons. What they think, how they act, what they say behind your back, the drama . . . nothing gets to you! It's because you know who you are. It's because you've stripped away the peeling of duality and claimed the core, which is divine. You've seen the angel inside, and you've said, "I know who I am. I am that I am!" Then you walk the planet differently, oblivious to those who you only barely tolerated before. That's the truth. Do you long for that day? Then take care of yourself, and watch everyone around you "change."

Question #5 – Get me out of this job!

"Dear Kryon: I can't believe where I'm working. It doesn't celebrate my magnificence, you know. It's not commensurate with my angel inside. Dear Spirit, get me out of this job so I can be a Lightworker!"

This is a review. We've said this in the past, but many of you have to hear it in context with all of the other things involved. What do you think your work is here, Lightworker? Perhaps you've said this to Spirit: "I want so bad to be a Lightworker, but I just go to work. I come home tired, and I just go to work and I come home tired. What's this about? I sure don't like where I have to go, and I don't like the people who are there with me. I would never have chosen them as my friends. I'm the only one there who has any concept of higher consciousness. Everyone else just walks from place to place. I'm alone. I want out!"

I will tell you this, dear Lightworker: Do you remember when you gave intent to be a lighthouse? Do you remember at what point you said, "I'll do whatever it takes—to vibrate higher—to experience the love of God"? Well, here you are at the very place where you're doing the most good and you can't wait to be removed! [Laughter] Maybe you're the only light there at that workplace. Maybe it's dark there. The metaphor is this: Imagine the lighthouse, anchored, standing tall on the rocks. The large ocean-going vehicles feature their masters searching for a path into a safe harbor. There you are, shining the only light! Metaphoric, oh yes. But that's the way it is!

You shine a light that illuminates places that would normally not be illuminated if you didn't stand there, anchor! Did you think of this? Let me tell you something: The energies of this year [2002] feature a storm that has increased. It batters the lighthouse more. It makes it harder for the masters of the ships in the dark. The power of the sea is awesome, and there you stand, anchored, with a guiding light. Blow after blow hits you, and what are you asking? Imagine if the lighthouse keeper said, "I'm tired of this, I want out. Put out the light and get me out of here!" It's free choice, you know. You could do that. But for those of you who wondered if Spirit was listening to your pleas, the answer is yes. We have been all along.

What you're enduring is not permanent, so the answer is this: Celebrate where you are—every day. Regardless of your goal, what you wish for, what you think may be happening, celebrate the way it is now. Does this sound familiar? Is it the answer to another question in this series? Yes. Be compassionate with everything around you, because the compassion creates an action, an interdimensional action. It increases your light; it tells Spirit about your energy. It sends out your name. It calibrates you to the rest of us. Did you know that?

When you ask to be removed from such a place, do you mean it? It's very much like question one, is it not? We say, endure it for the duration. It won't be that long, and as you walk it, walk it in celebration and honor. How many of you have the courage to come home and thank God for where you are, where you work, and the people there? Don't you think we know where you are? Don't you think we walk next to you the whole time? We do.

Question #6 – When do I get to the next level? I'm tired of this one.

"Dear Spirit: When am I going to go to the next spiritual level? I feel like I've been stuck at this level for a very long time. I want to go to the next one."

Of course this relates to question five, question three, and question one, does it not? It's all the same, you know. It's perception of where you are. You keep expecting that the next level is going to be something that's a far cry from where you are . . . a nice place that has less energy expended? Perhaps one where you're happier and more joyful? Do you know why we call you a Lightworker? Do you understand that this is work?

Regarding that next level: I'd like to tell you something profound. Do you know why you're exhausted and often despondent? It's because you've just gone to the next level! You didn't expect that, did you? Here you sit at the very place you're asking to be taken to! Here's a fun example: Do you remember what it was like in school? At whatever grade level you were, if you sat next to someone two grades higher, you might have glanced at their textbook. Wow! You didn't understand anything. It looked too hard! Secretly, inside, you might have said, "I hope I never have to do that lesson; it's just too hard. How do they understand all that? How am I ever going to do it when I get to that level?"

Let me tell you something: This planet of yours just skipped a grade! The difficult books are open, and you're climbing uphill. You're learning a new language. It's the language of communication. It's the language of how to feel joyful under these new "hard" circumstances. It's the language of tolerance! How do you calibrate to something that's interdimensional, that seems to exist in a way that you can't identify or see? This is hard! Yet it will become easier and easier as the earth moves into an energy that's more commensurate with your vibration. That's what's going on as the grids shift, pulling the energy of the planet into a new calibration and alignment.

Congratulations! You're at the next level, working with the book that always seemed too difficult, and you're indeed working with it. Is it any wonder that we marvel at you and your lives? How can we explain that it is *you* who are the heroes of this new energy? You walk from here to there making a difference for the entirety of Planet Earth, all the while asking when you're going to make a difference!

Question #7 – I'm worried about my young adult children.

"Dear Spirit: I have children who are almost grown. At least they think they are. I'm losing contact with them. They don't pay attention to me anymore. I fear for them. I don't know what to do. I've been a good parent and a Lightworker. I've tried to show them love, but they don't listen. I'm afraid for them as they walk into a new Earth. I don't know what they're into or what they might do. I don't know—I just don't. What can I do?"

Well, dear one, let's take first things first. Why don't you sit down and let us hug you for a while? There's nothing for you to do at this moment except to understand some spiritual dynamics. We say this, mother and father: When they were small children, you opened your jar of love and you poured it into that child. For all of these years, your jar poured and poured. Here is new information, yet intuitive. It's also ancient information and lasts forever.

Every single Human Being, as a child, has a jar that's empty, ready to be filled. Whatever the energy is of the parent around them, that jar is permanently open during childhood and will be filled with whatever energy and whatever light or dark goes on within the parent. Now, if you've filled that child's jar with white light, and if you've given them love—a responsible spiritual home—if they've been able to see how love works, then you stand clean in this. Oh, you may worry about them, and that's a typical Human fact. That's where we come in as family to help you . . . to sit next to you and hold your hand and say, "It's done. Your work is finished."

Whatever happens now is their choice, and it's the way of it. You know that. It was the same with you. But here is what you may not have known: Even after you may be gone, that child still has the free choice to reach down and open that jar and discover you! Do you understand what I'm saying? There comes a time in that child's life when they may wish to open the jar. And if they do, they'll discover the love you gave them! They'll start experiencing the memories and the responsibility issues—the things that you told them were the truth. They'll experience the now of you, the truth of what you taught, even if you're not here . . . even if you're a long way away. That is an axiom . . . a rule. It is forever.

The jar is full, and that's the way you send them out . . . prepared and ready, if they don't see it. You haven't failed. It's free choice for the child, but if they wish to open the jar, they're going to find the love that you gave them. And the beauty of this is that from your wisdom, they'll take the jar and they'll pour its contents into their children. Therefore, this is your lineage . . . that what you give a child today may be good for many generations down the line. Sometimes you only see the immediate problems and challenges, never understanding how profound you affect the energy of those who follow you. We speak in love . . . just wanting you to know and understand this . . . to capture for a moment the compassion of what may happen in a special moment with that precious soul who entrusted their childhood to you . . . when they someday open the jar.

Question #8 – How do I talk to my body?

"Dear Kryon: I have heard you say that we can talk to our cells. What does that mean? How do I do that? There are those in graduate status in this room who have come in with situations where they had to talk to their cellular structure in order to still be here."

The ones you speak of [in the seminar of the day] have learned that their enlightenment is not in their heads. Every single cell knows everything! That means your toe, your knee, and your elbow are important—as important as is the crown chakra, that creative spark at the top where you think your spiritual wisdom is happening. It isn't, you know. There are those in this room who are living extended lives right now because they learned a long time ago what it's like to recognize the divinity in every cell within their body—every one.

So the invitation is open to examine that very issue within you and start learning to communicate with yourself. This is much like question two, is it not? You're always wanting to communicate up, aren't you? What about communicating in? Did you know that the more you talk to your cellular structure about who you are and your divinity, the more the communication with family and Spirit will increase? You know it's all tied together, don't you? Your DNA is what is the issue, for all of it carries all the information . . . not just the amount at the top of your head within your brain.

Begin to understand the wholeness of this episode called ascension, spiritual communication, and co-creation. All of it requires a "whole-body" experience. Gone are the days when everything that you are seems to reside at the top of your head. For years we've told you that this was coming . . . and now it's here. The ancient yogis knew it, and showed you how to involve the whole body. Now you're going to find it necessary even to communicate, much less to heal yourselves! Meditation is not an exercise of the brain. It's an exercise of the Human Being— all of it! It's an exercise in compassion, and every cell will know you're in touch. It's a new language you're learning. And that's the truth . . . and that was question eight.

Question #9 – Why are some healed and some not?

Appropriately, questions nine and ten are about healers. Healers in this room and reading this have learned something, and I will tell you in a moment what they've learned. Here's a question that they may have asked and that you may have asked.

"Dear Spirit, I'm a healer. I perform the same energy balance on different people, yet there are totally different reactions. Some are healed, and some are not. Am I doing something wrong?"

Here's what experienced healers will tell you: Healers don't heal; they balance! There's nothing you or anyone else can do on this planet to heal another person without their entire and total consent and intent. But what you can do, lighthouse, is to shine your light so bright that they'll find that safe harbor called "healing" because you balance them to the degree that they can move forward on their own.

You've anchored your light, healer, and you've balanced the person. It's up them, is it not, to decide whether the balancing is sufficient for them to move forward? And this is free choice. So do not be in a position where you admonish yourself for a seeming failure . . . ever! You're doing the work of Spirit, and some of you are doing it in a profound fashion. Yet there are many who will get up from your healing table and never "see" what you do. They'll never feel any of it. They'll go on their way because they chose not to open their compassion, or actively chose not to be healed at this time.

There is a scenario about synchronicity, about co-creation, that isn't always what you think. Sometimes, many of you stay in a certain position or in a condition of nonhealing, waiting for something else to align itself, so that when you finally go for that condition of healing it's going be better than ever! We've said this before. Sometimes a "no" from Spirit at the present means a celebration later. And how would you know that, dear linear person, dear healer? How would you know if you had planted a seed of balance that would later bloom into an amazing flower? The answer is, you don't.

Here is something else for those who regularly sit before energy healers. You go to healer after healer, perhaps involving process after process, then you do something very interesting, dear linear Human Being. If you got a "no" from Spirit [no healing took place], you often throw away the healer, and the healing process . . . and you never return to it. Let me ask you this: If you planted a seed, then gave it two days and nothing happened, would you then throw away the pot, the soil, and the gardener? No! Instead, you often wait . . . knowing about the seasons . . . knowing the way these things work.

Those healers are still around, and the processes they use do work! Perhaps the energy didn't seem to work on you? Well, perhaps you weren't ready yet. Perhaps the timing of everything around you wasn't appropriate. Perhaps your individual path didn't have the wisdom to accept the "whole body" experience yet? Wait, and try again. Don't throw anything away, ever!

Human, are you listening to this? It isn't just with healing. How about the vision you've had of something you feel you should be doing . . . but nothing happened? Did you throw away the idea just because it didn't seem to work? You're not honoring the interdimensionality that we've been teaching you. You must work the linear against the nonlinear! Try it again. Understand that just because it didn't work at the moment you tried it on your linear track, that doesn't mean it's over! Honor the vision and the love that went into it. Honor timing, and the incredible amount of work that goes into preparing to fulfill your greatest intent. What a shame it is to have all the answers just an arm's length away, but unavailable because you thought that the door was linear and could only be opened one time!

Question #10 – Is it appropriate to heal someone who can't decide for themselves?

"Dear Spirit, I'm a healer. Is it appropriate and proper to work a healing on a Human Being who doesn't seem to have the ability to ask for it? This would be a Human Being, for instance, in a coma. It would also be a person in a mental state where they're not balanced. What's the difference between an appropriate life lesson and interference? Is it proper?"

So it would seem that the Human Being in front of you has their free choice "muted," and you ask the question of the appropriateness of a forced healing? There are two answers here: (1) Remember that you don't heal; you balance. Is it therefore appropriate to turn on a light on a dark room? Do you force the occupants to see? No. You enable them to choose! Therefore, the question is, really, "Is it appropriate to balance without permission?" (2) Every Human Being that's imbalanced or is unconscious has a piece of pure balance in every single cell. If the Human brain is in dysfunction, quite often the other cells (billions of them) are fine . . . and they're yelling for balance— every single one! This is no different than when the brain is awake and other parts of the body are in trouble . . . they hurt! Pain is the great communicator of biology to alert the brain that correction and balance are needed at a given area. It's the same in reverse. If the Human is in a comatose state, the cells in the body are trying to balance. They wish to be awake! There's a cry of intent in the brain to the unbalanced person to be balanced. This is often the reason for their anxiety. Although they may be dysfunctional, they're also often depressed, since part of them wishes to be whole . . . but they can't express it.

They may not be able to say it, and they may not be able to communicate it, but that's the truth, for the Human body desires the balance that you call "normal." When "normal" is not there, even though you may not hear it come out of the mouths or even out of the eyes, every cell craves it and asks for it. So, *yes*, it is appropriate that you would work and balance that person. *Yes*, it is appropriate to send light into a dark area. It's not forcing anything. It's only illuminating. Remember this: Sometimes you're the catalyst for an awakening of that Human, which never would have occurred unless you had done something. Sometimes you're their synchronicity! You're their angel! Think about it the next time you pass by someone who seems to be in a state that's beyond conscious reach. Put the energy of balance around them. Send light into them, and then let the free choice of their cells do its work.

Question #11 – Is it proper to heal those around me?

A third healing question comes from a non-healer. It comes from the Lightworker who sees those around him who he wishes to help.

"Dear Kryon, dear Spirit: I have relatives and friends, and I have joyful, spiritual information for them. I have healing for them. I have so many things that I've learned about the way things work. I could help make them whole; I could help make them feel better. I could give them exercises and information, and I might even give them a book that could help. What is it I should do? Is it appropriate? Kryon, you've said that this new energy is non-evangelical. Then what should I do?"

Lightworker, this is perhaps the most profound question of them all. You're the commensurate Humanitarian, are you not? You've learned compassion for self and for others. You're more alert to inhumanity than many, and you grieve harder for the earth than you ever did before. The answer is as it always was: You take care of you. Does that seem like a non-answer? Let me give you the mechanics, and you decide.

The higher the lighthouse stands, the farther the light shines and can be seen. The more anchored the lighthouse is, the less the storm will affect it. As you walk this planet sharing this light, you're going to shine into areas that are dark. The dark areas are where that ever-present "free choice" will be, which is so revered by us all . . . and so pivotal for those around you.

Do you have a relative who lives with you? Perhaps it's a friend whom you love and cherish? And everything within you wishes you could help them—but they're not interested? I'll tell you how they might be interested. Let them see you! Let them see you "live what you believe." Celebrate the job that you don't like. Become tolerant of the person who's intolerable. Smile a joyful smile from day to day—and mean it. Celebrate your life! Heal your body and talk to your cells. Then maybe, just maybe, that person will come to you someday, and say this: "Although I may not believe what you believe, I can see that it's working for you. Where do I begin? How can I have what you have?" Oh, family, don't you long to hear those words? You know who I'm talking to here, don't you? And that's the answer. Could it be so simple? Who said that was simple! Taking care of yourself, vibrating higher, going into ascension status . . . that's not simple. That's work.

Question #12 – How many steps are there in the ascension process?

"Dear Kryon, how many steps are there to ascension? I'd like a definitive answer, please. I've heard many versions."

Here's the truth: There's only one step. One. That's it. It exists at that point in time when you give intent to move past where you are—to go to the next level—to allow permission to change your vibration. That is the "ascension beginning."

Each Human Being can then intellectualize all they wish to about how many steps it may take for them to get to that goal. They may climb any number of rungs they wish. They may go through whatever procedures to achieve the same goal. Some may go through two, some may go through twelve, and some will say it's just too hard—too many steps, and stop. So the real answer is that there's one step—the step where the Human Being says to Spirit, "I'm ready. I want to go beyond where I am and move into a lighter, higher vibration." Then let your own free choice decide what you wish to do, and how many steps you wish to climb. The one step of intent starts the process, and the rest is variable depending on the individual.

Question #13 – Is shining your light into dark places considered an invasion?

"Dear Kryon, what is the appropriateness and the integrity of shining our light into areas of the earth, whether it's at the job or in the family, when it wasn't asked for? I want to be honest. I want to have integrity. I want to be a Lightworker, but isn't this evangelistic? This isn't about healing. It's about living ordinary life."

Here is something we've given you before, but here it is again. You can't hear it too much! It's the core issue of your lives. It's the guiding principle behind what you do and why you do it. It's also similar to question #11.

You show up in a dark place and hold the light. Those who are in that place, searching for a path, are doing their very best. Suddenly, however, they have more choices than they ever did before, due to the light being shown. This is not evangelistic. They don't know your name or what you stand for. All they're aware of is that they can now see better! Instead of forcing your truth on them, or even speaking at all, instead you're giving them choice. They, like you, have free choice to go where they wish. But now they have better light in which to make their decisions.

Let me ask you this, lighthouse: When the master of the vessel steers his grand ship into the safety of the harbor because the lighthouse showed the way, does he leave his ship and run to meet the lighthouse keeper? No. They never meet. The light didn't convince this captain of anything, either. It simply gave him the choice to see something that was in front of him. He made his own choices when he steered his ship with his own hands.

Indeed, it's appropriate to illuminate those paths that are dark and those places that need illuminating. Speaking of this, would you like to know where the best places you could illuminate right now, are? Right this minute—right this instant? Earlier today you were shown the profound influence that science now admits is part of Human consciousness. You're actually beginning to see what "the light" might be!

Today, direct your Human consciousness and the light that it gives into the darkest areas of the planet. Take it to the Oval Office of your land! Don't force an energy there; instead, simply place it there as wisdom. Take it to those areas that need it the most. Why not take it to Kashmir right now? There's much going on there. Why not take it into Palestine and Jerusalem right now, for there's much going on there. Why don't you take it to the mothers of all of these who are wondering what the future will bring for their sons and daughters ten years from now? They need it! Why don't you give them love and hug them while you're at it. All of what I've said is possible. It's what a Lightworker does. It's what Human consciousness is all about. It's interdimensional and awesome in its power to create change through illumination.

Question #14 – Kryon, are you leaving at the end of the year?

"Dear Kryon, we understand that you're leaving at the end of this year when the grids are done. In the first book, you talked of this. Is this true?"

In 1989, we gave you information that we were here to help set the grids and that many were involved. This was "The Kryon Group" we spoke of. We indicated the arrival time and departure time of that group. We also told you that the energy of Kryon has always been on the planet. I set the grids originally, and I am a permanent fixture here. I did not arrive in 1989, but rather, the grid entourage changing-group did . . . in response to your changing of the planet's goals. That is the group that will leave at the end of this year. That is the energy that will depart, but I remain as I always have been, in service to the family who sits before me.

My energy is just like yours: It's angelic, yet it's part physics and part love. And that, dear Human Being, is also the energy at the heart and the center of every atom in the universe. It's not a dichotomous situation, since both belong together, intertwined. For it was the love of God that created the planet . . . all the spiritual and physical attributes together. I remain on this Earth until the last Human. Then and only then will I depart.

We raise from where you are and begin to retreat back to the crack in the veil that you allowed to take place today. Someday you might think about this meeting. You may ask yourself, who came to see whom? Know that this day, this entourage, came to see you, and some of you know that, for you have felt it this very day. And so it is.

Kryon

"Questions from Readers"

Formerly seen only in
In The Spirit E-Magazine
(**www.kryon.com**)

Chapter Fourteen

"Questions From Readers"

Here are questions from the readers of the Kryon books.
These questions and answers have only previously been seen
in the "Q&A" section of the extensive Kryon Internet
E-Magazine, In The Spirit. Want to see more? Go to
[www.kryon.com]

Question:

Dear Kryon: I've been given a water filter that uses magnets in the filtration process as an attachment to the plumbing pipe. The filtering system claims to generate Pi water, also known as living water. Should I use this type of filtration sparingly due to the magnets utilized? Also, what about magnetic mattresses and chairs?

Answer:

Let me talk about these things once again. The use of magnets to alter substances and to create cellular stimulation is in a beginning phase on your planet. You're just starting to realize that they change and influence the matter and biology around you.

There are several things that you should be aware of. Without full knowledge of what you're doing, you might accidentally be altering or "signaling" your body to do things you didn't expect. The makers of these devices—including the chairs you rest on and sit on—are of good integrity, but their integrity does not automatically give them full knowledge of the details of magnetic influence on cellular structure.

At this infancy of your development, you're only aware of the stimulating attributes of the magnetics. You don't actually know what's happening, or the layers of DNA that are affected. You do know that they seem to stimulate and seemingly help some situations. You're also aware that a person can actually feel them working.

To stimulate your cellular structure for hours and hours with small passive magnets is an extremely coarse way of giving your cells information. Someday you'll discover just how elegant the cell needs to be to see these forces—fine-tuned to awaken them into very specific activities. Magnetic cell balancing and attunement is a refined process that needs to see active "designer fields," not an avalanche of random magnetic polarities. You're throwing the entire lower spectrum at them in a crude method. It would be like discovering herbs for the first time and taking them all at once in large doses, with the idea that one of them might help you.

We suggest that you honor your body's internal balancing system. If you feel intuitively that the system you have chosen is helping you, then use it only 50 percent of the time. Magnetics is a powerful tool! To willingly sit in a generic magnetic field as a "normal" situation is foolish. Use the system to stimulate your body into normal balancing behavior. Spend half your time with it, then let the body recover or balance, according to what it wishes. Then, just in case you're accidentally giving your cells less than positive signals, they have time to correct and balance. In case you're sending it healing signals, then the body can complete and enhance that.

For those who say, "It's helping . . . I can feel it," I say this: You can get the same reaction with a stimulating drug. What you don't understand yet is that magnetics is even more potent than chemistry.

Question:

Dear Kryon: I've recently read that Planet X will be returning to our solar system in approximately 14 months, and will cause terrible events to happen to our planet . . . a pole shift, earthquakes, floods, volcanic eruptions. It will put the earth into darkness for decades, and there will be a 90 percent loss of human life due to starvation and all the other catastrophes. This planet is supposed to come around every 3,600 years, the last time being during the time of the exodus out of Egypt. Many ancient cultures left accounts of this huge red planet causing devastating loss of life. I am asking you, Kryon, to please tell us if this is going to happen.

Answer:

Dear ones, again we give you the short answer: no.

Does this sound like the "new Earth" to you? Does this sound like the new path of reality that we spoke of? Does this sound like grand hope for the planet? Do you really think the Kryon messages of the last decade would have left something like this out? This is the old energy—fear-based information that we spoke of almost 12 years ago, which originated from soothsayers and fearmongers who wished to create disturbances in the light and feed on the results. We have told you this: Beware of those who would rob you of your hope, for they diminish your light by planting seeds of fear within you. These same forces will tell you that Kryon is evil as well.

Remember some of the recent prophecies of the past? What about the grand alignment of planets pulling the earth out of orbit? Remember the comet and the trailing pieces? It was to disgorge evil forces as it went by. Remember prophecies about the "three days of darkness" as your earth passed into the astronomical attribute called the Photon Belt? Remember Armageddon? How quickly many of you forget the things that "didn't happen" as you willingly grab on to other fears about new things that won't happen either. Do you really think that decades of astronomical observations from thousands of sources would somehow have kept this a secret from you?

It's time to put the pieces together, and see the reality that you've changed the paradigm of Earth, including the old prophecies of destruction, doom, and horror. Go inside and ask your Higher-Self. It will hug you and give you the same answer that I have.

Concentrate on the problems at hand that you can see. This is where the light is needed. Don't cast your energy to the fear of the things you can't see, giving away your power. You are needed, Lightworker . . . to use your light for the existing clearing of the current situations.

Question:

Dear Kryon: You have channelled that the "real" work of Kryon begins in the year of the five (2003). What is the "real" work of Kryon after the spiritual aspects of the grid are finished?

Question:

Dear Kryon: The grid is almost ready and should be activated at the end of 2002. What would the effects of this grid be on us? Will we feel different? P.S. Thank you for all the amazing work you're doing!

Answer:

Over the years, we have only set the stage for Earth's potential. We told you that the magnetic grid is the engine of cellular communication. We told you that the grid is also responsible for helping to posture the veil . . . your duality.

When it's finished, the teaching begins. What did it affect, and how can you now use the new gifts and tools that have been put into place? What are the new attributes? Will you feel different?

You should be feeling it now! Many have complained that what they got used to spiritually now moves away from them. This is what will stop, as the grids settle down and bring stability to your spiritual process. Soon, you'll be more comfortable with the new feelings.

These are the real teachings of Kryon. In 2003, we'll begin describing what the new grid attributes are.

Question:

Dear Kryon: I'm a hypnotherapist who desires to call forth the highest and best within each client. I've studied what my teachers have taught, but I'm left "wanting." I feel as though I'm being called from within to do my work quite differently than all the books and classes about hypnotherapy have stated. No matter why a client comes into my office, I find myself desiring only to discuss what they've "forgotten," telling them that they are already whole and loved. I find myself not wanting to discuss the issue that brought them to my office at all. I want to call up from within them, their truth. If we truly honored ourselves and others, wouldn't our problems disappear? We would simply choose not to overeat, abuse drugs/alcohol, be depressed, etc.

Answer:

Dear healer, everything you've said is correct. Over and over we've stated that the core information . . . the miracles . . . the physics . . . and event the ascension information is stored in every cell. Part of what we're doing with the magnetic grid is to make it more available as the veil lifts slightly in this new energy.

But look at your question. It's not about the Humans who come to you, but rather it's about you! It's about your frustration to go through layers of a system that's not fine-tuned, in order to help those who come to you to "see" this reality.

The answer? Ask for help to create a system using your gifts and tools to open a window of remembrance for those who sit in front of you. Slowly lead them into self-discovery, letting them know that they have the answers and the storehouse to find them.

What you need is what we're asking every enlightened Human Being on the planet to create" patience.

Know that you're dearly loved.

Question:

Dear Kryon: I'm a mother of a seven-year-old son diagnosed with autism. I've worked with energy for what seems to be all my life. During the past five years, I've been getting concepts that I don't really understand. Your channeling has been helping. However, perhaps those of you who read this (I trust it will be read by whomever Spirit intends) may have encountered this as well.

Here goes...my son's magnetic system does not feel the same as ours. Is there a possibility that his DNA may have different magnetic structures than non-autistics? I can almost see this in my mind as strands running through some sort of chrysalis-type prism. Okay, I know that sounds nuts. I also feel this same thing around dolphins. He is particularly drawn to the calls of humpback-whale recordings. Is it possible that the cetacean connection to autism is in the magnetics? His communication (still nonverbal) has been progressing in leaps and bounds over the past year. Are the magnetic grid alignments becoming more compatible with autistics' systems?

Answer:

Dear one, for you and the others who work with these

children, I honor you! We told you earlier that they are mostly savants. These children are indeed born with DNA differences of the kind that are magnetically enhanced. The difference is that they are more geared to an interdimensional existence rather than the 4D existence that you live in. So, yes, this is a magnetic cellular attribute. Some are even calling autistics "rainbow children." Your intuition is correct. Here's more.

(1) They wish to communicate and live out of linearity. They don't understand things in a row or in a line. They'll do far better with overall concepts that steer them to a pseudo-linear action, so that they can live in your world. If it were possible, they would love to communicate without "in-a-row," linear verbal speech. They would rather do it all at once using a "thought group." Their frustration is that everything around them is boxing in their expansiveness, and they have to stop and make sense of it.

Can you even imagine what it would be like to be born in a world where you had 3D, and everyone else had 2D? Let's say there was no depth—only height and width. You wanted to "reach inside" things, and you could see how—only to have an invisible wall stop your hand each time you tried, or stop your mind each time. You couldn't even walk around! Others around you would call you retarded, as they watched the funny kid who couldn't navigate in a simple 2D world. You would spend most of your time looking at things, trying to decipher if what you were seeing was true or not for the reality you were in.

(2) They tend to live partially in a reality that Humans don't see or understand. Where are they mentally, you sometimes ask, as they stare off into space. The truth? They're actually seeing and participating in interdimensional attributes of life . . . or trying to. They also can "see" the other life on Earth—the life that you don't even acknowledge yet. More on this some other time.

(3) They're attuned to the energy of the dolphins and whales, but more specifically, the dolphin. There has actually been research on this from your scientists, so it's not as odd as it sounds. There's communication at a distance between autistic children and these sea mammals. If they ever actually establish a one-on-one relationship to a single animal, it lasts a lifetime.

(4) Yes, the grid system of the planet is going to make them more comfortable . . . and you less comfortable. We've been channelling over the last year about becoming interdimensional. Perhaps it's time that Humans moved a bit in the direction of the autistics, instead of teaching them how to exist in yours.

Question:

Dear Kryon: As one who is soon to embark professionally on a path as a spiritual healer/facilitator, I'm wrestling a bit with the question of "healing"—that is, the significance of discovering the root cause of illnesses, emotional distress, ineffectiveness, powerlessness, etc. So much material has been given in the past about the impact of childhood traumas, and now we hear so much about how a person can be impacted negatively by past-life traumas. Personally, I believe "remembering" can aid in releasing charged/negative energy, but somehow I feel that this may not be necessary to healing anymore. Perhaps it once was in the "old energy"? My passion is to help others "remember who they are" and in that remembering, therein lies the power to self-heal.

P.S. May I say how very much I love the Kryon energy/spirit and feel such appreciation for what the Kryon entity/spirit/group is doing for humans and Mother Earth? I also love and appreciate Lee Carroll's courage and willingness to channel the wonderful Kryon messages. My heart overflows with love.

Answer:

Dear one, as so many of you are now starting to realize, what we told you over a decade ago is coming to the forefront. Yes, there is much in the cells that affect what you think and do. There is some information "stamped" into your interdimensional DNA that shouts to you of your past, and much that shouts to you of your present. The idea of "remembering" who you are and who you were is still very important.

What we're now teaching, however, is that it's no longer necessary to identify the exact parts of these remembrance items one-by-one. Instead, the new gifts of Spirit are creating a shortcut through all of this within the new powers of the Human Being. The grid is also playing its part in all of this. We don't wish to diminish the work of self-discovery, but there's so much more to do now than to spend a lifetime ... revisiting the last lifetime! Therefore, we've begun teaching about the "attunement to the cosmic lattice," and the "neutral" gift. We're encouraging Humans to vibrate at such a level that they may create a situation of clearing that's so profound that the old vows are neutralized, and the DNA is awakened. This is the Human becoming interdimensional . . . something we've spoken about over and over in these last months.

This creates the kinds of changes within a Human that are seen by everyone around them . . . an increase in wisdom, joy, and integrity . . . a health boost, and yes, even the ability to slow down aging. It's about pure intent, and always will be. Pure intent is a compassion catalyst that creates a unique energy that was used by shamans and gurus. It's the secret to a long, joyful life, and one that helps the planet. It creates the true Lightworker.

Regarding remembering: The Human who tries to fly on his own will fail. The Human who remembers that he is an angel will soar to the heavens.

Question:

Dear Kryon: Very often I talk to you. I have faith that you hear, even though I'm just a tiny little individual here in Australia. For a long time, I've wanted to serve humanity, and I somehow know that's what I'm supposed to do (or choose to do prior to coming). In my service (working at a hospital here in Western Australia), I do lots of different work, such as serving patients meals, cleaning the ward, etc. I love my work, and it is a joy, but sadly, I find that some people choose to run me down, insisting that I should be sitting in an office and putting my office skills to good use. I don't agree. However, I would like to know that I am in my contract, doing what I contracted to do, because I don't want to finally get home without achieving my purpose. Thank you for loving me, Kryon.

Answer:

Dear one, earlier this year I channelled a message just for you. It was called "The Ordinary Human." You say, "I am just a tiny little individual." There is no such thing to God. Your perceived smallness is your duality trying to tell you that in 4D, you appear small. It's a higher power within you, however, that knows better.

As you walk in that place where you think you're not honored, and where you think you're doing mundane things, I want you to remember that with each step, you illuminate dark areas wherever you go. People who will never meet you are blessed by your passing by, and those whom you stop and touch are blessed by your willingness to help. Stay at this job as long as it is possible, knowing that you're never alone, and that you're indeed in your contract for now. Follow your passion!

Blessed is the Human Being who understands the term Lightworker, and what it really means.

Question:

Dear Kryon: It's been proven that a single cell cannot survive and function without external help. It has receptors that communicate with the outside world, and without this communication, the cell stops functioning and eventually dies. Since we're talking about the lowest common denominator for biological life as we know it, one would presuppose that Spirit in one form or another is the communicator.

Kryon, you tell us that each of us has a group of family entities that are with us for our life of experience on this plane of existence. We, in a biological sense, are made up of millions (or billions) of cells, each with its own communication facility. Does this mean that we have millions (or billions) of spirits to assist us in our life experience, and if so, does this redefine the function of our Higher-Selves, and perhaps the structure?

Answer:

The question is a wonderful one, for it exposes what we've told you is the unexplainable. One or many? How many? How much? None of these questions are answerable, since we've been telling you that the interdimensionality of what you're being asked to experience is completely foreign to your consciousness. You still want to take an angel, put skin and wings on it, and give it a name. Every angel that ever visited Earth is a legion of energy. It has tendrils to every piece of God in the Universe. It is in communication with all of God, even with one voice. It is everywhere, yet only in one place.

Therefore, the answer to your question is yes. It's a definition we've been teaching you for the last six months. Also, know that your original premise of Spirit being the "link" of cellular communication is also correct. Do you remember what happened with the yogi who died? He laid in state for two weeks before his cells knew he was dead! What was going on? It was cellular communication at its highest . . . all connected to The Cosmic Lattice in a way that brought about communication with Spirit and the body, but the former was the most profound.

Those billions of spirits you spoke of have an interdimensional body, which in 4D looks a lot like one entity. Such is the way of your reality. We've told you that Kryon is a group—but not as you think. It's not a group with many names. It's a group with one name. You are the same, and all that is within you also has this same property.

If I told you that I loved you, would you ask, "How many loves are you giving me?" Would you ask, "What are the elemental parts of the love energy, and how many are there?" You could, but the answers would be comical to your brain. The 4D Human wishes to linearize, compartmentalize, and categorize everything it experiences. When you eat soup, do you count the soup molecules in each spoon? Or do you say, "The soup in the bowl is one soup, representing billions of soup parts"?

You can see by our answer that we're beginning to broach the core issue of God. As you grow in your enlightenment, you're going to realize eventually how the "family" is connected to you outside of your immediate 4D experience. You're going to realize that the true cellular connection is God.

Question:

Dear Kryon: As we begin to experience interdimensional energies, what changes are occurring in our physical body, especially to the pineal and thymus glands? How will these changes manifest in our day-to-day reality (if at all)? What symptoms might we experience as we hold more light?

Answer:

Eventually you'll find an awakened thymus. This may be noticed in about a decade, if at all. As to what symptoms you might experience? Not all of them are positive, but neither are they as you grow up:

You might experience occasional headaches, ringing in the ears, unusual sleep patterns, being overly tired (sometimes), an increasing awareness of the feelings of others, increased sensitivity in certain situations in crowds, a change in musical and/or art preferences, and a realization that some of the friends you've selected may not serve you anymore.

Question:

Lately I've been unable to tolerate certain situations—for example, going into a store or mall where there's a lot of confusion and noise. The same goes for certain kinds of music. I've also had problems around certain people, where I've had to leave their presence for the same reason. I told a friend recently that it's as if "my cells hurt" when I'm exposed to certain things. What's going on? Is it because I'm vibrating at a higher level? Will this pass, or will I always be so sensitive?

Answer:

The answer has already been given in the question above, but also know that none of these things are permanent. You're in a physical learning situation, and many may temper with time. The symptoms that may remain, however, are the new preferences in music and quality of friendship.

Question:

Dear Kryon: I've had profound experiences with my animals and animals in general all of my life. In recent years, I have to say that they've represented my strongest link in the Universe to "God." The animals in my life today have healed me and given me strength to go on in more ways than I can express in words. I believe that they're sent, or perhaps come to Earth, as volunteers and teachers for Humans. Can you give us more information on how everyone can learn from and communicate with the animals in their lives? Also, please comment on "their karma," as compared to "our karma," and how this concept interfaces with the potential for future planetary peace and evolution.

Answer:

We've mentioned before that certain animals are here completely for the Human experience. Not only do they teach you about the way Earth works, but some are actually designed to give you unconditional love. They also teach you communication.

Animals don't have karma in the same way a Human Being does. Instead, they have purpose. It's difficult to explain, but they're here to serve the planet, and to balance it for you. They incarnate, but they have only one purpose, and that is to support the planet so that you may be enhanced. The ones you call pets, which you love dearly, incarnate back to you personally if you will allow it.

As you can imagine, there are many kinds of service that these creatures offer, but the ones you believe are "sent," indeed are.

Question:

Dear Kryon: In which direction do we place our head when sleeping? One channel suggests that it helps to place our heads pointing to the north. But there's no elucidation as to whether this is applicable globally, or if it's only relevant to the northern hemisphere. I definitely did feel different when I slept with head toward the north when I was in India. Now I'm in Tanzania, which is in the southern hemisphere, but quite close to the equator. Do I now keep my head pointing north or south when sleeping? Or is it that it simply doesn't matter which way it's directed?

Answer:

Your question is a good one, since it shows that there may be a misunderstanding about this. Sleeping with your body positioned in a certain direction, and also certain body exercises (including spinning) are for temporary balance only. They're not considered as instructions for a lifetime.

About the north and south? Yes, try to point your head to the pole that's closest to you for a few nights. When on the equator, it won't matter. What does this say to you about the equator? There's much hidden here about some of the consciousness setups on the planet, and where the most unbalance and unrest is. Those on the equator will have the hardest time creating and maintaining balance.

Question:

Dear Kryon: About the Merkabah: Is the breathing technique the only way to connect to my Merkabah, or can I accomplish the same thing through other methods? If so, kindly enlighten me about those method(s). Also, is smoking, apart from being a "health hazard, also detrimental to spiritual progress?

Answer:

There are many Merkabah-enhancing techniques, and breathing is one very good one. That one is about oxygen, and the effect of intent combined with living oxygenation. Another is the attunement to the lattice, which is also scientific [and which has been discussed at length]. Still another is the alignment of cellular memory, which is just being learned, and hard to itemize the way you might wish it to be. Many more ways are coming, and as the grid shifts to accommodate your new abilities, they'll be revealed.

Your habit of smoking in itself is not detrimental to spiritual progress. However, anything you willingly do to shorten your life span sends a message to all the cells in your body, as well as your spiritual helpers, that you don't expect to live a full life. That tells your cells that you're not here to take full advantage of the gifts you're given.

This is the same for those who overeat, or who willingly give their physical bodies a challenge in other areas with any other type of substance abuse. For some time now we've told you that you're able to dismiss the most severe habits without the trauma that's normally associated with it. It's up to you, as it always has been. Let the teachers see this . . . that they should be an example to others as far as what can be accomplished.

Question:

Dear Kryon: I have a question that seems somewhat silly to me, but I'm curious. I've been reading in Chapter 7 of Book Six about life colors. I'm very interested in healing with color, sound, and touch. How much are we affected by the colors we choose to wear or have around us? For example, if I wear a color that doesn't harmonize with my skin or eye tone, or if I dye my hair red if it's supposed to be brown, do I create disharmony and imbalance? I don't believe this is connected with life colors, or is it? At any rate, I'd still like to know how important it is for us to wear, or have harmonizing colors, around us.

Answer:

Dear one, the use of colors and the attribute of life colors is all related to healing and the work of your intent. You can't harm your body energy by wearing mismatching colors or cosmetically changing the colors of hair against its normal state. You also won't unbalance yourself if you do this. You might create a reaction from others, however! [Kryon joke]

Understand that the color information is given to enhance the energy around you. Therefore, it's a grand tool. By wearing specific intuitive colors that suit you for the day, you can enhance your balance for that day. It always changes, since you always change, and it "shakes hands" with the astrological setup that belongs to you. Therefore, you may benefit one day from wearing a color that's in harmony with your life color, and also the astrological aspects. Sometimes it's quite profound, and it can help balance you on a day that might be difficult. Other times, it just "feels good." Use your intuition as you select your colors.

This is not a complex subject. It's easy to learn, and much has been written about it by others. The study of color for balance is one of your greatest gifts.

Question:

Dear Kryon: I had once asked you a question about a very dear friend of mine who's been sentenced to a Southern prison for 20 years. He's innocent of the crime that he's been incarcerated for. He's very much a human being of great light. Is there anything he can do to be free of this experience—to change it? A visualization, *or a certain type of energy work that he can do for himself so he can be freed? Thank you!*

Answer:

Those who suffer the injustice of other Humans have profound contracts to be here—to be in places where they can effect change. It is their life lesson. To be free? It can't happen until they're free from the mental anguish and the feeling of being the victim. Once they free their consciousness from all of it so that they're truly fine with the thought that this is their job on Earth, then the other 4D things around their situation may begin to be cleared if that's their intent.

We recommend trying some of the new energy techniques that are coming into their own at the moment, one being the EMF Balancing Technique. The idea is that as goes your peace, so goes your life. If you can truly be at peace with your contract, then you can see the bigger picture. That allows wisdom to decide if you're "needed" where you are, or if it's best to move on.

Look at this: It's a total empowering situation that puts the Human in control of their own reality. This is what we teach.

Question:

Dear Kryon: The first question is one that I'm sure every quack asks, but I'll ask it any way. In 1990, in our spirit group, I channelled an entity who called himself Kryon. At the time, I had never heard of him. I saw myself looking through what I interpreted as a "screen door." I had not heard of the grid at that time. I channelled information briefly, then as one member of the group sought personal information, the energy was quite clear that all questions must be of a universal nature. That was in southwest Alabama. I have never channelled that entity again. I've received information from other channels, but not Kryon. What was that channelling? What was the significance of it?

Answer:

Indeed you have validated your own experience! You never heard of my energy, yet you named it correctly. You also didn't know about the grid, yet you "saw" it. Was it real? Yes. Was it Kryon? Yes.

Anyone can occasionally "pull in" the energy of Kryon, and we encourage it. So this is what happened to you. We love it when this occurs, and we honor the time that is ours with you. We cherish the times when it happens, and again tell you that it is given as validation that you are family! Celebrate with us whenever it happens.

You are dearly loved. There's nothing that says that the Kryon entity or any other will be permanent in your energy, so don't think anything about it if you move on to other things. The only permanent Kryon channels are the nine I've indicated in my past writings. Here is a fact I have never shared, and one that will help you to validate the Kryon energy from others who say they are Kryon channels: If you find a Human who claims to be a world-Kryon channel (one of the nine), and you wish to know if he/she is valid, that Human will be channelling only Kryon. If other entities occasionally are present, they'll be part of a Kryon message.

You are dearly loved!

Kryon

"The Rainbow Filter"

Dealing with an Expanded Consciousness
An Article by Jan Tober

Chapter Fifteen

"The Rainbow Filter"

Dealing With an Expanded Consciousness
An article by
Jan Tober

My understanding is that on March 8, 2002, an asteroid the size of Orlando came closer to Earth than the experts would have preferred. On that day, I found myself around people with very frayed nerves! The asteroid pass reminded me of how people are affected by unusual energy situations. At the end of that day, I sat with my good friend Karen Wolfer, who had shared the day's experience with me. I asked her to take notes as I began to channel some information regarding our new expanded energy fields, and how they interact with normal 4D reality (*4D* is the new term for what used to be 3D. It's now height, width, depth, and time).

We both acknowledged that an expanded Human who comes into a "normal" situation is very much like the asteroid we experienced . . . passing by and affecting others.

During my interesting day on March 8, I experienced my guides and angels watching me to see how I would work with the energy of those around me. Later, I was reminded that we are all "making it up" as we go along, or being "in the now." I was also reminded that we've never before carried this much spiritual energy on the planet, and we're learning how to be as comfortable as possible with it. The only message that came through from my guides during the experience was: "Stay centered and even with everything and everyone. Place your intent that truth will prevail."

Later, as I began a full channelling session, I was told that what we all learned that day was to "be still, and gently wrap our ever-expanding auric field in an iridescent rainbow filter." This "filter" allows those who look at us to see our energy in a comfortable way, instead of the way many of us are being "sensed." It's "The Rainbow Filter," allowing those around us permission to pull out the colors from the filter that will enhance their own situation. Therefore, it enables those around us to relax and be safe with who we are.

We're slowly realizing that the vibrations we carry as Lightworkers sometimes have actual 4D effects wherever we walk. We are "sensed" as different and without the filter, those differences could be anything . . . even perceived as dangerous depending on the mind-set of the observer.

Since the 9-11, many are in positions of security and stewardship . . . guarding places and events. This has created an extra energy of awareness on their part, and their "antennae" are up, looking for those who might stick out . . . or who are different. Guess who often matches those parameters? We do!

Some of you are asking, "Really?" Can we really affect physical things around us? Let me tell you what we've experienced and what others *are* experiencing just in the physical alone: Many have told us that their new fields are setting off car alarms, draining batteries, and (for us) three hotel fire-alarm evacuations in one year during Kryon group overnight stays! If physical things are being affected this way, think of how consciousness is being affected in the emotional and light-bodies of those around us.

The Rainbow Filter actually looks like a very fine mesh or veil. This process allows you to radiate your full light, while allowing others to perceive only the colors or the amount of light that's comfortable for them.

You might ask, "How do you activate this filter?" Before you go into a very structured situation (airport, business, etc), ask if it would be appropriate to activate the filter. Then (if you get a yes), place your intent, and visualize a beautiful rainbow veil mesh around your being. This is *not* a protective energy or a shield of defense. Instead, this is a creative, active process that allows comfortable interaction with you and others.

Remember what Kryon said about the new energy? He said we're moving from the metaphor of the immune system to the thymus system—from "fight and destroy" to "tolerate and unify." The Rainbow Filter, therefore, fits well into this new energy, allowing you to move around in a more expanded state with ease. In this new process, you're also helping others to feel peaceful around you, and certainly more peaceful in general.

This will help you filter your energy field so you won't disturb other beings or electronics. In addition to this, remember that you may be somewhat "invisible" to certain Human Beings. So consciously place your intent to being "visible" when needed. Being "invisible" actually means that you're seen but not noticed. That is, you're neutral on a person's "radar screen." Being "visible" means that you wish to be noticed for who you are.

The urgency I experienced regarding the channelling was similar to what I experienced around "The Death Phantom," in that it seemed very important to publish this information and share it with the readers. (see *Kryon Book Eight,* page 286). Since this message, I've been investigating how others are using The Rainbow Filter, and what changes they're noticing. From their reports, it seems to have greatly improved their interactions with other adults, children, animals, and potentially challenging situations. It also seems to help one's mental attitude and sense of well-being as well.

We all have to walk day to day in this new energy. Together, we're all learning the best ways to create solutions as we go, making it a win-win situation for everyone. The potential here is to create more peace in our lives and for those around us. May peace prevail on our beautiful planet!

Namaste,

— Jan Tober

From the writer:

So you think perhaps becoming "invisible" to the attention of others may be a silly idea? Want to hear a real life experince that will warm your heart about this exact thing?

Read on . . . to the story of Fété and Clément and their miraculous escape from a very dangerous place.

— Lee Carroll

You have to ask yourself at some point: "Why did I come back, knowing that this was the time when all the prophecies would converge to create Armageddon?" We say it's because there was part of you that knew that in reality, change could happen. Because at the cellular level, you knew how things work! You knew that you had the power to change it, and you did.

Now you sit in the new Earth with a promise of new energy, one that is seemingly tearing itself apart with change at the moment, bringing down the old foundation so that it can rebuild on level ground.

Kryon

"The African Experience"

Intro by Marc Vallée
Told by Fété and Clément

Chapter Sixteen

"The African Experience"
Life's Amazing Synchronicities
by Marc Vallée

Life has its many surprises. Some are of a somewhat challenging nature, but others are so sweet. In November of 1999, I was invited by a group from the Ivory Coast to speak to them in the context of my work as a publisher of spiritual books and my involvement with a nonprofit organization called "Convergence." In *Kryon Book 7*, I have shared a few words about this organization's connection with the *Council of Elders* project.

During my first journey discovering Africa, and my bond with this land, my hosts told me about a Congolese couple (Clément and Fété) who had just left the Ivory Coast and were now residing in Montreal, and said that I had to meet them. So, following their guidance, I contacted them, and this was the beginning of a beautiful friendship.

The synchronicity here is quite interesting, for Clément and Fété had heard about the Kryon teachings when they were in Kinshasa. In fact, they had read many books from Ariane Publications that Fété's sister in France had sent them. Clément was a university teacher over there, and he also worked for the Intercontinental Hotel as a general manager. Fété was a businesswoman who had also built a library of spiritual books and owned an African art gallery. They also published a newsletter called "Le Bosquet," meaning "the bush," that the initiate recognizes as the symbol for a source of wisdom. So not only did we connect through the teachings that Ariane publishes, but they became important counselors for the Convergence project. Now we work quite closely together.

Convergence's main goal is to help Western societies realize the wisdom of many of the indigenous values, and to see the importance of considering them in our choices as both a society and in our paths as individuals. We believe that Western society is somewhat lacking in "managing" world affairs and would gain a lot by considering the ways of the indigenous peoples of this planet. It's time now for the present to blend with the past if we are to succeed in creating a sustainable future. The "natives" not only recognize and feel the consciousness in nature and Mother Earth, but they know how to create a sacred space, allowing life to fulfill its potential. We understand that not all is perfect in the indigenous ways, but it's fundamental that we work together to conceive a better world for our children.

So Convergence is now in the process of establishing study centers (we hope to eventually be active on the different continents) to contact and build trusting relationships with the elders of these indigenous communities and bring them to play in guiding roles in our social choices.

For some reason, circumstances caused us to open our first center in Abidjan. The people over there welcome the ideas of Convergence, and we are now working on a conference project for this fall (2002), and we will be visiting villages for a more profound field experience. So we now have a true base for our project in a house that has been renovated, we have more than 2,000 books donated by publishers in France and Québec, and a little Internet cafe. We are ready for the important work ahead.

Clément and Fété have been guiding us throughout the entire process. We even went to the Ivory Coast together in May 2001.

This special meeting of souls would not have been possible if Clément and Fété had stayed in Kinshasa. The reason they came to Montreal is explained in the text that follows. It is a very touching story. Clément is a Tutsi, and for this reason he was caught in ethnic-cleansing events. Faith and hope finally overcame atrocious moments that the couple went through in the Congo, and the teachings of Kryon played a special role here. They are now on the advisory committee of Convergence and enjoy life here in Québec. Fété even likes to walk outside on those beautiful winter days when a gentle snow falls on Montreal. She likes to say, "Where you are sown, you must grow."

For more information, to receive our newsletter, or to make a donation, please contact us. Our director, Joëlle Currat, will be pleased to answer you.

Convergence
1217, Bernard av. West, Suite 101
Outremont, Qc
Canada, H2V 1V7
514-279-0911 - Email: <fconver@cam.org>

P.S. By the way, on that first trip in November 1999, I met a beautiful Ivory Coast woman named Siame, whom I married a year later. This vision of Convergence is dear to her heart.

Marc Vallée

"The Presence of Kryon in Our Life Experience"
by
Fété and Clément

The following story was presented live April 28, 2001, at the Kryon Conference in Montréal, Québec, Canada, in front of 950 people. Fété and Clément took turns speaking.

Fété:

The wonderful experience we are pleased to share with you very briefly today occurred during the civil war that broke out in an African country in 1998.

Clément:

We can now call that experience "wonderful" because we understand the messages and teachings of Kryon that were sent to us at the very time when we most needed them. That was a great synchronicity, as Kryon frequently reminds us throughout his works. And you will realize the truth of that as you listen to our story.

Fété:

Flaming nationalism, coupled with tribal hatred toward an ethnic group that was supposedly at the root of the rebellion, led to a real manhunt. Like many of his people, Clément was arrested and immediately transferred to a military camp where prisoners were being executed as they were brought in.

After four days of fruitless searching, I had no idea what had become of Clément. Was he alive or dead? Finally I met a soldier* who agreed, for a price, to track down Clément in the dungeons and, thanks to his intervention, I was able to locate Clément.

That same soldier later agreed to serve as a go-between for a discreet exchange of correspondence and took a little bread and water to Clément. Through him, I made an arrangement with the jailers to ensure Clément's protection: Every time that those who were to be killed were supposed to be taken from the dungeons in the middle of the night, Clément would be moved. That saved Clément's life—he was hauled out of a cell just 20 minutes before 172 others who were detained with him were executed.

Two weeks after his arrest, I was informed by an acquaintance, a Western businessman,* that the capital was about to fall. According to his informants, the rebels were already in the suburbs of the capital, and he strongly urged me to find a way to negotiate Clément's release, as there were already plans to massacre the prisoners if the capital should be taken. What he meant was that I should pay whatever it took to get Clément out. In the electric atmosphere of the time, it was absolute folly to consider such a thing.

Throwing caution to the wind, I took the risk and against all odds, I managed without too much trouble to get Clément out with 40 other prisoners for 10,000 American dollars. Not knowing where to hide him, since most of our friends had fled to the country or preferred to keep a safe distance, we decided to go where no one would logically suspect him to go—to our own house. We lived on a main street, next to national police headquarters and a college with 10,000 highly politicized, hostile students. Clément and the children, who were also in danger, spent their days up in the stifling-hot attic and could only come down late at night to eat and sleep, going back up at the first light of dawn. There, in a nutshell, is the situation we were in before Kryon entered our lives.

Clément:

To make a long story short, during this time of deep despair, we received from my two young sisters-in-law, who were living in France, books that they said would help us "understand the meaning of what was happening" to us. It was then that we came to know Kryon. With lots of time on my hands, I was the first to meet Kryon. I immediately felt in complete symbiosis with his truth and the energy that flowed from every word. I realized then that in the situation of distress and total abandonment in which we were immersed, these teachings were the most marvelous gifts that life could offer us. I understood, above all, that I now held in my hands the keys that would open the new portals of my new life: obtaining the Kryon neutral implant, co-creation, being certain of the presence of guides, and the constant observation of synchronicities.

I urged Fété to read Kryon as quickly as possible, and she did so, but she was so preoccupied with finding a country that would offer us asylum, making the outside of the house more secure, and with her own work, that she kept on postponing the practice of Kryon techniques. I immediately requested the neutral implant [a Kryon *intent*-related gift] and began co-creation. As you may guessed, one of my first co-creations was to make us secure on the physical level; the second involved leaving the country for North America, Canada, or the United States. I realized much later that Fété had carefully avoided the neutral implant. When I insisted, she replied, "Frankly, don't you think we have enough to worry about without adding more worries for three months? It's pure folly, don't you think?"

Fété:

At the time, I was going around to the embassies of some Western countries looking for a country that would take us in. In my search, I turned naturally to Canada. The response was evasive and disappointing—the embassy had received many applications and was awaiting instructions from Ottawa. The U.S. had closed its embassy and evacuated all the staff to a neighboring country. Switzerland agreed to take us, but retracted soon afterwards on the pretext that Kosovars were arriving there in massive numbers. It was so urgent for us to leave the country that I turned to other African countries, starting with the country that was most peaceful at the time— the Ivory Coast—which gave us visas right away, while a neighboring country gave us transit passes.

I also obtained permission to leave from the political authorities (which required a total of eight signatures). Clément and the children were discreetly transferred from the house to a center guarded by the Nunciature to await their departure, along with about 30 others who were in the same situation. The day before they left, war broke out in the neighboring country through which they were to travel, and the borders were closed. Talk about misfortune! Despite my discouragement, I took further steps to get new exit papers.

Clément:

I realized immediately that the Ivory Coast was not our final destination. While we were waiting, the buildings where we were staying were attacked by nearly 200 armed soldiers. Treated roughly and publicly humiliated in front of a furious crowd that wanted the soldiers to burn us at the stake, we were all taken away in big military vehicles and driven to the same military camp where I had been held before.

Despite the spectacular raid and the brutality of the operation, I accepted events with serenity and even with some humor because I knew that with my new neutral implant and various co-creations, I was invulnerable. It was the same for Fété.

Although she was terribly shocked by events, she did not despair at any time. Now that she understood Kryon's messages, she was confident, for she realized that our lives were not in danger, but we were simply in the process of accomplishing what was meant to be done.

Fété:

Regardless of the danger for my own life, I went immediately to the camp to make sure they were really there. Then I started searching for another soldier* to communicate with them. Once that was done, I started to try to get visas again. This time, I went to the South African embassy. Thanks to the personal intervention of the United Nations Human rights representative,* I obtained visas in half a day. The minister in charge of this sensitive dossier promised to get Clément and the children out of prison and have us escorted to the airport.

The next day at 5 P.M., the minister's personal secretary asked me to join him at the camp where he was completing the exit formalities. When I arrived at the camp, I found Clément and the children in the prison building, but my joy was short-lived. We had a big problem—it was impossible to leave the camp with the sun shining so bright. The bright rays of our guiding star were literally laughing down from the sky, and it was unthinkable to dare to travel through the frenzied streets of the capital without being noticed. Besides, it was not a good idea to stay at the camp till nightfall, as some crazy soldier might simply fire his gun at us. What to do?

I recalled Kryon and, completely forgetting where I was, the soldiers and the circumstances, I sent an urgent call to my guides. I screamed out that they couldn't give with one hand and take with the other… now it was their turn to do the work, for it was far beyond my limited human intelligence.

What happened next could only be poured into the golden vase of marvelous gifts that heaven, through our guides, gives us in the most poignant moments of our existence. In less than five minutes—I repeat, less than five minutes!—a small gray cloud formed and passed before the sun, while a fine rain began to fall. The first drops fell on totally desiccated soil, releasing steam that would be our salvation. We dashed into the car and the windows fogged up in less than five minutes—just long enough to cross the camp and reach the exit, which merged into a main street that was very busy at that time. We were able to reach our house ten minutes later without mishap and without being observed. Then the rain stopped.

We never went to South Africa because our passports were confiscated while we were en route to the airport, escorted by the U.N. representative and the representative of the Minister of Human Rights.

Clément:

South Africa was not to be our final destination either, so it was back to square one. The minister in charge of our file gave us all the official authorizations we needed to go home, while strongly urging us to remain extremely discreet for our own safety.

Fété and the children were very discouraged, but that only lasted half a day, for the next morning Fété received a call from the U.N. human rights representative telling her to go to the Canadian embassy. Ottawa had finally responded and we could start the process. Fété decided to ask for the neutral implant.

In view of where we lived, we co-created protection for our house together, making it invisible to hostile onlookers. From that moment on, we observed the permanent presence and action of our guides at our side. The teachings of Spirit appeared more clearly to us every day. We knew then that we were progressively accomplishing our destiny and that all we had to do was trust. We agreed to let ourselves be guided by Spirit and established a true partnership. Our fear abated as we understood that we were fulfilling the most difficult part of our life contract, which we drew up ourselves, in which serenity and patience had become our best companions and accomplices.

A profound sense of justice and fairness came over us. We lived our daily lives fully and with great serenity. The feeling of being the victims of an informal machine or infernal forces left us.

Fété:

In this state of mind, we lived out the rest of our captivity. Having, in effect, understood the meaning of our experience, there was no room for anger or rancor. Our executioners were simply brothers who were playing their own roles as best they could to help us fulfill our own life contract. The suffering that arose from being away from our friends and relatives and from being betrayed by a worker was dulled, with no regrets. I had resumed the normal pace of my everyday activities. Since I was in contact with the outside world, I was the ears and eyes of the whole family. This time was lived like a state of grace. I was very much aware and felt in the depths of my being extreme gratitude to the Universe, which was giving me the privilege of living the fullness of my own experience in full awareness.

Clément:

The consular procedures took a long time, and while we were waiting to leave the country, we felt that we still had something important to do. Fété and I, among other things, were running a magazine on African traditions. Under the circumstances, I was unable to move around, so I put my time to good use by summarizing the essential messages and teachings of Kryon for publication in our magazine, *Le Bosquet*, and Fété distributed the issue to as many people as possible, free of charge.

She brought together 11 very talented and famous poets— she herself made it an even dozen. Together, they published a collective work on peace and the advent of fraternity in Africa. A few days later, Fété received a call from the U.N. representative telling her that the U.S. was willing to take us and we should get ready to leave within a few days. Later that afternoon, the Canadian consul called to tell her that our visas had at last gone through! How's that for synchronicity?

Our co-creation was realized beyond all human understanding! Just a few days before receiving this terrific news, we had received *The Journey Home* from my sisters-in-law, and all of us devoured the book. The children and I finally left the country on September 8, 1999. Despite my urging to leave together, Fété wanted to stay another month to settle some business. I'll let her tell you what happened to her.

Fété:

In fact, I was never able to settle anything, because I was recaptured by the security services, who let loose on me in the most unimaginable way. As you can imagine, they had been looking for me for a long time. Most of my time was devoted to helping with the searches that took place in our home and my office, as well as replying to all sorts of accusations about an attack on national security of which I was supposedly guilty. Exhausted and totally worn out, I finally understood the teaching: When it is time to leave, you must stand up without hesitation and follow the call of destiny with confidence. The ray of light for me in this sordid time was the sincere joy shown by the head of security and his assistants when, at their request, I handed over a box full of writings on the awakening of conscience, as well as several copies of the latest issue of our magazine.

Clément:

Despite the fact that Lee Carroll stated that he only channels Kryon for the European/American culture (French Book Four, p. 306), I would like to stress that only language and culture can throw up barriers to exchanges and communication. And even in this specific case, Kryon's message knew nothing of cultural boundaries and was stronger than the sound of cannon fire and automatic weapons that resonate continually on the soil of Mother Africa. The message reached us even in our damp, unhealthy dungeons in the very heart of Central Africa.

Fété:

Kryon's message was the beacon lighting our way through darkest night, slowly guiding our footsteps to the new harbor where we dropped anchor. Since then, an eternal feeling of gratitude and indescribable joy have taken up permanent residence: the serene joy of knowing for sure that things are well founded and fair, and the joy that resembles an outburst of laughter when you discover at last the extraordinary beauty that lives behind the dramatic comedy that is life. That joy is nothing other than love of life . . .

Clément:

. . . and a feeling of total confidence and abandonment in the arms of Spirit, who, in the new era, takes the commands in our cockpit.

This is what the works of Kryon have meant to our new destiny. We encourage everyone to keep their minds wide open so that they can grasp the permanent intervention of Spirit in their daily lives.

Fété & Clément

* The asterisks indicate all the people who have been angels for us.

Kryon News and
Products

Chapter Fourteen

The End Times

White   **Kryon Book One**

The First Kryon Book

The first Kryon book, and the one that started it all. This book continues to be one of the best selling of the entire series. Although written in 1989, it sets the stage for all that we are experiencing now.

"The simple manner in which the material is presented makes this a highly accessible work for newcomers to Metaphysics"

■ *Connecting Link* **magazine** - Michigan

Published by Kryon Writings, Inc • ISBN 0-9636304-2-3 • $12.00

Books and tapes can be purchased in retail stores, or by phone
~ Credit cards welcome ~

1-800-352-6657 - <kryonbooks@kryon.com>

Don't Think Like a Human

Blue　　　　　　　　**Kryon Book Two**

Channelled Answers

The second Kryon book, published in 1994. This book was the first one to begin to ask questions about how everything worked . . . mostly asked by the channel—an audio engineer!

"This read is a can't-put-it-down-till-the-last-page experience"

■ *New Age Retailer* - Washington

Published by Kryon Writings, Inc • ISBN 0-9636304-0-7• $12.00

Books and tapes can be purchased in retail stores, or by phone
~ Credit cards welcome ~

1-800-352-6657 - <kryonbooks@kryon.com>

Alchemy of The Human Spirit

Fuchsia   **Kryon Book Three**

Human New Age Transition

Kryon Book Three was published in 1995. It contains much explanation of formerly difficult Kryon attributes (such as the implant), and also broaches base-12 math. This is the book that begins the science sections, common to all the books that follow it.

"The Kryon channelled messages are growing to be as valuable as the Seth teachings"

■ *The Book Reader* - San Francisco, California

Published by Kryon Writings, Inc • ISBN 0-9636304-8-2 • $14.00

*Books and tapes can be purchased in retail stores, or by phone
~ Credit cards welcome ~*

1-800-352-6657 - <kryonbooks@kryon.com>

The Parables of Kryon

Kryon Book Four

New Soft-Cover Edition!

A book of 20 of Kryon's parables. Some have asked, "Are these parables also in the other Kryon books?" The answer is, only half of them. Ten are only found in this book, complete with the channel's interpretations.

"For anyone who is ready for the next evolutionary step, this information from Kryon is invaluable. It is both self-healing and planetary healing . . . Kryon really lets us know that all is well and we have work to do"

▌ **Louise L. Hay**—best-selling author

Published by Hay House • ISBN 1-56170-364-8
ISBN 1-56170-663-9 • $10.95

Books and tapes can be purchased in retail stores, or by phone
~ Credit cards welcome ~
1-800-352-6657 - <kryonbooks@kryon.com>

Partnering with God

Green　　　　　　　　**Kryon Book Six**

Practical Information

The sixth Kryon book, published in 1997, is packed with practical information, science, and an introduction of the new kids . . . The Indigo Children!

*"If you liked the original Kryon series, you are going to love this book!—Probably the most practical Kryon book yet, all 400 pages of **Partnering with God** are packed with the love of God for Humanity . . . a stirring read!"*

■ *The Leading Edge Review*

Published by Kryon Writings, Inc • ISBN 1-888053-10-0 • $14.00

Letters From Home

Violet   **Kryon Book Seven**

Messages from the family

The seventh Kryon book, published in 1999, is the largest of them all. Filled with loving messages from what Kryon calls the "family," it represents Kryon channellings from all over the world. If you need to recommend a Kryon book for a first-time reader, this is the one!

"If you are new to the best-selling Kryon series, this book will stand on its own. These inspiring and powerful messages are a beacon of light as we enter the New Millennium!"

■ *The Leading Edge Review*

Published by Kryon Writings, Inc • ISBN 1-888053-12-7 • $14.00

Passing the Marker

Cream   **Kryon Book Eight**

Understanding the New Millennium Energy

The Eight Kryon book, published in 2000. This book is filled with channellings before and after the millennium shift (year 2000). It prepares us for what is ahead, and reveals what is now obvious after the fact. Kryon speaks of the potential of "Spiritual Rage," and defines the new times with a phrase: "No more Fence-sitting!"

"Read about new gifts and tools, new energies and potentials for the Earth - even new dimensionality! What are the latest scientific advances that fit right into what Kryon told us could happen 11 years ago? . . . also a full alphabetized master index of all eight of the former Kryon books. Profound messages are given, some of which are very startling."

   ■ *The Leading Edge Review*

Published by Kryon Writings, Inc • ISBN 1-888053-11-9 • $14.00

Books and tapes can be purchased in retail stores, or by phone
~ Credit cards welcome ~

1-800-352-6657 - <kryonbooks@kryon.com>

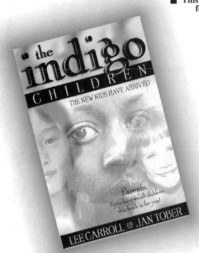

An Indigo Celebration

Lee Carroll and Jan Tober

More Messages Stories , and Insights From The Indigo Children

A continuation of the Indigo subject, but with a twist. The book on the left introduced the Indigo Children to the world and became a best-seller. This book examines experiences of parents and children. Warm and fuzzy, and also profound.

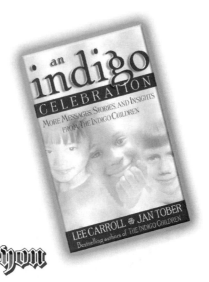

This book took me by surprise - it took me back through my own memories of parenting an Indigo. I got to reexperience my amazement at hearing my young son cry out to me to stop stepping on his toes, as I stood six feet away! It touched me deeply, brought tears to my eyes, gave me the urge to go out and run around the block in the rain in celebration of the child within. A healthy, inspiring read.

■ **The Light Connection - San Diego, CA**

Published by Hay House • ISBN 1-56170-859-3 • $13.95

Books and tapes can be purchased in retail stores, or by phone ~ Credit cards welcome ~

1-800-352-6657 - <kryonbooks@kryon.com>

Jan Tober's

Teknicolour Tapestry

Teknicolour Tapestry - A full album of beautiful channelled lyrics and melodies, accompanied by world-class musicians Mark Geisler (on Celtic harp and violin), Ron Satterfield (specific orchestrations), and best-selling Canadian New Age artist Robert Coxon on keyboard.This full album contains 9 songs, and over 50 minutes of uplifting energy - meditative listening for relaxing. Self empowerment is the theme, but healing is often the result.

On compact disk only

Published by Kryon Writings, Inc. • ISBN 1-888053-07-0 • $15.00

Books and tapes can be purchased in retail stores, or by phone
~ Credit cards welcome ~

1-800-352-6657 - <kryonbooks@kryon.com>

Kryon at the United Nations!

In November 1995, November 1996, and again in November 1998, Kryon spoke at the S.E.A.T. (Society for Enlightenment and Transformation) at the United Nations in New York City. By invitation, Jan and Lee brought a time of lecture, toning, meditation, and channelling to an elite group of U.N. delegates and guests.

Kryon Book Six, Partnering with God, carried the first two entire transcripts of what Kryon had to say . . . some of which has now been validated by the scientific community. *Kryon Book seven, Letters from Home,* carries the meeting in 1998 (page 289). All three of these transcripts are on the Kryon website [**www.kryon.com**].

Our sincere thanks to Mohamad Ramadan in 1995, Cristine Arismendy in 1996, and Jennifer Borchers in 1998, who were presidents of that bright spot at the United Nations. We thank them for the invitations, and for their spiritual work, which enlightens our planet.

Would you like to be on the Kryon mailing list?

This list is used to inform interested people of Kryon workshops coming to their areas, new Kryon releases, and Kryon news in general. We don't sell or distribute our lists to anyone.

If you would like to be included, please simply drop a postcard to us that says "LIST," and include your clearly printed name and address.

The Kryon Writings, Inc.

#422
1155 Camino Del Mar
Del Mar, CA 92014

At Home
with
Kryon

Get together for a personal afternoon or evening with Kryon and Lee Carroll . . . in the comfort of a cozy living room or community center with a small group of dedicated Lightworkers. It's called *At Home with Kryon,* the latest venue for joining in the Kryon energy. The special meeting starts with an introduction and discussion by Lee Carroll regarding timely New Age topics, then it continues with individual questions and answers from the group. Next comes a live Kryon channelling! Group size is typically 50 to 70 people. Often lasting up to five hours, it's an event you won't forget!

To sponsor an *"At Home with Kryon"* event in your home, please contact the Kryon office at 760/489-6400 - fax 858/759-2499, or e-mail <kryonmeet@kryon.com>. For a list of upcoming *At Home with Kryon* locations, please see our Website at [http://www.kryon.com].

Kryon Live Channelled Audio Tapes

▶ **Ascension in the New Age** - ISBN 1-888053-01-1 • $10.00
Carlsbad, California - "Kryon describes what ascension really is in the New Age.
It might surprise you!"

▶ **Nine Ways to Raise the Planet's Vibration** - ISBN 1-888053-00-3 • $10.00
Seattle, Washington - "Raising the planet's vibration is the goal of humanity!
Find out what Kryon has to say about it."

▶ **Gifts and Tools of the New Age** - ISBN 1-888053-03-8 • $10.00
Casper, Wyoming - "A very powerful channel. Better put on your sword, shield
and armor for this one."

▶ **Co-Creation in the New Age** - ISBN 1-888053-04-6 • $10.00
Portland, Oregon - "Tired of being swept around in life? Find out about
co-creating your own reality. It is our right in this New Age!"

▶ **Seven Responsibilities of the New Age** - ISBN 1-888053-02-X • $10.00
Indianapolis, Indiana - "Responsibility? For what? Find out what Spirit tells us
we are now in charge of . . . and what to do with it."

▶ **The Lemurian Tapes** - ISBN 1-888053-02-X • $10.00
Hawaii - These three channellings were given on the USS Patriot, on the 2nd annual Kryon
Cruise. September 11th was right in the middle of this event. (Release scheduled for late
2002)

Music and Meditation

▶ **Crystal Singer Music Meditation Tape** - ISBN 0-96363-4-1-5 • $10.00
Enjoy two soaring 17-minute musical meditations featuring the beautiful singing
voice of Jan Tober.

▶ **Guided Meditations Tape** - ISBN 1-388053-05-4 • $10.00
Jan presents two guided meditations similar to those delivered at each Kryon seminar
throughout the United States and Canada, with beautiful Celtic harp accompaniment
by Mark Geisler.   Side One: "Finding Your Sweet Spot"   Side Two: "Divine Love"

▶ **Color & Sound Meditation CD** - ISBN 1-888053-06-2 • $15.00
A complete color/sound workshop — an exercise to balance and harmonize the chakras. Jan
guides us through the seven-chakra system using the enhancement of the ancient Tibetan
singing bowls.   Side One: 30-min meditation   Side Two: 12-min meditation

▶ **Teknicolour Tapestry** - ISBN 1-888053-07-0 • $15.00
A full album of beautiful channelled lyrics and melodies, accompanied by world-class
musicians Mark Geisler (on Celtic harp and violin); Ron Satterfield (specific orchestrations);
and best-selling Canadian New Age artist Robert Coxon on keyboards. This full album
contains nine songs, and over 50 minutes of uplifting energy—meditative listening for
relaxing. Self-empowerment is the theme!

Kryon Audio products

continued . . .

Music, continued

▶ **I have the feeling I've been here before** - ISBN 15882 008722 • $15.00
This is a jazz album, but very healing! Jan Tober's past included touring with some of the
jazz "greats" in American history, among them *Stan Kenton* and *Benny Goodman*. Her vocal
talents still remain grounded in the healing properties of music of all kinds. This album
features Jan singing soft jazz favorites of the past with world-class guitarist Jeff Linsky. It's
the kind of album you put on for your friends during dinner, or listen to with earphones
while enjoying the intimacy of soft love songs of the past.

Kryon Audio Books

▶ **"The End Times"** - *Read by Lee Carroll*
Published by **Audio Literature** - ISBN 1-57453-168-9 - $17.95

▶ **"Don't Think Like a Human"** - *Read by Lee Carroll*
Published by **Audio Literature** - ISBN 1-57453-169-7 - $17.95

▶ **"Alchemy of the Human Spirit"** - *Read by Lee Carroll*
Published by **Audio Literature** - ISBN 1-57453-170-0 - $17.95

▶ **"The Parables of Kryon"** - *Read by Lee Carroll & Others*
Published by **Hay House** *and scored with music!* ISBN 1-56170-454-7 - $16.95

▶ **"The Journey Home"** *Unabridged !* - *Read by Lee Carroll*
Published by **Hay House** - *a six-tape set!* ISBN 1-56170-453-9 - $30.00
(seven-hour listening experience)

Books and tapes can be purchased in retail stores, or by phone
~ Credit cards welcome ~ 1-800-352-6657

Index
"The New Beginning"

Book Index

Index

Index

Index

And so it is that we say good-bye, but not for the final time, for there is no final time. We will see each of you again in the Hall of Honor, where we will call you by name. We will wink at one another and remember the day we met, where you all gathered together, pretending to be something else.

And so it is that we have a hard time retreating from you. It has gotten harder and harder to close these communications, the closer you get to finding who you are. The visits from family on this side of the veil are something we look forward to in a way you'd never imagine. Again we say, you have no concept of who came to see whom here today. We knew you'd come, and you did. And in your intent, you've allowed the energy of Spirit to surround you—the loved ones to surround you. And in that energy of love, we have all basked, and we have loved you and washed your feet this night.

And so it is.

Kryon